1992

Dance and the Music of
J. S. Bach

Music: Scholarship and Performance

Thomas Binkley, general editor

Dance and the Music of J. S. Bach

Meredith Little and Natalie Jenne

Indiana University Press
Bloomington and Indianapolis

In chapter 7, the translation by Patricia Ranum of Father François
Pomey's "Description d'une Sarabande dansée" is reprinted from *Early
Music* 14/1 (1986) by permission of Oxford University Press.

The paper used in this publication meets the minimum requirements of
American National Standard for Information Sciences—Permanence of
Paper for Printed Library Materials, ANSI Z39.48-1984.

Manufactured in the United States of America

Library of Congress Cataloging-in-Publication Data
Little, Meredith, date.
    Dance and the music of J.S. Bach / Meredith Little and Natalie
Jenne.
        p.   cm. — (Music—scholarship and performance)
    Includes bibliographical references and index.
    ISBN 0-253-33514-0 (cloth)
    1. Bach, Johann Sebastian, 1685–1750—Criticism and interpretation.
    2. Dance music—18th century—History and criticism. I. Jenne,
Natalie, date. II. Title. III. Series.
ML410.B13L52   1991
784. 18'82'092—dc20
                                    90-42362
                                       CIP
                                       MN

1 2 3 4 5 95 94 93 92 91

To the memory of our remarkable
teacher and dear friend,
Putnam Aldrich

CONTENTS

PREFACE

In an age when it was fashionable to dedicate works of art to wealthy patrons or rulers, Johann Sebastian Bach offered his *Clavier-Übung* to "lovers of music, for their spiritual enjoyment and for the refreshment of the mind."[1] For almost three centuries lovers of music have responded to Bach's creations with a sense of their romance, drama, adventure, and "intrigue with surprising resolutions." And, as lovers will, they have invariably searched for greater intimacy, for more knowledge about the structure of the music and more understanding of its inner qualities.

Clavier-Übung I and II contain seven large-scale works for keyboard—six Partitas and *Overture in the French Style*—which together include forty titled dances (seven allemandes, seven sarabandes, six gigues, four correntes, four menuets, three courantes, three passepieds, two gavottes, and two bourées, "Tempo di Minuetta," and "Tempo di Gavotta"). Scholars agree that the Partitas illustrate Bach's complete mastery of the technical and structural features of Baroque dance music, as well as his consummate genius in bringing Baroque musical forms to a profound degree of expressiveness. Hundreds of titled dances by Bach have been preserved, and many more have undoubtedly been lost, including some that may have been part of the numerous symphonic and chamber works which have not survived.[2]

It is clear that Bach devoted a significant portion of his life to the composition of dance music and that it was a serious interest for him. Yet until now there have not been any books which discuss structure and style in his dances, nothing which shows the choreographic origins of his dance forms, and no studies tying Bach's dances to those of his predecessors and contemporaries. Furthermore, there is no satisfactory history of Baroque dance music, and no comprehensive discussion of structure and style as it developed in dance forms in this period. Even the few books which deal with a single dance type, such as the allemande[3] or gigue,[4] treat only art music in a descriptive fashion and do not touch on such controversial but important topics as performance styles and the essential rhythmic characteristics of the dance.

The present book speaks to these needs by applying new information and analytical tools to characterize Bach's pieces with dance titles. At the same time it is also a source book on the structure and style of Baroque dances in general, with suggestions for performance. Part I lays the foundation for our discussions of Bach's dance music. The first chapter describes French Court dance practices in the cities and courts in which Bach lived, since most of the dance forms he used were choreographically alive and flourishing in Germany during his lifetime. The second chapter sets up terminology and defines the procedures used in Part II of this book. A new set of analytical tools is necessary in order to discuss dance music with precision. For example, the bourée until recently was still considered "a piece in quick duple meter with a single upbeat,"[5] even though this vague description fits numerous pieces which would never be considered bourées. Our system of analysis for temporal structure and dance rhythms enables one to make specific statements about particular places in particular pieces and to compare one piece structurally with another.

Part II presents the characteristics of the dance forms used by Bach, combining information from choreography, harmony, theorists' writings, and the music of a variety of seventeenth- and eighteenth-century composers. All of Bach's titled dances are discussed. On some there is little comment, while others, more typical of Bach's mature style, require detailed analysis. The extraordinary variety of Bach's realization of the dance "ideal" demands this comprehensive approach.

As a personal word of advice, we urge readers not to intellectualize rhythm. Many problems arise when rhythm is analyzed as a thing to be understood by the mind, rather than as an activity perceived primarily by the body and only secondarily by the mind. One aim of this book is to encourage a feeling for the rhythms in Baroque dances so that the full strength of their vitality may be experienced, remembering that Johann Matthias Gesner once described Bach as a conductor by noting that he was "full of rhythm in every part of his body. . . . "[6]

We are deeply indebted to the many people who have helped us in our work over the last fourteen years, donating gifts of ideas and criticism as well as encouragement. In particular, we thank Wendy Hilton for her help with the dance sections. Other friends and colleagues who contributed substantially to aspects of the text are: Don Franklin, University of Pittsburgh; Robert Marshall, Brandeis University; Herbert Myers, Stanford University; Kurt Petermann, Akademie der Künste der DDR, Tanzarchive, Leipzig; Newman Powell, Valparaiso University; and Erich Schwandt, University of Victoria, Canada. Our families also gave consistent, indispensable support: Edward and Hilda Jenne, Milton and Louise Jenne, and John Little.

The dedicated staffs of numerous libraries helped, too, including those at The Newberry Library, Chicago; The University of Chicago Libraries; The Library of Congress; The Stanford University Libraries; The University of California Library; The Sibley Library, Eastman School of Music; University of Arizona Special Collections; The New York Public Library; The British Library, London; Bibliothèque Nationale, Paris; Musikbibliothek der Stadt Leipzig; Staatsbibliothek Preuszischer Kulturbesitz and Deutsche Staatsbibliothek, Berlin; and Sächsische Landesbibliothek, Dresden. Finally, we acknowledge generous financial assistance from The American Philosophical Society, The Aid Association for Lutherans, and The American Council of Learned Societies.

PART I
Introduction

CHAPTER 1

French Court Dance in Bach's World

Germany was still recovering from the severe economic and social disruptions of the Thirty Years War when Bach was born in 1685. The Treaty of Westphalia had officially ended the bloodshed in 1648 by stipulating that the princes of each of the over 300 states and other political units would decide the religion and laws to govern their own areas of control, with free cities, such as Hamburg and Leipzig, excepted. The long period of reconstruction from the civil war was to last over a century, embracing all of Bach's life. Many German courts and cities imported culture from France and Italy as part of a peacetime cultural competition, striving to build brilliant, elegant centers of civility which would outshine those of their neighbors. The standard biographies of Bach contain little about French influence, yet French culture was a forceful presence in most of the places in which he lived and worked.

For example, Bach would have encountered French language, music, dance, and theater while he was a student at the Michaelisschule in Lüneburg in 1700–1702. Though at school he studied traditional subjects, such as orthodox Lutheranism, history, and rhetoric, he shared room and board with the aristocratic young men who attended the Ritterakademie in Lüneburg. Karl Geiringer writes:

> The Academy was a center of French culture. French conversation, indispensable at that time to any high-born German, was obligatory between the students; and

Material in this chapter was originally presented by Meredith Little at the 1985 Aston Magna Academy, "J. S. Bach and His World," held at Rutgers University.

Sebastian with his quick mind may have become familiar with a language which he had no chance to study in his own schools. There were French plays he could attend and, what was more important, French music he could hear, as a pupil of Lully, Thomas de la Selle, taught dancing at the Academy to French tunes. Most likely it was de la Selle, noticing the youth's enthusiastic response, who decided to take Bach to the city of Celle, where he served as court musician.[1]

Bach visited the court at Celle many times; it was a "miniature Versailles" in its recreation of French culture, according to Geiringer. As an impressionable teenager, Bach probably encountered Lully's music as played by the excellent French orchestra; the keyboard music of composers such as François Couperin, Nicholas de Grigny, and Charles Dieupart; and possibly ballet and French social dancing as well.[2]

Most of Bach's titled dance music implies a connection to French Court dancing. Minuets, gavottes, passepieds, courantes, sarabandes, gigues, and loures were frequently performed at the courts and in the cities where Bach lived.

FRANCE

French Court dancing, a symbol of French culture, was especially in favor in Germany. This graceful, balanced, refined, and highly disciplined style was "invented," as it were, or given its classic characteristics, by dancers working at the court of Louis XIV from the 1650s on.[3] The technical achievements of this style—for example, turnout of the legs from the hips and the five positions for the feet (Fig. I-1), and the calculated opposition of arms to step-units (Fig. I-2)—were an obvious, stunning improvement over any other dance form in Europe. French Court dancing was not a fad, but the beginning of ballet. It was internationally accepted even as it was being invented and codified in France, not only in Germany but in England, Scotland, Spain, Portugal, Czechoslovakia, Holland, and Sweden, later spreading to Russia and the European colonies in North and South America.

Under the strong, central rule of Louis XIV (reigned 1661–1715), France experienced an especially prosperous and influential period of her history, unlike Germany with its many small, competing states. Louis XIV was a life-long lover of aristocratic dancing. Even as a youth he and his friends dressed up in fanciful costumes and danced in ballets for their own entertainment. A ballet required the support services of scene designers, costumers, singers, dancers, poets, and musicians. Every year at least one new ballet was presented, most often in the season between Christmas and Lent. It was usual for a ballet to be organized around a theme, such as the seven liberal arts, or an event from classical mythology, such as the birth of Venus. Ballets normally did not have a strong central plot, but consisted of a series of vocal airs loosely organized around the theme. Sung by various characters, these airs were interspersed with dances (*entrées*) performed by various characters dressed in fanciful costumes.[4]

Aristocrats at the court of Louis XIV also enjoyed social dancing, using the same steps and movement styles as ballet but wearing formal dress instead of costumes. Elegant ceremonial balls were held to celebrate important events of the realm, such as a military victory, the signing of a treaty, the marriage of a socially prominent person, or someone's birthday. They often occurred after an evening of theater or other recreation. But unlike social dancing today, these events were carefully planned and rehearsed, and only the best recreational dancers performed, while the assembled company watched and admired.

The king sat at the head of the room, with members of the court arranged around him according to rank. He and his partner danced the first dance, after which everyone else in the royal company danced, one couple at a time, again in order of rank. The dancing couple began at the foot of the room facing the king; the musicians were usually behind them or in raised galleries on the side of the room. Every dance began and ended with a formal *Reverence* to one's partner as well as to the king. Almost all of the dances—minuets, courantes, gavottes, and other forms—consisted of special written choreographies which were memorized beforehand; other members of the court had learned the same choreographies and would know if they were performed correctly. Courtiers practiced daily in order to present a graceful picture while they danced. Other spectators might watch the ball from bleachers behind the central area but would not participate in the dancing.

In addition to these "grand balls" there were innumerable occasions for dancing, at court and at the private estates of noblemen. There were masked balls, with gaily costumed participants, at which a masquerade would be presented—a scene from a ballet, or a scene with dancing and singing invented for the party. The *jours d'appartement* took place on special evenings at the king's palace, with dancing and other entertainments, such as gambling and billiards.

> During the six-month period between 10 September 1684 and 3 March 1685, the beginning of Lent, there were at the court alone: 1 *grand bal;* 9 masked balls; 16 *appartements* that definitely included dancing; 42 other *appartements* that almost certainly also offered dancing; and at least 2 evenings of comedy that included dancing between the acts by courtiers.[5]

It was the French dancing masters who created the ballets, ceremonial balls, and masquerades. For ballets they choreographed the dances, rehearsed the ballet corps, coordinated the dancing with the music, and often

Fig. I-1: From **Rameau:Maître**. a. *Reverence* before dancing (p. 62); b. First posture of *demi-coupé* (p. 71); c. Second posture of *demi-coupé* (p. 72); d. Third posture of *demi-coupé* (p. 73); e. Fourth posture of *demi-coupé*, balancing on one foot (p. 74); f. The five positions for the feet.

a.

b.

c.

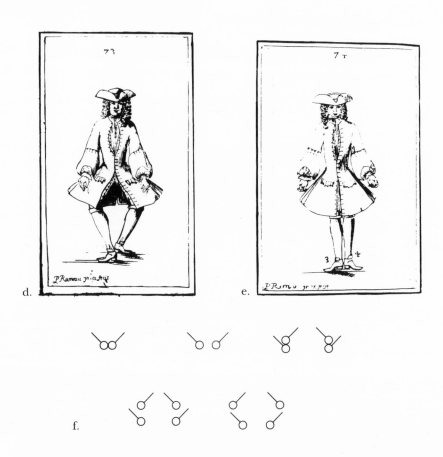

performed in the productions. For the ceremonial balls, dancing masters were in charge of seeing that everyone observed the rituals, and at the proper time. The short theatrical presentations at masquerades also needed careful production. Dancing masters gave daily lessons to able aristocrats, including the king himself, to ensure that all the participants knew their parts and that the balls and ballets would be as magnificent as possible. In addition to teaching dancing they instructed courtiers in deportment, such as the proper way to bow to a superior or to an inferior, how to do honors in passing, what to do when introduced at court, what to do with one's hat and sword, and so on. There were precise rules which, when followed, resulted in elegance and the appearance of gentility, the height of civilized behavior.

The technique of French Court dancing has been preserved, happily, through numerous dance manuals as well as a notation system which could record particular choreographies.[6] The technique was based on a strongly centered carriage, with the back straight (but not stiff); a long neck support-

Fig. I-2: "Une Dame de la Cour de Pélée,"
watercolor on parchment. Courtesy Musée
Carnavalet, Paris.

ing a balanced head, which was tilted neither downward in submission nor
upward in haughtiness; and arms and legs which moved without hunching
the shoulders or bowing the back. The elegant ease and noble bearing of a
dancer in motion is shown in Fig. I-2.

The dance technique emphasized turnout of the legs from the hips because it enabled the dancer to look his best to an audience, and the courtier
his best to the court, even in sideways movements which may appear awk-
ward without turnout. The five positions for the feet (Fig. I-1) meant that the
legs would always move in an ordered, prescribed fashion rather than in
haphazard ways. Additional order occurred in duets, where the dancing couple moved through symmetrical, balanced floor patterns, performing the
same steps at the same time but on opposite feet.

The ideals of the French style were inspiring. They included *douceur* (kind-
ness, sweetness), *bonté* (goodness), *honnêteté* (integrity, decency), a beautiful
body and a beautiful spirit, and "a certain majesty," as well as order, balance,
hierarchy, and discipline. Above all these was "nonchalance," which for
dancing means that beyond the straight back and balanced head the body is
relaxed but at the same time ready for any action or movement. One scholar
has called it "an 18th-century cool."[7] As a French ideal it was taught along
with dancing.

GERMANY

French Dancing Masters

Many of the competing German courts hired French dancing masters, preferably Parisian, to lead them on the pathway to elegance. The dancing master would give instruction in French dance technique and the latest dances from Paris, and would also teach deportment. These niceties were necessary for anyone who wanted to be presented at court and participate in its activities, because one had to know specific rituals for bowing, taking off one's hat, and other genteel behavior. Bach must have learned these rituals, for he was presented at court many times, and he participated in the activities of numerous courts. The French dancing masters were in demand in German cities and courts as part of the effort to rebuild the economy and enhance the general well-being after the havoc of the Thirty Years War. By teaching gracious behavior as well as dancing they instilled a sense of pride and competence in society, especially as middle-class persons began to use body language as an avenue to a better life. The French dancing master functioned as the Master of Ceremonies for important social occasions in Germany, just as he had in France.

Research by Kurt Petermann has revealed that the Leipzig directory of 1701 listed three French dancing masters, but by 1736 there were twelve, out of a total listing of about 20,000 persons,[8] and there were undoubtedly many others who did not appear in the book. It would also be interesting to have a list of French dancing masters in Germany during the period 1650–1725. In Renate Brockpähler's (admittedly incomplete) list of dancers associated with ballet composition in opera performances in Germany up to 1753, of the forty-seven men listed, two names are Germanic, eight are Italian, and the rest are French.[9]

A better measure of the importance of the French dancing master in society can be found in a book published by Christoph Weigel in 1698.[10] Its 212 plates illustrating the different occupations in Germany at the time are presented in order of rank. The first plate, for example, is of "The Regent." Weigel divides the occupations into three main types: the *Regierstand*, or ruling and organizing work, such as that of the Regent, the general for war on land, and the admiral for war on water; the *Lehrstand*, which includes teaching, medical, legal, and business people; and the *Belustigenden Künstlern*, or peasants and middle-class workers, which include stone masons, pearl workers, printers, foresters, musical instrument makers, etc. At the end, and outside these three groups, is the lowly gravedigger. The French dancing master is in the second group (Fig. I-3), along with doctors, lawyers, and businessmen; his picture appears next to those of the fencing master and ball-game master. Thus Weigel, an influential publisher, shows the French

Fig. I-3: "The Dancing Master," from Christoph Weigel, *Abbildung der Gemein-Nutzlichen Haupt-Stände* (1698 edition), plate 72. Courtesy The Huntington Library, San Marino, California.

dancing master to be a respected professional with an important position in German culture by the late seventeenth century.

French Social Dancing

French social dancing was an important cultural event in Bach's Germany. Ceremonial balls and other French forms of social dancing were widely performed in German-speaking courts and cities, including those in Saxony. By the early eighteenth century the custom of formal balls in the French style was beginning to be enjoyed by middle-class persons as well as by aristocrats. Dancing masters in Leipzig, for example, held weekly balls at their studios to give students a chance to perform their choreographies, with the French rules of precedence and decorum strictly upheld. References to such dancing abound in memoirs, dance manuals, travelers' reports, and letters, but at this writing there is no systematic study of French social dancing in Germany during this period. Angelika Gerbes summarizes the ideas of the German dancing master Gottfried Taubert on formal balls:

> Balls were gatherings expressly for the purpose of dancing. . . . [They] were given by high-ranking nobility at their courts, by ministers of state, by lesser nobility, and also by burghers. Since the bourgeoisie strove to imitate the court life, the balls were also imitated as much as possible. These balls could be held either in regular dress or in costume. The latter were considered to be more fun. He who gave the ball was designated King of the Ball, and the lady in whose honor the event took place was the Queen of the Ball. She was presented with a bouquet by the "King" and was the first to be asked to dance by him.[11]

French Theatrical Dancing

The more affluent courts and cities had even more elaborate activities involving French dancers, including works for the theater, such as opera and ballet. Many courts were able to do this by the second half of the seventeenth century, and many more had incorporated such activities by the early 1700s.[12] French ballets and operas require a large assemblage of people for their production, and an even larger audience with the refined taste to enjoy them and to make such an effort worthwhile. Yet many German courts invested in this recreation.

In Württemberg, which includes Stuttgart, Prince Eberhard-Ludwig had a "divertissement à la française" produced at court in 1684, a ballet-opera entitled *Le Rendesvous des Plaisirs*. It had many scene changes, with dancers chosen from among the ladies-in-waiting; the Prince (age nine) played the part of Eros.[13]

In Celle there was French theater, music, and dance, especially after a peace treaty was signed by Duke Georg Wilhelm and the king of France in 1679. Duke Wilhelm put on festivals and diversions in the style of Versailles, including operas and ballets performed in a 500-seat theater. The court of Celle, along with the courts at Osnabrück and Hanover, supported a band of French violinists, which, when put together, totaled twenty-four, the number of string players chosen by the French Court composer Jean-Baptiste Lully for ballets and operas in Paris. The band played for four months of the year at each court, performing in theatrical works as well as for social dancing. This was first reported in 1669 by Samuel Chappuzeau, a Frenchman traveling in Germany.[14] Ballet at the court of Hanover was highly praised even in Paris; the French journal *Mercure galant* of April 1681 reviewed the ballet *Le Charme de l'Amour*, which had been performed at the court of Hanover, and found it admirable because it "imitated so gallantly all the manners and customs of France."[15]

In Kassel both Wilhelm VI (reigned 1649–63) and Wilhelm VII (reigned 1663–70) fostered a strong interest in French culture at their courts.[16] Some of the music used for ballets and social dancing has been reprinted in a modern edition, Ecorcheville's well-known *Vingt Suites d'Orchestre.*[17] Numerous courantes, sarabandes, gigues, galliardes, and branles are included, as well as a few minuets, passepieds, and a bourée, a repertoire dating from about 1650–68. Both Wilhelms maintained close contact with French culture. Members of their courts danced with great enthusiasm at home and abroad, visiting Paris and other courts often and in turn receiving visitors from all over Europe. In 1664 the Elector of Brandenburg was welcomed to Kassel by a mythological masquerade in which all the court took part. French ballet emerged even near courts under the influence of the Viennese, who officially espoused the Italian culture and opposed the French. In Vienna, ballet was performed at the home of the French ambassador. The music library in Kroměříž (now a part of Czechoslovakia) holds dances composed by Lully for Cavalli's opera *Ercole Amante;* but, interestingly, the music is entitled "Balletti francesi à 4 del S. Ebner." In other words, this music by Lully, written to accompany the French dances between the acts, is credited to the composer Wolfgang Ebner, the official Italian ballet composer at the court of Leopold I in Vienna.[18]

French ballet was also produced in Berlin, where Jean-Baptiste Volumier was violinist, dancing master, and composer of ballet music from 1692 to 1708. Although none of his music survives, one of his efforts was the ballet music for the marriage opera of Crown Prince Friedrich Wilhelm I in 1706, *Der Sieg der Schönheit über die Helden.*[19]

The court of Berlin was rivaled only by the Saxon court of Dresden, which Bach visited many times.[20] Dresden had one of the most elaborate, splendid, and expensively maintained courts in Europe, outside of Paris. An interest in French dance can be documented as early as 1620, when the German dancing master Gabriel Mölich was sent to Paris for training. Ballets with dancing in the French style were produced all through the seventeenth century. For example, *Ballet von dem Paris und der Helena,* mounted in 1650, had five acts, each of which contained several ballet entries. This and the many other ballets at Dresden appear to be analogous to the types of court ballet being done in France at the same time, although a lack of music and dance texts makes real comparison impossible.

In 1694 Friedrich August I came to power at the age of twenty-four. He was to foster French music and dance even more than did his predecessors, attracting the illustrious performers and composers who motivated Bach to visit Dresden so many times during his life. In the first year of his reign

Friedrich August reorganized his artistic forces, sending away a troupe of Italian actors but retaining the French dancing master Charles Dusmeniel. In 1696 a French theatrical group from the court at Hanover performed for him during Carnival, and by 1708 he had made a special trip to the Low Countries to recruit his own troupe, a hand-picked group of French singers, actors and dancers from Lille. It consisted of a director plus seven gentlemen and six ladies for singing and dancing, four violinists, a decorator, and a prompter. New dancers arrived soon after, and by 1717 the company had more than doubled.

Some musical theater productions at Dresden have French titles, but a majority are Italian, leading scholars to conclude that Italian influences outweighed the French there. However, French dances were performed between the acts and after the conclusion of Italian operas, according to court records. When Bach attended the performance of Johann Adolf Hasse's opera *Cleofide* in September 1731, he undoubtedly saw French dances.

Theatrical presentations featuring French dancing were not confined to the wealthy courts; student dramas in Leipzig also indulged in this elegant style, according to the dancing master Samuel Rudolph Behrens in his 1713 book, *L'Art de Bien Danser, Oder Die Kunst wohl zu Tantzen*. The first part of the book consists of an introduction to French Court dancing, describing posture, positions for the feet, and the dances of the day, which apparently were bourées, courantes, sarabandes, minuets, and other French dances. However, the author also offers a rare glimpse into "native" German practices—the "Inventiones" of local dancing masters and their students. For example, No. 21 is "Ein Balet, worinne die vier Complexiones der Menschen vorgestellet werden" (Ballet of the four complexions, in which each of the four humors [e.g., melancholy] forms one of the entries). The scenery and costumes are vividly described, although no music or dance survives in notation. From this treatise one learns that French dance has passed well beyond the aristocratic courts and penetrated the middle-class world which surrounded Bach in Leipzig.

French Dancing Masters: Friends of Bach

Bach knew personally or knew the work of three eminent French dancing masters in Saxony: Johannes Pasch, Pantaleon Hebenstreit, and Jean-Baptiste Volumier.

Johannes Pasch (1653–1710) was raised in the Dresden court, where his training in French Court dancing began when he was a very young child. He made many trips to Paris to study dancing, but his career was in Leipzig, where he taught French Court dancing for almost forty years and was highly respected as a dancer and a choreographer. His dancing was favorably compared by his contemporaries to that of his Parisian teacher, Pierre Beauchamps, who was also the personal dancing master of Louis XIV. Pasch attended Leipzig University but did not receive an academic degree. Two treatises by Pasch have survived; both reveal a fascinating glimpse of dance practices of the day.

Beschreibung wahrer Tanz-Kunst, of 1707, shows Pasch to be well versed in philosophy and rhetoric as well as dancing. He defends French Court dancing from the attacks of pietist writers, describing it as "the true dance art," and arguing that the graceful movements are not only morally uplifting and lead to noble actions, but are in agreement with philosophy, mathematics, and theology. A well-regulated dance is natural and useful to man, and only its misuse becomes immoral.

His other extant treatise is *I.H.P. Maître de Danse, Oder Tantz-Meister.*[21] This forty-four-page pamphlet, dated 1705, contains four French choreographies set in a notation somewhat different than that used in Paris, for example, in Feuillet's *Recueil de Dances.*[22] Two dances have concordances with the Paris repertoire. Despite the notation, their steps and floor patterns are unchanged from the Paris originals, with no adjustments for German taste. This Leipzig publication clearly indicates a demand for authentic French choreographies.

Pantaleon Hebenstreit (1667–1750) is better known today as a virtuoso instrumentalist at the Dresden court, where he played exquisitely on the violin and the "pantaleon," a large dulcimer of his own invention. He had supported himself in Leipzig during his student years by teaching French dancing; in 1698 he became dancing master at the court of Weissenfels and, in 1708, at the court of Eisenach (Bach's birthplace). He became one of the court musicians at Dresden in 1714, and was a friend of Bach's.

Jean-Baptiste Volumier (c.1670–1728) was also one of Bach's good friends. A Belgian who had been brought up in the French court, he was a dancing master, violinist, and finally Konzertmeister and composer of music for ballet entries at the court in Berlin before coming to Dresden in 1709. He had introduced French violin techniques to the orchestra in Berlin (1692–1708). At Dresden he had much the same duties as at Berlin, and as Konzertmeister (1709–21) he presided over an orchestra which became internationally famous. Quantz stated that he never heard a better orchestra than the one at Dresden under Volumier.[23] Interestingly enough, some of the scores from this orchestra still exist in the Dresden Sächsische Landesbibliothek, with French ornamentation, slurs, and other performance indications written into the music; some of the first violin parts bear the name "Woulumier" (Fig. I-4).

Clearly, Bach had ample opportunity to see, to know, and to appreciate French dancing and dance music. We may fairly conclude that French Court dancing and French influences were an intrinsic, important, and graceful component of Bach's world, and that his titled dance music reflects the noble and subtle movements of early ballet. The extent of ballet's influence on his music will be the subject of Part II of this book.

Fig. I-4: Volumier's personal copy of "Premier Dessus de violon," used for Dresden performances of the chaconne from Lully's *Acis et Galatée*)Sächsische Landesbibliothek Ms. Mus. 1827-F-31, p. 11). Courtesy Sächsische Landesbibliothek, Dresden.

CHAPTER 2

Terms and Procedures

Rhythm, according to the ancient Greek writer Aristoxenus, is an activity, not a thing.[1] In earlier times the word "rhythm" was used as a verb—"I will 'rhythm' these notes" or "I will 'rhythm' these harmonies." Thus, to "rhythm" something was to give it an organization, a shape, a form, and a distinctive life. In Baroque dances, one would "rhythm" in the context of a particular meter and tempo.

METER

Meter is usually thought of as duple, triple, or "compound." Actually, all meters are hierarchical; that is, they operate by the cooperation of several levels. The activity one perceives at these levels—the "rhythming" of the meter, if you will—involves varying degrees of motion and repose, most importantly of the beat. We have adopted the terms *arsis* and *thesis*, first used by the Greeks and later by Marin Mersenne in his *Harmonie Universelle* (Paris, 1636–37), to describe this phenomenon. Rhythmic activity on a metric level may be more or less arsic, or more or less thetic. In discussions of rhythm and meter in Baroque dances we use "A" to signify a more arsic place, and "a" for a less arsic place. Similarly, "T" refers to a more thetic place, and "t" to a less thetic one. For example, see Fig. III-2.

Table I shows the metric levels in the Baroque dance types, using the most commonly notated time values in each dance, with the most common time signature. Numerical descriptions of these levels appear in the column labeled "Metric Structure." For the bourée, "II" signifies two half notes to the measure; the first "2" means that half notes are divided into two quarter notes, and the second "2" that each quarter note is divided into two eighths. The arrows at the top of the column to the left show how each type of dance may have been conducted in Bach's day, according to instructions from numerous French[2] and German[3] writers of the period. In this book we call each movement of the conductor's arm a "beat," so that, in the bourée, there are two beats to the measure, shown by the Roman numeral "II." This is the level of the beat, or the metric level in which beats occur. In a time signature of 2 or ¢ the duration of a single half note is one beat, ready to be grouped with other beats into measures and, eventually, into a phrase.

A problem often arises for performers when several time signatures appear in a given dance type. In the pieces entitled "gigue," for example, the beat is the dotted quarter note in a signature of $\frac{6}{8}$, but it is the dotted half note in $\frac{6}{4}$. This may not seem like much of a problem, but gigues were also notated in $\frac{12}{8}$, $\frac{3}{8}$, $\frac{3}{4}$, 3, and other signatures; furthermore three distinct types emerge, which we identify as "French gigue," "Giga I," and "Giga II."[4] Before playing a "gigue" notated in 3, a performer must first locate the level of the beat, or, in other words, find out what note value represents one beat. This identifies the metric structure and avoids the possibility of projecting the wrong level of meter. We designate the three lowest levels of metric significance by the terms "beat," "pulse," and "tap," the last being the lowest level of significance. Notes below this level are always ornamental and are never separated from each other by slurs or other types of phrasing techniques.

In Baroque dances the level of the beat, by our definition, is capable of at least two levels of subdivision, shown in Table I by the pulse and tap levels. Beats in Baroque dances are usually grouped by twos or threes into measures, although in some sarabandes and correntes and in most minuets there is only one beat to a measure. The pulse level is the lowest level that can be syncopated. This fact is useful in determining the level of the beat, since syncopations do not appear in the tap level. In addition, the pulse is the lowest level of metric significance in which units may be replaced by a dotted rhythm. For example, a quarter note can be replaced by a dotted eighth and a sixteenth. Conductors occasionally indicate pulses by an arm motion when a special effect, such as a ritard, is needed.

A good conductor will not indicate the tap level, a subdivision of the pulse, by an arm movement. A tap is the smallest unit that can make an essential contribution to the perceivable rhythmic hierarchy. Subdivisions of taps are not of rhythmic significance but are ornaments or melodic flourishes which are not "counted" or "measured" by the listener. The tap is the lowest level that can be consistently dotted, and it is the normal level for *notes inégales* in Baroque dance music. It is also the lowest level that can be articulated. The articulation patterns given in manuals which describe the bowing, tonguing, or fingering of Baroque instrumental music never use a level lower than the tap.

With these definitions in mind one makes some useful discoveries. First,

TABLE I

Metric Levels in Baroque Dances

Dance type	Usual time signature*	Usual note values and metric levels*	Metric structure
Bourée Gavotte Rigaudon	2, ¢, [2/4]	beat · pulse · tap	II-2-2
French gigue Giga II Canarie Passepied	6/8, 12/8	beat · pulse · tap	II-3-2
Loure Forlane Siciliana	6/4	beat · pulse · tap	II-3-2
Giga I	12/8, 12/16, 24/16	beat · pulse · tap	II-2-3
Minuet	3/4, 3	beat · pulse · tap	I-3-2
Sarabande Polonaise Chaconne Passacaglia Corrente	3/4, 3	beat · pulse · tap	III-2-2
Courante	3/2	beat · pulse · tap	III-2-2

*Most dance types may be found in more than one time signature, and several occur in more than one metric structure (e.g., corrente may also be I–3–2 or I–3–3; sarabande may also be I–3–2).

harmony changes in Baroque dances occur most frequently on the beat and pulse levels; they occur infrequently on the tap level, and then only in a brief, transitional sense. Second, in Baroque songs the text syllables occur most often on the beat and pulse levels. They occur on the tap level or below only in a type of "patter" song in which the individual words are not rhythmically significant. Finally, the dance steps of the extant Baroque dances coincide most often with the beat and pulse levels of the music. Dance steps use the tap level only for special effects in highly ornate theatrical dances.[5]

TEMPO

Although metric structure often can be derived from notation, tempo cannot. It is disturbing to many musicologists and performers to be unable to "prove" this or that tempo for a particular piece, and scholarly literature is full of efforts to give exact, or fairly exact, metronome markings to each dance type.[6]

One line of research points out that information may be derived from time-words such as "adagio" or "vite." Irmgard Hermann-Bengen offers hundreds of such instances,[7] though it is still difficult to assign a precise metronome marking to these time-words. Some composers use the time-words in such personal ways that their meaning is no longer clear to us. The basic problem, however, is in determining the level of meter to which the time-word refers. For example, the courante is a slow dance if one thinks of half-note beats, but if one counts by quarter-note pulses, as did Muffat,[8] the courante is indeed fast.

Another kind of approach to the tempo problem is through choreography. As soon as dancer-scholars began reviving French Court dancing in the 1960s they were besieged by musicologists, who were not interested in dance style or phrase lengths or affect or the beauty and grace of the dances, but in tempo. They remembered that some sixteenth-century dances, such as the simple five-step galliard pattern, or "La Volta,"[9] appear to have one perfect tempo for dancing, with little variation in range because of the leaps of the dancers. Donington's phrase rang in their ears: "Once having danced the volta yourself, you know the tempo for the rest of your life";[10] and those who had, indeed, danced La Volta (including the present authors) could only agree. But the French Court dances are proving to be a different case. A range of tempo is possible, just as in music. Beginners usually prefer faster tempi since the careful articulation of step-units by *plié* (bending the knees) is difficult; it is easier to slight the *pliés,* hardly articulating at all. But Wendy Hilton, combining erudition and a formidable technique, prefers tempi which at first seem quite slow but which strongly project an aristocratic dignity and elegance.[11] Other dancers have chosen different tempi according to their own artistic perceptions. Thus it appears that choreography in itself proves nothing conclusive about tempo—it only makes suggestions, along with the time-words. Yet a decision about tempo is at the same time a decision about affect (or character), metric structure, and which metric levels one wants to project most strongly. Table II presents the spectrum of dance tempi from the fastest dances to the slowest. The chapters on each dance type offer fuller discussion of tempo issues.

TABLE II

Relative Tempi of Baroque Dances from Fast to Slow

Rigaudon,* Passepied, Canarie*
French Gigue, Giga II, Bourée
Loure, Forlane, Gavotte, Giga I
Minuet,** Chaconne, Passacaglia, Corrente
Polonaise
Sarabande, Courante

*Does not occur in Bach.
**In the sense of three "temps" per measure; see below, chapter 5, for a thorough discussion.

CHARACTER

Much has already been written about the concept of affect, or character, in the eighteenth century.[12] Friedrich Wilhelm Marpurg stated in 1749 that "all musical expression has an affect or emotion for its foundation."[13] Johann Philipp Kirnberger sums up this idea explicitly:

> The term *Gemüthsbewegung*, which we Germans give to passions or affections, already indicates their analogy to tempo. In fact, every passion and every sentiment—in its intrinsic effect as well as in the words by which it is expressed—has its faster or slower, more violent or more passive tempo. This tempo must be correctly captured by the composer to conform with the type of sentiment he has to express.
>
> Thus I must admonish the aspiring composer above all that he study diligently the nature of every passion and sentiment with regard to tempo, so that he does not make the terrible mistake of giving the melody a slow tempo where it should be fast, or a fast tempo where it should be slow. However, this is a field that is not limited to music, and that the composer has in common with the orator and poet.
>
> Furthermore, he must have acquired a correct feeling for the natural tempo of every meter, or for what is called *tempo giusto*. This is attained by diligent study of all kinds of dance pieces. Every dance piece has its definite tempo, determined by the meter and the note values that are employed in it.[14]

ARTICULATION

The core of our approach to Baroque dance music is that rhythm and articulation grow from the performer's conception of phrases. Most of the dance types consist of phrases of a definite length and shape. One might even be tempted to say that there was a "prescribed" length and shape because of the widespread use of these characteristic phrases, except that the word "prescribed" implies that someone made up the rules and that everyone else followed them. On the contrary, the nature of these characteristic phrases was not clearly described until after 1750, when writers such as Marpurg and Kirnberger (both students of Bach and keen admirers of his music) set forth the basic concepts of dance rhythms. In Bach's time the dance rhythms represented a convention in the composition of music, a convention which may be derived not only from Marpurg and Kirnberger but also from studying the dance music of the major and minor French and German composers of the day. In addition, the writings of theorists contain many assurances that recognizable, model dance rhythms did exist. For example, Michel L'Affilard, in an early eighteenth-century treatise on sight-singing, presented vocal airs which he said were "models" for dances and could be used "when one wishes to sing or play other dances of the same kind."[15] L'Affilard also indicated breathing places in the airs which correspond exactly to the dance phrases and serve to delineate them for the listener.

THE NOBLE STYLE OF DANCE

Dance phrases are made up of steps, not tones, as in music. In order to understand phrasing and articulation in a dance style one must become familiar with the step vocabulary of the style. In the French noble style of dancing the performer moves by steps and springs grouped into step-units. A step is a transference of weight from one foot to another. A spring is a rising into the air followed by a landing. A step-unit is a grouping of two, three, or occasionally four steps into a unit which normally fits with one measure of music. A single step with several actions (such as bend and rise) is also a step-unit. Table III lists the most commonly used step-units and their manner of performance. The analytic symbols show the quality of the principal actions of each step. These symbols are used in the dance examples of each chapter to show exactly where the transference of weight occurs in relation to the music.

The step-units are almost invariably preceded by a *plié*, or bending of the knees. This is a definite motion downward; English writers called the *plié* a "sink."[16] The *plié* serves as a preparatory gesture for each step-unit and thus sets it apart from preceding ones. A *plié* is usually performed to the pulse of the music preceding the "downbeat" of a measure.

The downbeat itself is normally marked by either an *élevé* (rise) or one of the many types of springs. In the *élevé* the dancer rises from a *plié* onto the ball of the foot and normally straightens both legs. For example, in the *demi-coupé* the dancer bends both knees in a *plié*, moves one foot to a new place, transfers the weight of the body onto that foot, and straightens both legs

TABLE III

Steps and Step-Units Commonly Used in French Court Dancing

The following analytical symbols show the quality of the dance steps and the way they fit with the music:

Λ *plié*
v *élevé*
⌐ *jetté*
~ *glissé*
| step without bend or rise
ⅈ step without change of weight

Step or Step–unit	Performance
Demi-coupé v Λ	*Plié,* rise onto the ball of the stepping foot.
Pas marché |	Walk on ball of foot; no bend or rise.
Pas glissé ~	Walk, as in *pas marché,* but slowly slide foot to position.
Jetté v ⌐	Bend both knees and spring from one foot to the other.
Tems de courante v Λ~~	Bend both knees, straighten and rise on the supporting foot, and slide the other foot to position slowly.
Pas assemblé v ⌐	Bend both knees, spring off one foot, and land on both feet.
Pirouette v Λ	Bend both knees, straighten and rise on both feet, and turn.
Pas coupé v Λ | or v Λ~	*Demi-coupé* plus *pas marché* or *pas glissé* (many different forms).
Pas de bourée v Λ | |	*Demi-coupé* plus two *pas marchés.*
Pas de menuet v Λ v Λ | | v Λ v Λ | v Λ Λ ⌐ | v ⌐ v ⌐	Four steps set to two measures of music. There are many varieties; the most common are: 2 *demi-coupés* and *pas marchés* 2 *demi-coupés, pas marché,* and another *demi-coupé* *contretemps de menuet*
Contretemps de gavotte v ⌐ | |	*Plié,* hop (on one foot), and two *pas marchés.*
Contretemps ballonné v ⌐ v ⌐	*Plié,* hop (on one foot), and leap onto the other foot.
Jettés v ⌐ v ⌐	Two *jettés* set to one measure of music.

Jettés chassés	Two springs from one foot to the other, with one foot "chasing" the other.
ʋ ⌐ ʋ ⌐	
Pas de sissonne	*Plié* spring from one onto two feet, land in *plié*, spring onto one foot (land in the following *plié*).
ʋ ⌐ ʋ ⌐	
Glissades	Two *pas coupés* in one measure of music (the effect is that of four quick steps).
ʋ ʌ ∼ ʋ ʌ ∼	
Pas de courante	*Demi-coupé, pas coupé.*
ʋ ʌ ʌ l	

while rising onto the foot that moved. Fig. I-1 shows a *demi-coupé* in slow motion. Basically, it is an elegant bend and rise, the bend usually occurring with the last pulse of a measure and the rise coinciding with the first pulse of the following measure. In dance terminology the combination of bend and rise was known as a "movement."

In the *sauté* the dancer springs from a *plié* onto one or both feet, thus transfering the weight of the body, so that the basic movements are "bend, spring, and land." Again, the *plié* is a preparatory gesture, and the landing from this spring marks the transference of weight and the chief accent of the step. Springs are usually part of a step-unit, but two or three together may also occur in one measure of music, each one preceded by a *plié*. The springs may be of several kinds, e.g., a leap from one foot to the other (*jetté*), a jump onto both feet (*pas assemblé*), or a hop from one foot to the same foot, for which there is no special term in the French treatises.

The *pas glissé* makes an impressive, beautiful step because the foot slides, or glides, to its new place rather than simply moving there. A *glissé* is a slow, sustained effort which is especially elegant to see. A step-unit using a *pas glissé* often marks the resting place in a dance phrase if more active steps have preceded it (as in the opening phrase of *La Bourée d'Achille*, Ex. III-1). Step-units which use this gliding movement include the *pas coupé*, which is composed of a *demi-coupé* and (often) a *pas glissé*, and the *tems de courante*, composed of a bend, rise, and *pas glissé*. This is the slowest and most sustained of the step-units, a noble gesture unique to French Court dancing.

Turns add grace to the steps, especially when they are *pirouettes*. From the *plié* one rises with the weight on both feet, the heels slightly raised from the floor and the legs straight, turning as little as a quarter turn or as much as a whole turn. In theatrical dances, turns of a once and a half around or more, with the weight on one foot, are commonplace for men by about 1700 and in dances for women by 1712.

The arms and hands add to the graceful picture by changing position, usually once or twice per measure. Fig. I-2 shows a dancer with particularly expressive arms and hands. The arms and hands make carefully controlled circular motions mostly below the shoulders. These motions are coordinated with those of the legs, so that during a *plié* preceding the downbeat of a measure the arms rotate inward until the palms face the floor; on the *élevé* the arms circle upward, usually with one arm higher than the other, and with the higher arm in opposition to the leg which moved. In Fig. I-2 the left leg is receiving the transference of weight while the right arm is in opposition to it and higher than the left arm, thus creating a graceful and balanced picture.

From all of this one can see that in most dances the step-units are structured to emphasize the downbeat of a measure of music. The *plié* articulates each measure and the *élevé* (or spring) accents the first pulse, enhanced and verified by the use of the arms and hands. But how are the step-units joined into phrases?

Rhythmically the step-units have a certain degree of flexibility. They can be performed in duple or triple meter simply by adjusting the amount of time given to each of the actions following the initial *plié* and *élevé*. They can also be done at various tempi, slower or faster. Many step-units are used in almost every type of dance—the *pas de bourée, tems de courante, pas coupés,* and *contretemps de gavotte,* for example. Furthermore, the step-units may be grouped into phrases in a great variety of ways, seemingly limited only by the choreographer's ingenuity. On the other hand, certain step-units were customary only in certain dance types. The *pas de menuet* was used only in the minuet and (in a faster tempo) in the passepied; the *pas de courante* appears only in the courante. In addition, dance types such as the gigue and the gavotte use primarily the lively springing steps, whereas the sarabande and the courante are characterized by the slow, sustained *tems de courante* and other steps with *pas glissé,* with only occasional springing steps.

As an example of how phrases are formed in French Court dancing, consider the step-units in the first section of *La Bourée d'Achille* (Fig. III-1). The two strains are four and eight measures long respectively. The first consists of two measures of *pas de bourée* and a *contretemps de gavotte,* followed by a *tems de courante* in measure 4. One may think of this phrase as three measures of movement (arsis) followed by one measure of repose (thesis). One may abbreviate the shape of the phrase as "aaAT," where "A" signifies a moment which is more arsic than those signified by "a." Because measure 3 is even more active than the two preceding measures, one might think of it as a "rhythmic climax," a place of greatest activity before the thesis measure. This step sequence is then repeated. The second strain features four *pas de bourées,* two measures of springs (*pas de sissonne*), another *pas de bourée,* and the thesis measure (*pas coupé,* one of the sustained steps). This is a true eight-measure phrase, with no place of repose until the end. One may show its shape by the formula aaaaAATT, with the rhythmic climax in measures 9 and 10. On a repeat of the music later in the piece, the second strain has a different set of steps, which might be thought of as atatAATT. Note that when the rhythmic climax occurs in the fifth and sixth measures of the phrase, the next measure becomes a reduction of activity leading to the restful *pas coupé.*

In all choreographies, the rhythms of music and dance form counter-rhythms at least some of the time. Counter-rhythms create further interest, heighten tension, and may take place on any level of rhythmic activity. An example of counter-rhythms on the level of the pulse may be seen in Fig. III-1, in measure 10, and in measure 6 in the repeat. The two voices of the music form a syncopation, but the rhythm of the dance steps does not. On another level the cadences or points of repose in dance figures do not necessarily coincide with the end of a strain of music. For example, many passepieds and minuets contain dance figures which are accompanied by two bipartite pieces of music. The end of the first piece of music may coincide with the middle of one of the dance figures. This contributes to the forward movement of the piece, avoiding any feeling of repose until the final cadence in the music, which occurs simultaneously with the ending posture of the dancers at the foot of the room, where they began.

Having established our basic definitions and symbols, we return to L'Affilard's concept of dance models. In the present book a dance rhythm is a phrase, usually several measures long, which is characteristic of a certain dance type. The dance rhythm has a specific length and shape in most of the dance types. The length is verified by both harmony and rhythm; the shape consists of frequently used patterns of motion and repose (arsis and thesis). We derive the dance models and the characteristics of the dance types by means of theoretical writings, choreographies, the harmonic patterns of the music (i.e., the arsic and thetic qualities of the harmony), and the various articulation signs composers have added to their pieces. Each chapter in Part II contains a model for the particular dance type it discusses, as well as documentation for the dance model and the usual characteristics of the dance. But lest the reader doubt that these "invisible themes" really existed, consider the words of a leading eighteenth-century theorist and one of Bach's students and admirers, Friedrich Wilhelm Marpurg.

In 1762 Marpurg published *Clavierstücke*, a collection of keyboard pieces, with a practical introduction "for beginners and advanced players" which provided the most detailed and analytical description of a dance form by any eighteenth-century writer. The following quotations speak for themselves; they indicate that our approach to dance music is not original but was already conceived in the 1760s. Marpurg's ideas about hierarchy are set forth in the section entitled "On the Different Types of Composition for Keyboard, and the Organization of Rhythm in a Piece":[17]

Each piece is made up of paragraphs, periods, and phrases.

Each small section of a composition that includes a few measures and is separated from what follows by a point of repose is called a phrase. Two or more of these, of which the last ends with a half-cadence, is called a period; and two or more periods, of which the last ends with a full cadence, make a paragraph.

. . . If we disregard the half measure of two quarter notes with which the piece begins ["La Jeannette," Ex. II-1] and if we call the following whole measure number 1 and the next one number 2, and so on, then these points of repose in the

142, 958

second, fourth, sixth, and eighth measures and, indeed, at the beginning of each of these measures is clearly in evidence. The first point of repose occurs with the notes e-d-c in the second measure, and the second point of repose with b-a-g in the fourth measure, the third again with the first notes of the sixth measure, and the fourth with the full cadence which begins in the seventh measure and is realized in the beginning of the eighth. Since there are four points of repose, it follows that there are four phrases. . . . The first two phrases . . . ending with a half cadence, make a period, and the two last, namely the third and fourth, again make a period. These two periods together form a paragraph.

Before we continue the explanation of "Jeannette," I will define a full cadence, half cadence and *Absatz* [imperfect or feminine cadence]. . . . The full cadence occurs where the bass goes from the fifth to the tonic; the treble, however, either goes through the second or seventh to the tonic. Both last notes of the bass and soprano together make the interval of the octave and both must occur on a strong beat [*guten Tacttheil*], which one calls the caesura, or completion of the cadence. Examples of the full cadence one finds at the end of the Rondeau "Jeannette"; also at the end of the first and second couplets, and at the beginning of the fourth measure in the third couplet.

The half cadence is characterized by the bass moving from the tonic, fourth, or sixth to the fifth. The completion must, like the full cadence, fall on the strong beat [see Ex. II-2]. The two final notes in (a) and (b) make the interval of the fifth, and in (c) an octave.

The mark of the imperfect cadence is that the upper voice usually makes a third against the bass. They are frequently used in place of a half cadence. . . . In the first couplet of "Jeannette," as in the rondeau, there also are four points of repose, in the second, fourth, sixth, and eighth measures. But the first and the second points of repose end in the same way, seeing that the two final notes seem to make a half cadence. But this is not the case; we have only a plain imperfect feminine cadence. For the completion [of the cadence] falls not on the first, but on the second quarter note, and the second quarter note in a two-part beat [i.e., duple beat] is no beat, but a part of the beat and, to be sure, an inferior [i.e., weak] part.

The third point of repose in the first half of the sixth measure, where the completion falls normally, although it is delayed by an appoggiatura, can be taken for a half cadence as well as an imperfect cadence; a half cadence on account of the bass, or the latter because the point of repose happens with a third. Furthermore, the first two phrases form a period, as do the last two. If one wished to extend the first period to the third point of repose, that would be going against the correct procedure because the modulation changes after the second phrase. The two periods again constitute a paragraph and, indeed, the second of the piece.

The second couplet is constructed just like the first. This marks the end of the third paragraph of the piece. The second point of repose of the third couplet ends with a full cadence, and the fourth with a half [cadence], for the delay of the close does not change the essential nature of the half cadence. In this third couplet one finds, at the full cadence on F, the fourth paragraph of the piece, short, to be sure, but nevertheless a paragraph. For the result contains nothing but an interpolated period that stands for a preparation in order to return to the first paragraph, with which the piece closes.

Ex. II-1: "La Jeannette," from Friedrich Wilhelm Marpurg, *Clavierstücke* (1762).

Ex. II-2

Marpurg's analysis shows that he conceived of "La Jeannette"[18] as a carefully articulated work made up of parts arranged hierarchically. Phrases, with points of repose, make up a "period" (i.e., half of the strain in a rondeau) and two periods make a "paragraph" (i.e, a whole strain). In this rondeau the entire piece consists of four "paragraphs," the first repeated several times, since it is the rondeau section; the other three are couplets, which occur only once. The use of the word "paragraph" shows that Marpurg was thinking of a short, concise statement rather than a lengthy discourse, which would have contained many more than four paragraphs. He uses harmonic organization to delineate the structure of "La Jeannette," showing how cadences of different degrees of finality or lack of finality create a sense of order and hierarchy in the succession of phrases.

In the same book Marpurg goes further in his analysis by discussing the gavotte, in particular:

> The gavotte is a composition which is in common time and, of course, set in two sections, with the upbeat beginning with two quarter notes or their equivalent. The gavotte is composed from a simple [unaffected] easy melody, and it is restricted to an equal number of measures, which must, from section to section [phrase to phrase] be kept in even proportion to each other. The gavotte can begin with notes of equivalent value to two quarter notes, and they give the natural tendency to the whole meter [*Metro* = character of the notes in regard to figuration, progression, and movement. Cf. Marpurg, *Clavierstücke*, I, p. 8, paragraph 12]. One understands by this either four eighth notes (of which the first and third can be dotted and the second and fourth reduced to sixteenths), or a dotted quarter note with an eighth following, or a quarter note with two eighths following, or two eighths followed by a quarter or, finally, a half note.
>
> No gavotte can have fewer than four measures for each period or section. In general, there are eight measures for each section. If the first [section] closes in a related key, then in general one allows the second to consist of a single paragraph [two or more periods]; that is, within itself you do not modulate into a related key. If, however, the first section has its cadence in the tonic key, then the cadence in the middle of the second section falls in a related key.
>
> The completion of all cadences must always be masculine as required by the rule of the $\frac{2}{2}$ measure, and the closing note [of the cadence], therefore, without division of the downbeat, fills out the entire value of the half note to which it

belongs. However, one is sometimes allowed a feminine cadence; that is, to close on the second quarter note of the divided downbeat—but only in gavottes that are meant to be dances, and then only chiefly at a cadence in the middle of the second section [see Ex. II-3].

The *Metrum* can be constructed in various ways—with prevailing quarter notes, or prevailing eighths, or mixed. One can, here and there, employ a dot and other similar variations [i.e., dotted notes], the selection of which, as well as the beginning of the upbeat, is dependent upon the character and the movement which one wishes to give to the gavotte. The gavotte can be used to express all kinds of emotion in various degrees, both sadness and joy in different degrees and also in more or less faster and slower tempi.

This piece belongs to the smaller or lesser compositions, but its tempo and *Metrum* also have a place in longer pieces for singing and playing. Many rondeaus are composed the same as gavottes. An example of this is the "Jeannette" in the first part of these keyboard pieces. In addition, it is noteworthy that some composers use $\frac{2}{4}$ time instead of $\frac{2}{2}$. Basically, it doesn't matter as long as the tempo is clearly indicated by the required words. But the usual thing is to use $\frac{2}{2}$ time in the actual gavotte.[19]

Ex. II-3

Marpurg describes the gavotte as having "a simple, easy melody," an equal number of measures in the dance phrases (usually four- or eight-measure phrases), and a fairly predictable harmonic organization delineated by the cadences at the end of two- or four-measure phrases or at the end of the strain. Masculine cadences are normal, with feminine cadences occurring occasionally, and a wide variety of affects and tempi are in use. He refers to "La Jeannette" as a gavotte even though it is not so titled. All these characteristics concur with the ideas set forth in chapter 4 of this book.

Rhythm—"the activity of rhythming"—is indeed the key to an understanding of Bach's dances. As Johann Nicolaus Forkel wrote in 1802 in his well-known biography of Bach:

> The composers of Bach's time had an admirable opportunity to acquire the due and easy management of the various kinds of rhythm, by the so-called suites, which were then common instead of our sonatas. In these suites there were, between the preludes and the concluding jigs, many French characteristic pieces and dance tunes, in which the rhythm was the most important object. The com-

posers were therefore obliged to make use of a great variety of time, measure, and rhythm (which are now for the most part unknown), and to be very expert in them, if they desired to give to every dance tune its precise character and rhythm.

Bach carried this branch of the art also much farther than any of his predecessors or contemporaries. He tried and made use of every kind of meter to diversify, as much as possible, the character of his pieces. He eventually acquired such a facility in this particular that he was able to give even to his fugues, with all the intricate interweaving of their single parts, striking and characteristic rhythmic proportions in a manner as easy and uninterrupted from the beginning to the end as if they were minuets.[20]

PART II
Bach's Dance Music

Part II discusses all of Bach's titled dances. Although each chapter is uniquely organized according to the requirements of the individual dance type, certain features are present in most of them. Each chapter normally begins by setting out some of the most important qualities of the dance type, elucidating its characteristics, and distinguishing it from other similar dance types. Choreography comes next, with a discussion of character and tempo, relying heavily on writers and theorists from Bach's time, but also drawing on choreographic information. An example of an actual dance or part of a dance illustrates these points. Following that is the model dance rhythm which shows the essential temporal characteristics of the dance type, with discussion and examples. Next is a survey of the performance techniques useful in rendering dance music of this type, with information on phrasing, articulation, and rhythmic alteration, including bowing,[1] tonguing, and fingering practices wherever such information is available. All of this is illustrated with music by composers of Bach's time or before, using many different styles and including vocal as well as instrumental pieces, soloist as well as ensemble music.

We do not always repeat important information when analogous situations occur in several of Bach's dances in the same chapter. Thus, even if a reader is interested in only one piece, comments about other dances of that type may be helpful. The suggestions for performance arose from our understanding of performance conventions, choreography, and the structure and style of each individual piece.

Appendix A lists all of Bach's titled dances, in approximately chronological order. Unfortunately, many of them do not have firm dates and perhaps never will, despite much recent research. Our lists are as accurate as possible, relying particularly on *The New Grove Bach Family*.

Appendix B lists Bach's untitled dances, that is, works which appear to be based on a dance type but which do not bear a dance title. Though these lists are not exhaustive, they provide telling witness to the pervasive influence of dance rhythms in both the sacred and the secular music of Bach.

As sources of Bach's music we have relied mainly on the now out-of-date but easily accessible Bach-Gesellschaft edition, as improved by the Neue Bach-Ausgabe, and supplemented by facsimiles of manuscripts and prints from the time of Bach.[2] See the Bibliography for these sources and for the Bischoff editions of Bach's music, which we recommend highly.

We discuss all the titled dances used by Bach except the allemande and the siciliano. We exclude allemandes because by Bach's time they no longer reflected a particular dance form. In a study of allemandes of this period we discovered neither clear choreographic roots nor distinguishable recurring rhythmic patterns; nor did we find any choreographies. Natalie Jenne's article on the performance of Baroque allemandes offers an introduction to this often prelude-like form.[3]

We exclude the siciliano for the same reason; although earlier it was undoubtedly associated with dancing, the siciliano of Bach's time is essentially an aria without surviving choreographic roots. The six titled sicilianos by Bach appear only in sonatas and concertos, not in his Suites, Partitas, or any other works which contain other titled dances.

In numbering measures in musical and dance examples we follow the system of the Neue Bach-Ausgabe. Numbering begins with the first full measure, leaving any upbeats unnumbered. Second endings are not numbered, nor are repeats indicated by signs or double bars with dots. Numbering continues throughout the two or more written strains of a piece, but in rondeaus the rondeau section is numbered only once.

BWV 831/I

CHAPTER 3
The Bourée

The bourée is rhythmically the least complex of all the French Baroque dances. Its character was described by eighteenth-century theorists as gay (*gaie*) or joyful (*lustig*), and it is played "lightly" (*fort légèrement*), or perhaps "lightheartedly."[1] Johann Mattheson describes its gentle nature: "its essential characteristic is contentment, pleasantness, unconcern, relaxed, easy going, comfortable, and yet pleasing."[2] Bourées do not expose the depths of a composer's soul, but they do express a genuine, aristocratic *joie de vivre*.

The music to *La Bourée d'Achille* (Fig. III-1), a popular duet at court balls of the early eighteenth century, shows many of the bourée's characteristics at that time. The metric hierarchy (II–2–2) is duple on all levels, the beat is the half note, and harmonic change is primarily on the beat and pulse levels. Most bourées have a time signature of either 2 or ¢, with two half note beats to the measure. A few use the time signature $\frac{2}{4}$, in which case the beat is the quarter note.

Most eighteenth-century theorists describe the bourée tempo as fast in comparison with the other French Baroque dances, though Charles Masson specifies that both the bourée and the rigaudon have the same tempo as the gigue; i.e., bourée and riguadon beats move at the same speed as gigue beats.[3] Georg Muffat indicates that the bourée tempo is generally faster than that of the gavotte, even though both dances have the same metric structure.[4] Danced bourées employ many lively steps, such as the *pas de sissonne, jettés chassés,* and *glissades,* adding to its reputation as a fast dance. On the other hand, the Christoph and Stössel *Lexicon* (1737) describes the bourée as "a slow French dance" which had been in use for many years.[5] This comment

Fig. III-1: Music and dance in the first portion of *La Bourée d'Achille,* a ballroom dance choreographed by Louis-Guillaume Pécour, **Pécour:1700Recueil,** pp. 1, 10–11.

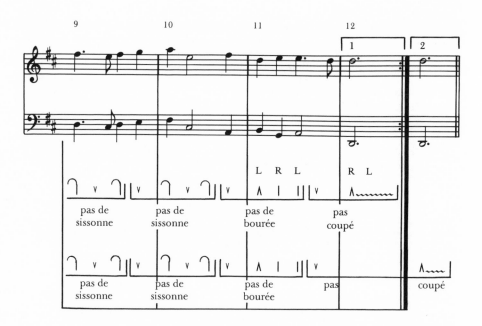

underlines the fact that the noble court bourée was indeed slower than the newer (possibly non-aristocratic or non-French) dances of the 1720s and 1730s, even though the bourée was generally faster than the other French Baroque dances. Some performers play the bourée extremely fast, but too fast a tempo will render the articulations of beats and pulses imperceptible, depriving the dance of its unique rhythmic qualities (see Fig. III-2 and Ex. III-1). A tempo of ♩ = MM 80–88 is not too slow for many bourées.[6]

In the bourée dance rhythm (Fig. III-2) the rhythmic-harmonic phrase is eight beats in length (four measures), preceded by an upbeat, usually two eighth notes or a quarter note. Beat 7 and the first half of 8 constitute the primary repose, or thesis; beat 3 and the first half of 4 provide a preliminary resting point, or secondary thesis.[7]

A thesis in the bourée has the value of three quarter notes, all on a single harmony (♩. or ♩ ♫♩ or ♫♫♩). The thetic quality is best achieved in performance by phrasing all three pulses together: ♩♫♩, not ♩.♫♩ or ♩ ♫.♩ (Ex. III-1d, measures 4 and 8; Ex.III-1f, measures 2 and 4). In fact, stepwise melodic figures in the rhythms ♩ ♫♩ and ♫♫♩ (Fig. III-1, measure 2; Ex. III-1c, measure 4; Ex. III-1f, measure 2) are virtual trademarks of the bourée since they mark the thesis of interior cadences so frequently.

The upper voice of measures 3–4 of *La Bourée d'Achille* (Fig. III-1) contains a characteristic bourée cadential formula: ♩ ♩ ♩. ♪ |♩.. An ornament on

Ex. III-1: Lower-level articulations in the bourée. a. Bourée with bowing indications,
Muffat:FS, Ex. 24; b. Bowing example from **Montéclair:Violon;** c. **Dupont:Violon,**
p. 34; d. First strain of *Bourée en Rondeau,* by Jean-François Dandrieu, with fingering
added by the composer; e. "Bourée Paysanne," measures 9–16, for viole and basse
continue, from Marin Marais, *Pieces de Violes,* Livre III (Paris, 1711); f. First strain of
a bourée for two instruments and basse continue, from François Couperin, *Les Na-*
tions, IIIe. Ordre (Paris, 1726).

T = *tirer,* or down-bow equivalent
P = *pousse,* or up-bow equivalent

Explanation of bowing in the bourée. Q. What do you say about the bourée? A. When it begins with two eighth notes take both of them up-bow; when [in the middle of the piece] there are two eighth notes between two quarter notes, take both eighth notes up-bow; when there are two eighths after a half note syncopation, take both eighth notes up-bow; if a quarter note follows the syncopation, take the quarter note up-bow also.

Explication du coup d'archet, de la Bourée. D. Qu'elle remarque faite vous de la Bourée. R. Lorsqu'elle cōmence par 2. croches, il faut les pousser toutes 2. et lorsqu'il y a 2 croches, entre 2. noires, il faut pousser les 2. croches de même. Lorsqu'il y a 2. croches, apres une blanche sincopé, il faut pousser les 2. croches, ou la noire qui est apres elle.

beat 6 (dotted quarter note in measure 3) is stylistically appropriate, as is a shortening of the eighth note leading to the thesis on beat 7. This intensifies the arsic nature of beats 5–6 and makes the thesis, by contrast, a place of repose.

Arsic measures very often consist of duple groupings of pulses, which, if carefully articulated, will contrast strongly with the thetic measures. For example, the first four measures of *La Bourée d'Achille* might be performed in this manner: ♩ | ♩ ♩ ♩ ♩ | ♩ ♫ ♩ ♩ | ♩ ♩ ♩ | ♪ | ♩.

The same technique works in the first four-measure phrase of Ex. III-1d, giving it a characteristic bourée identity. On the other hand, the composer may avoid an interior thesis by a change of harmony on beat 4, thus dividing the measure into twos even though a thesis was expected in measure 6. The phrasing of the second phrase thus contrasts with the first, answering it with duple groupings of pulses in measures 5–7 followed by a thesis only in measure 8.

A syncopation (♩ ♩ ♩) is also characteristic of bourées, and composers use them in several interesting ways. It is frequently heard in arsic measures to intensify the forward movement of the phrase. In the middle of Marin Marais' "Bourée Paysanne" (Ex. III-1e, measures 12–14) the composer himself marks phrasing which forces an articulation before the half note of the syncopation. Another usage, the less-intense syncopation-with-change-of-harmony, appears in Fig. III-1, measures 6 and 10, where it avoids an expected repose. A third usage is syncopation-on-the-same-harmony, as in measure 8 of the same piece, where it marks the dominant cadence in the

Fig. III-2: Model for the Bourée Dance Rhythm

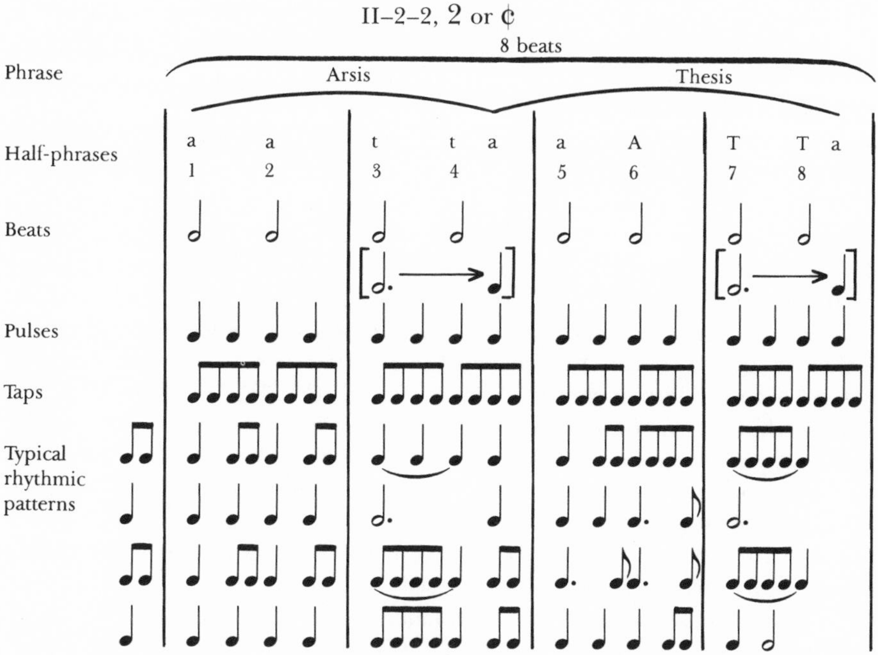

II–2–2, 2 or ¢

middle of the strain. See also Ex. III-1a, measure 2; Ex. III-1b, measures 4, 8, 10, and 14; and BWV 831/I, measure 4 (at the head of this chapter).

The French theorist Pierre Dupont offers special instruction for bowing the *syncope* (Ex. III-1c, measures 10 and 14); and Freillon-Poncein offers a specific tonguing pattern to wind players: ♩ ♩ ♩.[8] Both imply an articulation between the first and second notes of the syncopation.

Because of its active qualities syncopation is not used much in the final thesis of a strain, at least not in the eighteenth century. Jean-Baptiste Lully used syncopation at the end of the first strain in some bourées of ballets in the 1660s,[9] and this also occurs in contemporaneous bourées of the Kassel Manuscript[10] and in the two keyboard bourées in B major by Nicholas Lebègue in *Les Pièces de clavessin* (Paris, 1677).

Another characteristic of the bourée might be termed its "upbeat quality," which refers to an abundance of quick anapestic rhythms (♫♩), which are lively and forward-moving, creating a lilt to the rhythm from the pulse and tap levels. They are often effective with an accent at the end (♫♩) except when they are part of a syncopation; in that case they sound well with the accent at the beginning (♫♩), especially when the harmony is the same for all three notes. Of course, interesting cross-rhythms may be created by varying the articulation of such anapestic figures, especially in the longer bourées of J. S. Bach, such as those in BWV 807, 820, 816, and 996.

The bourée dance rhythm begins with an upbeat. To clarify the bourée structure it should be slightly detached from the note that follows, in the middle of a strain as well as at the beginning of the piece (Ex. III-1d, measure 4; Ex. III-1f, measure 2).

Ex. III-1 offers numerous examples of articulations in pulse- and tap-level rhythms in the bourée. They show that composers and theorists expected the performer to give rhythmic life to these levels as well as to the larger continuity of the four-, six-, and eight-measure phrases. Eighth notes often receive special attention. Muffat (Ex. III-1a) uses a separate bow stroke for each eighth or quarter note, but Dupont and Marais (Ex. III-1c and 1e) slur eighths together in pairs fairly often. Montéclair (Ex. III-1b) uses a different tap-level bowing in two different places (measures 7 and 13). Quantz states that "A bourée and a rigaudon are executed gaily, and with a short and light bow-stroke."[11] *Notes inégales*, when appropriate, may be applied to the tap level, or eighth notes.

The bourée dance rhythm as shown in Fig. III-2—its eight-beat length as well as its patterns of motion and repose—appears also in dance and poetry throughout the baroque period. The dance steps to *La Bourée d'Achille* (Fig. III-1) form four- and eight-measure phrases, a normal length, though sometimes one finds phrases of twelve or sixteen measures. Although balanced phrasing is normal in bourées, it is not an invariable characteristic, as in the minuet, gavotte, and sarabande.[12] The shape of a bourée phrase is that of a comparatively restful step or step-unit in measure 4, preceded by more-active step-units using springs and forward movement. The first important grouping of steps in the dance is by measure, which contrasts with the music in that the beat (or half measure) is a significant grouping of pulses and taps. The syncopation rhythm does not occur in the dance steps, so the music and the dance are always in counter-rhythm whenever syncopation occurs in the music (Fig. III-1, measures 6, 8, and 10).

Ex. III-2 shows a bourée in poetry, with the text carefully divided according to bourée structure. The syncopation appears in a thesis position, mostly in interior cadences. Its function, however, is not to create gaiety or excitement but to provide a place of temporary repose in the flow of words. The alternation of phrases with and without the syncopation gives balance to the poem (counting syllables): first strain, 7 8 8 7; second strain, 8 7 8 7.

Although the bourée was popular in early eighteenth-century French ballets and other theatrical works, it appears less often in French solo and chamber music. German composers of suites and symphonic music favored it more than did their French counterparts, and J. S. Bach wrote many of them.

Ex. III-2: A bourée song, from *Brunetes ou petits airs tendres,* Vol. III (Paris, 1711), arranged from Jean-Baptiste Lully's *Serenade* from *Ballet de l'Impatience* (1661).

Som-mes nous pas trop heu-reux Belle I - ris Que vous en
Mon coeur est sous vô - tre loy Et n'en peut ai - mer un

sem - ble? Nous voi - ci tous deux en - sem - ble Et nous
au - tre Lais-sez - moy voir dans le vô - tre Ce qui

nous ai - mons tous deux. La nuit des ses som - bres
s'y pas - se pour moy. La nuit est calme et pro -

voi - les Cou-vre nos dé - sirs ar - dens; Et l'A -
fon - de Nul ne vient mal à - pro - pos, Le re -

mour et les E - toi - les Sont nos se - crets con - fi - dents
pos de tout le mon-de As-su - re no - tre re - pos.

BACH'S USE OF THE BOURÉE

Twenty titled bourées by Bach have survived. But since eight of these pieces actually consist of two contrasting bourées, and the Bourée in BWV 1002 is followed by a *double* (variation of the same piece), one may say that the total number of bourées is actually twenty-nine. They appear in all four of the orchestral suites, in two of the English and two of the French suites for keyboard, in two of the solo suites for cello, and in the Partita for solo flute. The earliest are in keyboard works from Bach's Weimar years (1708–14); and the last two, in the Orchestral Suite in B minor (BWV 1067), date from the late 1730s.

The Bourée in the keyboard suite in G minor (BWV 822) may have been Bach's arrangement of another composer's piece;[13] typical anapestic rhythms characterize much of this piece. His next three bourées—in BWV 820, 832, and 996—are similar to each other in that all have a two-part texture with equal voices, frequent use of anapestic rhythms, and a structure clearly based on four- and eight-measure phrases.

Stylistically, the bourées in the English Suites BWV 806 and 807 are more mature and more highly developed. Although still in a two-part texture, both now have two bourées, the first with longer phrases and the second in contrasting French musette style (the simple harmony implies a drone bass, and the four-measure phrases are unusually clear). A harmonic *tour de force* (a series of harmonies which resolve only at the end of a long phrase), not in the previous bourées, appears in the first strain of BWV 807, Bourée I (measures 9–24) and in BWV 806, Bourée I (measures 25–40). Here Bach creates ambiguity by temporarily obscuring the four-measure phrase structure, using harmonies to weaken or avoid cadences in places where they would be expected. *Notes inégales* are appropriate in stepwise passages in both sets of bourées; the slurs in BWV 806, Bourée I may actually suggest this practice.[14]

The two bourée sets from the orchestral suites written in the Köthen or the early Leipzig days (1717–25) show Bach trying other new techniques, especially with syncopations. In BWV 1066, Bourée II, syncopation typically occurs in all three arsic measures of most four-measure phrases. In BWV 1069, Bourée I, the first strain has syncopation in measures 1–2 and 6 of an eight-measure phrase, and the second strain uses it in just as many measures in the phrase. In BWV 1069, Bourée II, the syncopation appears if one accents the first note of an ornamental written-out turn figure in the inner voices of the lower choir. BWV 1066, Bourée II, is quite French in its clearly defined, carefully cadenced four-measure phrases; whereas in BWV 1069, though the structure is always clear, it is enhanced by Italian-style orchestral practices such as the antiphonal use of three choirs in Bourée I and contrasting textures and rhythms, with brass and percussion absent, in Bourée II.

In the "Tempo di Bourree" of Partita I for solo violin, (BWV 1002), the bourée structure is clearly present and is a necessary grounding for Bach's variations in the *double*. In measure 12 of both pieces an articulation before beat 1 will emphasize the avoided cadence. In the *double* the articulations should be very clear, with syncopations clearly projected, in order to avoid performing an endless stream of undifferentiated sound. The bowings in this piece are rare in Bach's dances because they sometimes cross the bar line (i.e., measures 18–19 and 56–57).

In Partita III for solo violin (BWV 1006), Bach employs ambiguity, not in the middle of a piece (as in the bourées of BWV 806 and 807) but in the very first phrase—a bold gesture and a departure from "usual" bourée practices, including his own. It might be articulated differently on the repeat, with the exception of the thesis measure, which, to signal the bourée, must have the first three pulses slurred together. The solo violin uses a broken-chord technique to evoke a two- to three-part texture; sequences and echo effects abound; and one is far from the French bourée style except for the underlying harmonic structure. Bach arranged the same piece for lute (BWV 1006a)—without altering the ambiguous opening phrase—but weakened some of the cadences (e.g., in measure 4) to ensure forward movement.

More bourées in pairs, from about the same years in Köthen, occur in the cello suites BWV 1009 and 1010, as Bach again experiments with the problem of projecting four-part harmony with a single-voiced instrument. The clear French bourée rhythmic structure of these pieces may be made evident by the articulation techniques described earlier in this chapter. The Anna Magdalena manuscript, which was probably copied from Bach's without embellishment, gives bowings which underscore the dance rhythms. In no instances do these bowings cross the bar line, as they often do in the Bach-Gesellschaft edition of the music. In the manuscript the upbeat is clearly defined, but in the Bach-Gesellschaft edition it is obscured by the slurring of the upbeat *tirata* sixteenth notes with the following quarter note. In all the dances of the cello suites in the Anna Magdalena manuscript, none of the bowings cross a bar line.

Slight tempo changes will help to contrast the two bourées of each pair, should the performer find this desirable; for example, in BWV 1009 the second one might be played slightly faster than the first, and, conversely, in BWV 1010 the second might be played slightly slower than its predecessor. The slower tempo allows the syncopations to occur with elegance and breadth. For a graceful performance in BWV 1010, Bourée II, use an anticipatory space between the first and second notes of a measure with syncopation, adding an *agrément* on the second note (e.g., a mordant on the second note in measure 1 and a *port de voix* in the same place in measure 2). The performer may find that *notes inégales* add grace to Bourée II of BWV 1009.

The Bourée for solo flute, from BWV 1013, is a difficult piece with seemingly no place to breathe. Use of the bourée dance tempo will solve the problem, and the breathing may be artistically integrated into a nuanced rendition with graceful *agréments*.

The keyboard Bourée in the Suite in E♭ major (BWV 819) is in mixed French and Italian style, with numerous syncopations (in measures 1, 2, 3, 5, and 7) and two- and three-part texture; a tempo suitable for dancing will not be too slow for this stylized example (= MM 80–88).

The keyboard bourées from the French Suites BWV 816 and 817 are very similar to each other. Both employ two-part writing in Italian instrumental style, with harmonic sequences, broken chords, and melodies following chordal rather than stepwise motion; a rather fast tempo may be appropriate. Neither uses syncopation, but Bach anchors them to the old French bourée by rigid adherence to the dance rhythm. *Notes inégales* are effective in BWV 817 in the stepwise passages preceding major cadences (measures 9–11, 21–23, 29–32, and 36–39).

The two bourées from the Leipzig symphonic suites BWV 1067 and 1068 are similarly anchored to the bourée dance rhythm but also seem distant from French dance style. Bach's Italian embellishments include melodic and harmonic sequences, a flute solo with string accompaniment (in BWV 1067, Bourée II), and ostinato bass (in BWV 1067, Bourée I). Clues to the old bourée include frequent syncopations in BWV 1067 and anapestic rhythms in BWV 1068.

Bach's last titled bourée set for keyboard, Overture in the French Style, in B minor (BWV 831) is surprising after all his previous experimentation. Bourée I takes no liberties and would easily serve as a textbook model of this style, with all expected characteristics woven into a seamless work of genius; *notes inégales* seem appropriate for stepwise passages. But Bourée II is unique and unorthodox: it has an upbeat of three eighth notes and appears to be in the style of a prelude. Bach employs ambiguity, and the performer may use a slight fluctuation of the beat, to lead the listener far from the ballroom.

BWV 816

CHAPTER 4
The Gavotte

The gavotte was beloved as court dance and music for over two centuries. It was danced in one form at least by the 1580s and continued with various different types of steps and music through the 1790s. Part of its popularity undoubtedly derived from the great regularity of the music and a predictable rhyme and balance, which seem out of place in an era designated "Baroque." Yet the classic proportions of the gavotte, both as music and as dance, reached a high point in popularity during the "pastoral" craze of the 1720s and 1730s when those who lived in cities and courts idealized a simpler rural life, with shepherds and shepherdesses doing rustic dances outdoors to the accompaniment of bagpipes. It was during this period that Bach wrote most of his gavottes, frequently including pastoral references but always retaining the ideals of a calm balance and an expected rhyme, which are so characteristic of this dance.

The gavotte could express a great variety of affect, ranging from "tender" (Bacilly[1]) and "graceful" (Dupont[2]) to "joyful" (Mattheson[3]). Freillon-Poncein, the French oboist and flutist, described gavottes as "very slow and serious airs, whose expressiveness is very touching."[4] In 1740 James Grassineau wrote in his dictionary that the gavotta, or gavotte, is "brisk and lively by nature."[5] In Rousseau's *Dictionnaire de Musique* (1768) one finds that "the movement of the gavotte is ordinarily graceful, often gay, and sometimes also tender and slow."[6] Marpurg said it could be either sad or joyful.[7] Though contrasting, these are all generally moderate affects, not violent or extreme ones.

A great variety of tempi were used in gavottes, although still within a "moderate" range. Jean-Jacques Rousseau insisted that gavottes could be "fast or slow, but never extremely fast or excessively slow."[8] The Abbé Démotz, in 1728, said that it moves in two slow beats (i.e., two half-note beats to the measure).[9] In comparison with other French dances, Georg Muffat stated that it is not as fast as the bourée;[10] and Quantz mentioned that it is more moderate in tempo than the rigaudon.[11] Dupont, in 1718, said that the gavotte is also a little slower than the march.[12] Composers sometimes wrote tempo indications for the gavotte, probably because the dance music by itself did not suggest a specific tempo. For example, both François Couperin and Henri d'Anglebert wrote gavottes marked "lentement" or "tendrement."

In instrumental music there were at least two distinct national styles in the gavotte of the early eighteenth century. Mattheson described a French and an Italian type of gavotte. The latter, used especially by Italian composers, was written for the violin and featured "excesses," specifically a fast tempo and a virtuoso performance style.[13] Montéclair illustrated two types of gavotte, one marked "léger" with a time signature of 2 in which the eighth notes would have been performed *inégale,* and the other marked "presto" in a time signature of $\frac{2}{4}$ with instructions to play *Croches égales* (i.e., to avoid the *inégales* of the French style).[14]

Fig. IV-1 shows the opening measures of three early eighteenth-century gavotte choreographies, illustrating several forms of the dance. Fig. IV-1a has the opening phrase of a virtuoso theatrical dance, a duet for two gentlemen. The steps occur on the eighth-note level and include elaborate leg gestures and leaps. The dance rhythms are subtle and the steps are often ornamented. The music and dance relationship is complex, with almost constant counter-rhythms; agreement comes only on beat 8 (downbeat of measure 4). This dance is through-composed, meaning that new steps occur constantly, without repeated sections.

Fig IV-1b, *La Gavotte de Seaux,* a duet for a gentleman and a lady, is also through-composed but is a much simpler dance, intended for the pleasures of the ballroom. One step-unit is set per measure, and the *assemblée* on the first beat of measure 4 closes the phrase with music and dance in accord. Counter-rhythms between music and dance occur in measures 1–3, however; beat 1 of the music has no dance step, and when the dance enters the steps move to beats 2–3, 4–5, 6–7, with agreement finally on beat 8. The counter-rhythms were undoubtedly enjoyed by dancers once they had learned to be independent of the music, since the thesis, or arrival, occurs in both the music and the dance on beat 8.

The dance in Fig. IV-1c, for two gentlemen and two ladies, is simpler than either of the first two, and was probably taken at a faster tempo. It is entitled

Fig. IV-1: Music and dance in three French gavotte choreographies of the early eighteenth century. a. *Entrée pour deux hommes,* from Louis-Guillaume Pécour, *Recueil de Dances* (Paris, 1704), p. 148; choreography by Pécour, music by Lully; b. *La Gavotte de Seaux,* from *XIIe. Recueil de danses pour l'année 1714* (Paris, 1714) p. 3; choreography by Balon, music anonymous; c. *Le Cotillon,* from *IIIe. Recueil de danses de bal pour l'année 1705* (Paris, 1705) p. 1; choreography and music anonymous.

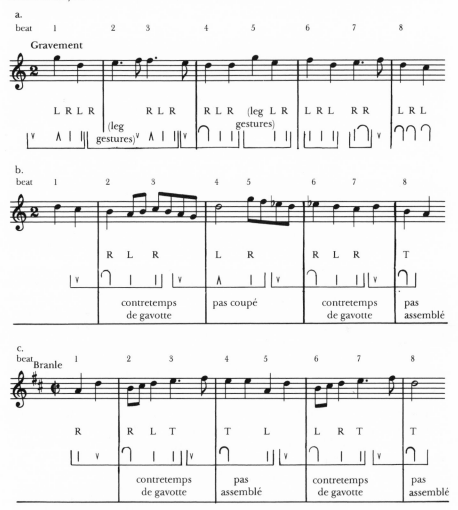

"Branle" and is actually an early form of contredanse, in which a few step-units repeat continuously throughout the piece. Furthermore, a step occurs on beat 1 of the music, which avoids the counter-rhythms. *Le Cotillon* is not labeled "gavotte," but the music is clearly of this dance type. These steps are so easy, the notator of the dance says, that one can dance this piece "without ever having learned it.''[15] *Le Cotillon* is a rondeau, a form used frequently in gavottes.

The metric structure of the gavotte (Fig. IV-2) is identical to that of the bourée, that is, duple on all levels (II–2–2). The beat is the half note, harmonic change is primarily on the beat and pulse levels, and the meter sign is 2 or ¢. Even though the bourée also has all these characteristics, the gavotte is quite a different dance because of its balanced, rhyming phrases and its slower tempo, allowing more possibilities for subtleties.

Fig. IV-2: Model for the Gavotte Dance Rhythm
II–2–2, 2 or ¢

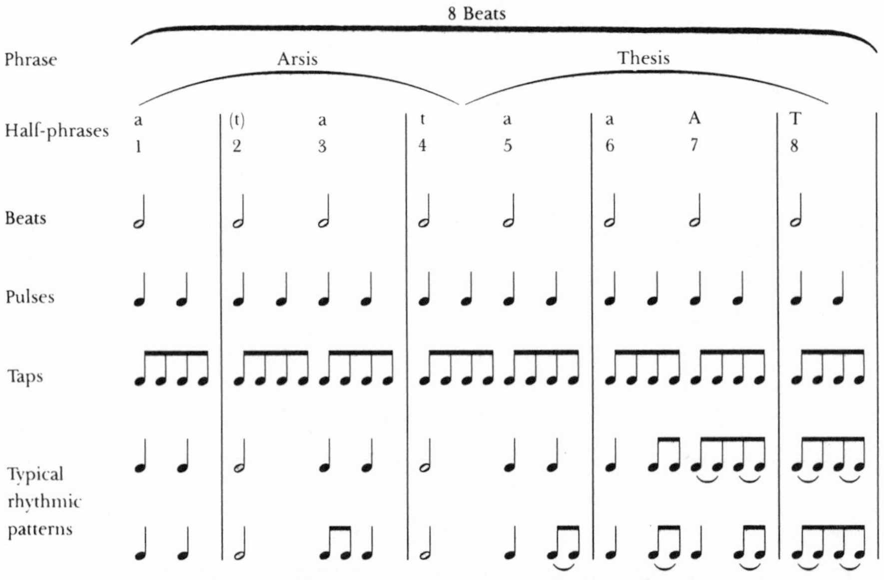

The gavotte dance rhythm consists of a rhythmic-harmonic phrase eight beats in length (four measures), divided into 4 + 4 beats. Normally, all phrases on a given level are of equal length. The grouping of beats by twos crosses bar lines. Since the phrase divides neatly in the middle (after the fourth beat), it may be thought of as "question and answer" or "statement and counterstatement." Beat 8 is the primary thetic point of the rhythmic phrase, and beat 4 is a secondary thesis. Marpurg's exposition on the gavotte (see chapter 2, above) is an eighteenth-century version of these same ideas, though Marpurg emphasizes the measure level, calling the eight-measure phrase the basic unit, instead of a four-measure phrase made up of eight half-note beats.

Because both the gavotte and the bourée have identical metric structures, the two dances may be difficult for the modern listener to distinguish if the performer does not clearly project their rhythmic differences: mainly that the gavotte begins in the middle of the measure and the bourée begins on the downbeat. In Fig. IV-2 the first beat of the gavotte dance rhythm comes before the first bar line; thus, the grouping of beats by twos occurs *across* the bar line. This is in contrast to the bourée, in which the grouping of beats by twos occurs inside the measure (see Fig. III-2). It is just this quality—the beats beginning in the middle of the measure to form a rhythmic unit across the bar, and moving in pairs to a thesis on beat 8—that distinguishes the gavotte most clearly from the bourée, in which the beats begin on the downbeat of the measure (after a short upbeat), form rhythmic units within the bar, and move to a thesis on beat 7.

This analysis is not a modern one but is rooted in the performance practice of the early eighteenth century. For example, numerous French theorists of the period describe the half measure of the gavotte as a "beat," i.e., one movement of the arm in beating time. Saint-Lambert said, in his 1702 harpsichord treatise,

> When pieces like these begin with half a measure, as in the examples of slow duple and $\frac{6}{8}$ time above, and if the measure is beaten in two as in these same examples, one must start to beat with the upbeat and not with the downbeat, as one does in other pieces. But if the piece starts with a quarter or a third of a measure, or sometimes less, as in the other examples, then one only starts to beat on the first note of the first complete measure. That which precedes it is played or sung while holding the hand in the air ready to fall on the first beat of the measure. Allemandes, courantes, gigues, rigaudons, and bourées are pieces of this last type.[16]

Freillon-Poncein, writing in 1700, made a similar statement in his tutor for the oboe: "The above [bourées] are not the same as Gavottes. . . . To succeed well with them, you must begin on the second beat of the measure, which is indicated with a 2, and count it very slowly."[17]

It is interesting to note that gavottes in the sixteenth century and well into the seventeenth began on the downbeat of the measure, not in the middle. This may reflect a different type of piece, or it may simply be another type of measure organization. Examples appear in Arbeau's *Orchésography*, Michael Praetorius' *Terpsichore*, the Kassel manuscript, the Uppsala manuscript and some seventeenth-century works of G. M. Bononcini (Opus 1, 1666), Arcangelo Corelli, and N.-A. Lebègue.[18] The internal phrase organization appears to be identical with that of later gavottes, though there are stylistic differences, such as the type of harmonies used. It is possible that composers changed gavotte music to begin at mid-bar in order to reflect the different rhythmic structure of the gavotte dance phrase and to distinguish it from the typical phrases of other duple-meter dances, such as the bourée, rigaudon, allemande, and La Mariée. It is also possible that a new and different type of gavotte was intended by beginning at mid-measure. One of the first composers (possibly the very first) to set the gavotte in the new manner was Jean-Baptiste Lully, whose earliest recorded gavottes are in the *Ballet des Plaisirs* (1655).

What articulations are appropriate to the basic rhythmic phrase of the gavotte? An articulation after beat 4 will create a perfect sense of balance in the two-member, eight-beat phrase. Ex. IV-1 shows a dance song by Michel L'Affilard in which the composer has added breath marks for the singer after every four beats, underlining the text and dividing the phrase into two statements which complement, or answer, each other. The bass part keeps the phrase moving forward so that the piece does not "stop" at this point. To emphasize the complementary nature of the two sections, the text has a "feminine" rhyme on the fourth beat ("ap*pelle*") and a "masculine" rhyme on the eighth beat ("ai*mer*"); the former helps keep the movement going, while the latter creates repose. For further contrast the thesis on beat 4 is marked by an *agrément,* and the thesis on beat 8 by a half note (long note). L'Affilard's dance-song, which is in rondeau form, continues in similar fashion throughout the entire piece, with a caesura (breath mark) for the singer after every four beats and a "masculine" rhyme in the text on every eighth beat.

Ex. IV-1: Gavotte song en rondeau, **L'Affilard:Principes,** p. 53.

Within the phrase, an articulation before beat 2 (the downbeat of the first full measure) serves as a "trademark" to indicate that the piece is, indeed, a gavotte. Numerous manuscripts and printed works of the eighteenth century even wrote this articulation, which is a definite break, right into the music. In Ex. IV-2 François Couperin includes it in both of the eight-beat phrases which make up the first strain of the piece (his sign for "leave a little space" is the vertical episema, seen in the upper voice on the notes preceding measures 1 and 5).

Another aspect of the gavotte which is shown in this example is the importance of each beat; Couperin's ornamentation clearly emphasizes the beginning of almost every beat by *agréments* of various sorts. Thus the beats do not "run together," but are clearly separated in a lightly articulated style. The

Ex. IV-2: First strain of a keyboard gavotte, **Couperin:Pièces,** I, 2 (1713).

exception is beat 3 of each phrase, which is deemphasized by tying it harmonically to beat 2 in both phrases in this strain; linking beats 2 and 3 builds
toward the release of tension in beat 4 and gives shape to the first four-beat
segment of the phrase.

The excerpts by Couperin, Saint-Lambert, and Dandrieu (Exx. IV-2–4) all
feature an ornamented dotted quarter note and an eighth note on beat 7, a
typical cadential rhythm used in gavottes. The performer may emphasize this
arsic situation, and thus intensify the phrase, by overdotting the quarter note
and shortening the eighth note; leaving a small space before the shortened
eighth note effectively heightens the tension.

In Ex. IV-3 the French theorist-composer Saint-Lambert has meticulously
provided fingerings for his keyboard gavotte; the use of the same finger on
two consecutive notes forces an articulation between the notes. Though the
amount of the space is unspecified in such an articulation, one may safely
assume that, if the notes in question are far apart on the keyboard, a larger
space will ensue than if the notes are close together. For example, there is a

considerable articulation in the bass between beats 3 and 4 of the phrase, probably in order to signal the thesis on beat 4. On the other hand, the articulation between beats 2 and 3 of the upper voice, being on the same note, would probably be very slight (even though a large articulation is theoretically possible), just enough to emphasize beat 3 but not enough to interrupt the forward motion. The same situation occurs between beats 4 and 5— a large articulation in the bass but a much smaller one in the upper voice, signaling both the halfway point in the phrase and the continuing forward motion to the thesis on beat 8. On beat 1 as well as beat 5 the consecutive 2–4 fingerings require detached pulses, which emphasize the arsic quality in these beats.

Ex. IV-3: First strain of a keyboard gavotte, **Saint-Lambert:Clavecin** (1702), with fingering by the composer.

Other kinds of gavotte articulations are suggested in a gavotte by Dandrieu, with fingerings and slurs by the composer (Ex. IV-4). Not only are the beats delineated by frequently grouping the pulses by twos (especially in the bass), but the quarter-note pulses are projected by grouping the taps by twos (as in the slurs and fingerings of the upper voice). This grouping of taps suggests use of *notes inégales,* which is specifically called for in French gavottes by Montéclair.[19] Normally the type of inequality is long-short. The Couperin gavotte even has *notes pointés,* an extreme form of *notes inégales,* written into the notation (Ex. IV-2, measure 7). On the other hand, the short-long type was undoubtedly used in gavottes on occasion. An interesting case is François Couperin's famous "Les Moissonneurs," from Ordre 6 of his keyboard pieces. It is surely a gavotte (though not so titled) and has the short-long rhythmic alteration clearly indicated in the notation.

The Italian style of gavotte writing mentioned by Mattheson[20] is illustrated in Ex. IV-5, a trio sonata for two violins and continuo by Arcangelo Corelli. The piece is in a fast tempo and begins on the downbeat of the measure, with contrapuntal, imitative part writing, four harmony changes per measure, and feminine cadences. The French characteristics just mentioned, such as the eight-beat (four-measure) phrase, careful sense of balance, and moderately

Ex. IV-4: Beginning of a gavotte by Jean-François Dandrieu, **Dandrieu:Pièces** (1715–20), with fingering by the composer.

slow tempo, are not present. The piece is entitled "Tempo di Gavotta"; among Corelli's published works, which typify the Italian style in many respects, are four pieces entitled "Gavotta" and seven called "Tempo di Gavotta." The "Gavottas" do have balanced phrases, are written in a fast tempo, and begin on the downbeat of the measure; two also have an eighth-note upbeat, and two have written-in *notes inégales.* A study of the gavottes of J. S. Bach reveals that he was well aware of both the French and the Italian styles in gavotte writing, though he clearly favored the French style.

Ex. IV-5: "Tempo di Gavotta," by Arcangelo Corelli, Op. 4, No. 3.

BACH'S GAVOTTES

Bach wrote eighteen titled gavottes, including the keyboard "Tempo di Gavotta" (in BWV 830) and two lute arrangements of gavottes written for other instruments. Since eight pieces consist of two gavottes played "en suite," the total number of titled gavottes is actually twenty-six. Gavottes were a frequent component of Bach's secular music; they appear in three of the four orchestral suites, two of the English and three of the French suites for keyboard, and two of the solo suites for cello. Their presence reflects the great popularity of the gavotte in the 1720s and 1730s, the period when Bach wrote most of his gavottes, and shows him to be in close touch with secular trends of his day.

All Bach's gavottes use the half note as the level of the beat, and almost all have a continuously clear sense of balance created by the setting of four- and eight-beat segments in a "statement and counterstatement" format. Thus, Bach often formulates for himself the problem of making an interesting piece while retaining many of the Classical features of the early eighteenth-century French gavotte.

The earliest gavotte, in the Suite in G minor (BWV 822), is an undistinguished keyboard piece probably arranged from the work of another composer. A different matter are the four gavottes in the two English Suites BMV 808 and 811, which show Bach already a master of the form. Both pairs are strongly in the "pastoral" mode, with Gavotte I in a minor key followed by Gavotte II in the parallel major and written in musette style. In BWV 808, Gavotte I, the French and Italian styles are mixed. French style appears in the clear four- and eight-beat phrase segments, numerous mordents, long *agréments*, and opportunities for *notes inégales* (e.g., measures 2–3 and 6 in the bass and conjunct portions of measures 10–14 in the upper voice). Italian style is seen in the many large intervallic leaps and outlining of chords in the upper part, the sweeping sequential passages (e.g., measures 27–32), and the extension of the gavotte rhythmic phrase beyond its four-measure length (e.g., the cadence in measure 18). Gavotte II is a tender musette, which some performers will choose to play slightly slower than the more-forceful Gavotte I. With such a simple melody, almost like a lullaby, the temptation to embellish is ever present; Ex. IV-6 shows one possibility for the repeat of the first strain.

Ex. IV-6: Possible rendition of the repeat of the first strain of J. S. Bach, Gavotte II, BWV 808.

In BWV 811, Gavotte I, in three-part texture, is based on a melodic idea that is carried over into the musette, which follows in Gavotte II. The constant Italianate running eighth notes in the bass line of both gavottes is interrupted only in measures 14–18 and 22–23 of Gavotte I, where the alto and then the soprano take the lead. And what a refreshing change! *Notes inégales* enhance the conjunct motion of these passages, contrasting with the previous eighth-note movement. The pulses of the opening subject in both gavottes should be articulated clearly, with a large space before beat 2, as in the Couperin piece (Ex. IV-2). The trill on beat 2 should be incorporated into all analogous passages, as the written-out terminations suggest (e.g., the sixteenth notes in measures 5 and 9).

The two gavottes in BWV 1066, another orchestral suite, are predominantly in Italian style. Both have avoided cadences, so that the phrase is not four but eight measures long, giving the pieces a buoyant energy. Several syncopations in Gavotte II, which are common in Italian style (see Ex. IV-5) but not in French gavottes, contribute to this energy. An allegro tempo, moderately fast in the Italian manner, works well in both gavottes, although the phrases should be articulated before beat 2 in order to project the "across the bar line" groupings of the gavotte. Two-note groupings on the tap level are indicated in Gavotte II, while in Gavotte I there are frequent four-note groupings. Though scored for seven instruments, both pieces have a four-part texture, Gavotte I with homophonic part writing and Gavotte II in modified antiphonal style—strings versus winds.

Another gavotte from Bach's Köthen years, from the Suite in D major (BWV 1069), is even more complex in its texture. There are three "bands"—strings, woodwinds, and brass—and no instrumental part consistently doubles another. The tempo will be a little slower than that of the gavottes in BWV 1066, since ornamental *tiratas* (e.g., measures 8 and 20 in the violins) and slide figures (measures 3–4 in the bass parts) must be inserted. This type of ornamentation sounds best if it is cleanly articulated—before the first and last notes of the *tirata,* and before each of the slide figures. The character is joyful and stately, enhanced again by frequent syncopations in the Italian instrumental style.

The secular cantata No. 202 ("Weichet nur, betrübte Schatten"), composed for a wedding, contains a lovely gavotte which is as perfectly balanced as any French dance by that title. After an opening statement by the oboe, the voice enters with a simple but elegant ornamentation, which Bach has written into the score. The syllabically set German text works as well as any French text in projecting the gavotte rhythmic phrases. Bach has chosen a text in which the strongest theses end the first half of the dance phrase (i.e., beats 4, 12, 20 and 28, as in "Zufrieden*heit*"), with lighter theses at the conclusion of the pattern (beats 8, 16, 24, and 32, using words such as "tage," "trage," and "helle"). Numerous other gavotte arias in the sacred as well as the secular cantatas of Bach testify to the popularity of this dance form in the 1720s (see Appendix B).

The longest of Bach's gavottes is in rondeau form and is for solo violin (BWV 1006). Its 100 measures begin with the rondeau section, a jaunty tune made up of a balanced dance pattern of 8 + 8 beats. Bach progressively expands through four couplets: the first couplet is 4 + 4 measures, the second is 8 + 8 + 8, the third is 16 + 16, and the fourth is 4 + 2 + 14 measures. The first couplet ends on the relative minor, the second on the dominant, the third on the secondary dominant, and the last in a deceptive cadence, which drives back to the rondeau.

The rondeau of this piece can be a gentle, delicate, subtle French gavotte if the violinist thinks in terms of a long phrase with articulations as in the French examples presented earlier (Exx. IV-2–4). Some violinists will enjoy playing with the rondeau section so that each reappearance is different. Bach's bowings throughout the piece are meticulously done.[21] They normally delineate the pulse by grouping two eighth notes together, except at thetic points, where they often reinforce the beat by grouping four eighths together. Where Bach wishes the movement to push ahead he also slurs 3 + 1 eighths (e.g., measures 3, 5, and 13). Bach's arrangement of this piece for lute (BWV 1006a) adds a variation in measures 82–85. A long trill on the g♯ pedal point replaces repetitions of that note in the violin version.

Bach's suites for cello solo contain two gavottes. These six suites are important because, according to Klaus Marx, they are the first solo works for cello written by someone who was not a cellist.[22] Bach clearly demonstrates the cello's ability to weave a polyphonic texture without the aid of other instruments. For example, in Gavotte I of Suite V (BWV 1011) the disjunct, Italianate figuration actually projects a three-voice texture. Whole chords are sometimes outlined in Gavotte II of the same work (e.g., measure 2), and the constant triplet figures seem to be a *double* in which the original piece is missing. In the charming, rondeau-form gavottes of Suite VI (BWV 1012) the chords are not only implied but are present as four-voice harmony, struck or arpeggiated in numerous places throughout both pieces.

Bach underlines the French origin of Gavotte I by frequently putting the heaviest, four-note chords on beats 1 and 2 of the gavotte rhythmic phrase, as if to verify François Couperin's articulations (Ex. IV-2) for shaping and giving weight to those parts of the phrase. The texture of Gavotte II varies from two to three voices, beginning as a kind of melody and accompaniment in the rondeau section and progressing, in the second couplet, to a broken-chord variation in musette style, still with an accompanying bass part.

Both of these gavottes succeed well as graceful elaborations of the "pastoral" idea; as such they are not "serious" pieces, but reminders of the gentle, simple pleasures. *Notes inégales* used in conjunct melodic passages will reinforce this concept; the use of contrasting meter signs (¢ and 2) for the two gavottes implies a tempo contrast—perhaps slightly faster in the second one.

These four gavottes for solo cello project the French gavotte phrase structure clearly, actually more than do the gavottes for solo violin. The two- and four-note groupings in the Bach-Gesellschaft edition are those of Bach manuscript P 26, a highly reliable source.[23] These slurs give life to the rhythmic phrases by sometimes emphasizing the pulse and sometimes the beat. The triplet figures of BMV 1011, Gavotte II, each have a separate slur, which projects the pulses of the gavotte. In all four gavottes the phrases will be enhanced and clarified by a definite articulation before beat 2.

The fifth cello suite (BWV 1011) is to be played in a scordatura tuning, in which the top string is tuned to g instead of a. This tuning enlarges the coloristic and technical possibilities of notes played on this string. It also makes fingerings easier in the key of C minor, but the effect on resonance and sonority is probably what motivated Bach to prescribe scordatura tuning.[24] The sixth cello suite (BWV 1012) is problematic because scholars are still debating what instrument Bach intended it to be performed on. Instrument specialist Klaus Marx believes that it could have been either a violoncello piccolo or a normal-sized cello with an extra e' string.[25]

The three gavottes in the keyboard French suites are all in bipartite form, and all have clear, balanced phrase structure. The Gavotte in French Suite IV (BWV 815) begins with four eighth notes, grouped by twos in the Bischoff edition, thus clarifying the two pulses of beat 1. The same grouping may be continued in order to project the pulse level throughout the piece, except for measure 15, which has a grouping by fours in the upper voice. In measure 4 the slurs imply a short-long inequality for the first four eighth notes; analogous places may also use this type of inequality (e.g., the first four notes in the upper voice of measure 12). It is interesting to compare this piece with Corelli's "Tempo di Gavotta" (Ex. IV-5). The main melodic idea, set in an allegro tempo with frequent use of imitation, is not unlike Bach's in the Gavotte of BWV 815.

BWV 815a is a "Gavotte II," which appears only in a later source of this French suite (see Neue Bach-Ausgabe V/viii). BWV 815a is immediately striking because of its length—it is the longest surviving gavotte by Bach except for BWV 1006 (for violin solo), which is in rondeau form. He achieves length by restating whole passages (measures 1–4, 5–8, 50–58), by sequential patterns (measures 43–45), and by a long series of suspensions (measures 37–42). In the latter two instances a three-part texture momentarily interrupts the prevailing two-part writing. This piece is Italianate: it has many sixteenth-note ornamentations cast in figures of turns and *tiratas,* and it uses imitation, which is uncommon in French gavottes but often employed by Corelli (Ex. IV-5).

The gavottes in French Suites V and VI (BWV 816 and 817) are both in a major key, with clear, symmetrical phrasing that is almost march-like in its stately simplicity. Conjunct eighth-note motion in the bass or melodic voices of both pieces sounds well as *notes inégales,* at least on repeats. However, the notated short-long inequality may add variety in some cadential measures (4 and 16) of BWV 817.

BWV 995 is a lute arrangement of the gavotte pair in the solo cello suite BWV 1011, discussed earlier. The new version is from the Leipzig years, 1727–31, and is dedicated to a Monsieur Schouster. Bach has changed the key from C minor to G minor, but, what is more important, he has added a bass line which greatly clarifies the sometimes ambiguous harmonies of BWV 1011 (e.g., in measures 4–8 of Gavotte I). The bass line especially enhances the "swing" of Gavotte II; cellists may find the underlying rhythms of BWV

1011 more quickly by studying the harmonies of the lute version. In addition, all performers may learn about variety in articulations by comparing the several manuscript versions of the cello suites with Bach's lute arrangements. For example, in measures 28–32 of Gavotte I the lute plays groupings of four eighth notes, whereas the cello version as published by the Bach-Gesellschaft (based on manuscript P 26) groups two eighth notes together.

French Suite III (BWV 814) contains an anglaise, which is labeled "gavotte" in some editions. The mistake could have occurred because Italian gavottas are in duple meter and usually begin on the downbeat of the measure, as does this anglaise.

The two gavottes from the Leipzig orchestral suite in D major (BWV 1068) succeed well in the tempo and articulation patterns of the French gavottes discussed earlier, but the trumpets, timpani, oboes, and strings create a more brilliant and forceful piece than the intimate expressions of, for example, the L'Affillard gavotte (Ex. IV-1). Although the phrase structure is consistently clear, and measure 4 of the first gavotte cadences "according to plan," the other intermediate cadences are usually weakened by movement in the bass line, strongly intensifying the forward momentum. This momentum is underlined by large leaps in the melodic line of Gavotte I, contrasting with the anapestic rhythms of the written-in mordent figures of Gavotte II. These figures are perhaps a nod to the naiveté of the "pastoral" style; articulating them clearly will enhance this quality.

Bach's "Tempo di Gavotta" from the sixth keyboard Partita (BWV 830) seems neither graceful nor French; it is unlike any of his other gavottes and much more complicated than the Italian-style pieces entitled "Tempo di Gavotta" by his predecessor Arcangelo Corelli (see Ex. IV-5). The phrase structure is unbroken by the nuances of French Court and theater dances, concentrating on pure "refreshment of the mind," as Bach wrote in his preface to the Partitas.[26] Numerous notational problems confront the performer, and we offer the following suggestions: 1. Assimilate the duple rhythms (dotted eighth- and sixteenth-note figures) into the triplet figures[27] so that they match and do not form counter-rhythms. 2. Play the opening duple figures of the subject as triplet figures; they appear as triplet figures in measures 13, 20, and 21. 3. Play the four sixteenths in measures 6, 14, 22, and 26 (♩. ♬♬) as (♩♩ ♫♫), or else as an unmeasured *tirata* figure, which is probably what it is. The resolution of the duple figures into some sort of triple configuration is only one of several options available to the performer, but it does give this gavotte a playful kind of "swing," which is not evident if simultaneous duple and triple figures collide.

Bach's final pair of gavottes, in the 1735 French Overture in B minor for keyboard (BWV 831) returns to the French simplicity and balance of his earlier dances but with fresh rhythmic nuances. Sixteenth-note *tirates* appear frequently in both upper and lower voices of Gavotte I; harmonic progressions yield surprises, as in measures 12–18; and the piece suddenly shifts to a higher register (measure 20). Gavotte II, by contrast, is entirely in the lower register of the keyboard and contains written-out mordents (measures 13–15) which, if accented at the beginning, produce "jazzy" syncopations against the bass and contrast with the more-normal gavotte rhythms (measures 21–23). Italianate syncopations also dot the landscape, but both gavottes end quietly and in French style, as if nothing unusual had ever happened.

BWV 1046

CHAPTER 5

The Minuet

The most famous of all the French dances was the minuet, and for many people it still serves as a symbol of the great elegance and nobility of seventeenth- and eighteenth-century France. The minuet was the only Baroque dance form to survive as a titled movement in the Classical symphonies and sonatas of the late eighteenth century, and this period is especially rich in source material for both dance and music. Eighteenth-century sources describing the minuet reveal both an amazing consistency for a period of over a century and considerable modifications made at different times and in different parts of the world—in England, Germany, Austria, Italy, Spain, Portugal, Russia, and the American colonies.[1] As a dance it penetrated many different levels of society, from the highest to the lowest, and was performed in a wide variety of styles, ranging from noble to artificial and mannered. As music it also exhibits a bewildering variety that has yet to be sorted out by historians; much of the variety is undoubtedly a reflection of dance styles now forgotten.[2]

The minuet was born in the aristocratic setting of the French Court of the 1660s. The theatrical works of Jean-Baptiste Lully contain ninety-two titled minuets composed as dance accompaniment for his ballets and other stage works from the 1660s until his death in 1687.[3] The minuet was a popular social dance at court at least by the 1680s, and stylized minuets were frequently heard in aristocratic solo and ensemble music from the late seventeenth century on, as the works of composers such as Louis Couperin, Henri d'Anglebert, Marin Marais, and Gaspard Le Roux testify. By the early eighteenth century minuets were enjoyed as social dances throughout Europe, including Bach's Germany. Minuet music continued in favor with the same audiences, appearing in suites as one of the "new" dances between the sarabande and the gigue. Perhaps as a sign of its growing popularity, the German writer Johann Mattheson gave it a larger coverage than any other dance in his 1713 *Das Neu-Eröffnete Orchestre.*[4] By 1752, a Frenchman, Jean Lecointe, could write: "I know nothing in the whole Art of Dancing more noble, more expressive, nor more elegant, than the Minuet. . . . The Minuet is in Fashion everywhere: They dance it both at Court and in the City: It is used all over *Europe.*"[5]

The extraordinary popularity of the minuet is reflected in a bewildering variety of reports, which sometimes appear to conflict. Until further research is done, it is wise not to place complete confidence in any one source. For example, the widely quoted French writer Brossard said in his 1703 *Dictionaire:*

> Minuetto, which means Menuet, or very gay dance, originally comes to us from Poitou. One ought to mark the movement, which is always very gay and very fast, with a sign of $\frac{3}{8}$ or $\frac{6}{8}$, as the Italians do. However, the practice of marking it with a simple 3, or triple quarter notes, has prevailed.[6]

This statement has been frequently cited and quoted, not only by writers in the eighteenth century but by present-day researchers. Some use Brossard's words to "prove" that the minuet "slowed down" in tempo during the eighteenth century, since it is easy to find references from the second half of the century which describe the minuet as a moderate or even a slow dance.[7] However, tempo is a slippery concept; some forms of the minuet may well have retained the tempo used at the court of Louis XIV, which many decades later would have seemed slow in comparison to newer dances. Furthermore, not all writers agreed with Brossard. Jean-Jacques Rousseau, in his article in the Diderot and d'Alembert *Encyclopédie* (compiled 1750–65), states:

> Menuet, kind of dance which, the Abbé Brossard tells us, came originally from Poitou. He says that this dance is very gay and its movement very fast. This is not quite right. The character of the Menuet is a noble and elegant simplicity; the movement is moderate rather than quick. It may be said that the least gay of all the kinds of dances used in our balls is the menuet.[8]

The issue of tempo is only one of many unsolved problems in the history of the minuet, and it is prudent to keep an open mind on this and many other aspects of the minuet's role in history. The discussion which follows will concentrate on the minuet during the time of Bach, citing sources which appear to be relevant to his music.

THE DANCE

Pierre Rameau's *Le Maître à Danser* (1725) contains a detailed description of the French social dance minuet of the early eighteenth century. The book is authoritative for the French style because it had the official approval of Louis Pécour, chief choreographer for the Paris Opéra. The following is a summary of his description:

After the usual bows to the king and to one's partner, the dancers proceed, using minuet step-units, to diagonally opposite sides of the dancing space. They perform several figures outlining a letter Z (Fig. V-1). The dancers themselves decide exactly how many Zs to do. Each Z uses six minuet step-units, each requiring two measures of music, so that each Z occupies twelve measures of music. After several Zs the dancers present right hands to each other in the center of the dancing space, turn a full circle around each other, and then return to diagonally opposite corners. The dancers then present left hands to each other in similar fashion, then turn a full circle around as before. More Zs may occur after the presentation of left hands. The climax is the presentation of both hands (Fig. V-2), after which the dancers turn two or more circles around each other before retreating together to make the bows to the king and to each other.[9]

The two-measure step-units of Rameau's minuet normally consist of four steps taken to the six quarter-note counts of the music (Fig. V-3). Each step-unit begins on the right foot. One of the most popular of the many types of minuet step-unit was the *pas de menuet à deux mouvements* (minuet step of two movements), which consists of two *demi-coupés* and two *pas marchés* (plain walking steps), falling on counts 1, 3, 4, and 5 (Fig. V-3a). Simple but charming counter-rhythms occur between the steps and the music. Another type of step-unit, the *pas de menuet à trois mouvements* (minuet step of three movements) also used two *demi-coupés* and two walking steps, but in a slightly different rhythm and with a tiny leap onto the final step (Fig. V-3b). A third type of rhythm occurs in the *contretemps de menuet* (minuet hop), which consists of a hop on the left foot on count 1, a gentle setting down of the right foot on count 3, a hop on the right foot on count 4, and a leap onto the left foot on count 6 (Fig. V-3c). This livelier rhythm with springs was used for variety and was often inserted in place of the normal minuet step-units. The counter-rhythms of the steps and the music are even more evident when the dancers perform a minuet hop. Thus the basic rhythms of the social dance minuet are contained in the two-measure step-unit, with the four steps often in various counter-rhythms with the music.

Another type of relationship occurs in the phrasing. Since the Z figures

Fig. V-1: Z figure in the minuet,
"The Fourth and Principal Fig-
ure of the Menuet," plate from
Rameau:Maître (c. 1725).

require twelve measures of music, and since minuet music generally consists of eight-measure phrases, the music and the dance would often fail
to coincide at the ends of phrases, leading to a pleasant tension which
would be resolved occasionally but not regularly.[10] A complete minuet
would require from 100 to 120 measures of music, meaning that a single
bipartite piece in phrases of, for example, 8 + 8 measures, would not
suffice. It was normal practice to use at least two bipartite pieces, repeating the first one if additional music was needed for the complete
performance.

Thus the minuet as a dance offered numerous subtleties in its relationship
with the music, not only on the phrase level but also within the two-measure
module of the minuet step-unit. These nuances are an important quality for
performers of the music to recognize. As Wendy Hilton states:

> In performance, the menuet derives enormous strength, beneath its controlled
> surface, from the hypnotic cross-rhythm between dance and music. The stressed
> rise of the second demi-coupé in the step-unit occurs one beat before the down-
> beat of the second measure of the music.[11]

Fig. V-2: Climax of the minuet, "Presentation of Both Arms,"
Tomlinson:Dancing (1735), Plate XII.

An understanding of these relationships helps to establish the tempo and style in minuets, such as some of those by Bach, which reflect the aristocratic French social dance tradition.

Other types of minuet were being danced in the early eighteenth century. Some of these were easier than the *danse à deux,* for example, the contredanse, in which two couples at a time used fixed, repetitive minuet step-units in following a prescribed floor pattern. Other dances were more difficult. Two surviving theatrical minuets are not only through-composed but also contain numerous difficult step-units not normally used in social dancing.[12]

Minuet music of the early eighteenth century has balanced phrases and a clear sense of rhyme, or question with an expected answer. In this respect it is similar to the gavotte; but the gavotte is in duple meter with phrases that

Fig. V-3: Three minuet step-units set to music by J. S. Bach, Minuet I, BWV 809. a. Pas de menuet à deux mouvements; b. Pas de menuet à trois mouvements; c. Contretemps de menuet (minuet hop).

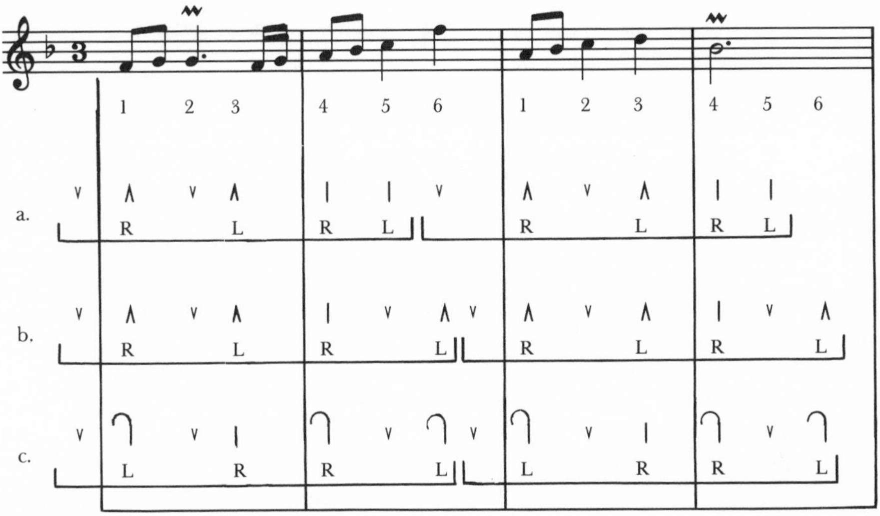

begin before the first bar line, whereas the minuet is in triple meter and its phrases commence at the beginning of a bar, with only an occasional upbeat. Both dances feature prominent counter-rhythms between the music and the dance—in the gavotte because the music phrases begin one beat before the downbeat and the dance phrases begin on the downbeat (see Fig. IV-1b), and in the minuet within the two-measure unit of the dance steps.

The minuet is of moderate character, as is the gavotte, and not given to extremes of passion, unlike the sarabande. Mattheson describes its affect as "moderate gaiety."[13] Much has been made of Brossard's statement that it is "very gay," and it is, indeed, gay in comparison with other triple-meter dances of the early eighteenth century, such as the courante or the sarabande. It did not necessarily "slow down" in later years; even if it kept the same tempo, it would have been considered slow in relation to the newer, faster, gayer triple-meter dances of the second half of the eighteenth century, such as the ländler and the German waltz.[14] The character most relevant for the time of Bach is moderate gaiety, cheerfulness, and serenity as a reflection of the nobility of the French style.

The question of tempo is important, but it can be dealt with only after a discussion of the various views regarding the way to beat time in the minuet. Musicians used at least two ways. According to musicologist Newman Powell, "the primary (and earliest) concept of the seventeenth and eighteenth centuries, . . . seems to have been that the simple ternary measure constitutes only one true beat—a concept expressed the most clearly in the *tactus inaequalis*

Fig. V-4: Three ways to beat time in the minuet, J. S. Bach, Minuet II, BWV 825.

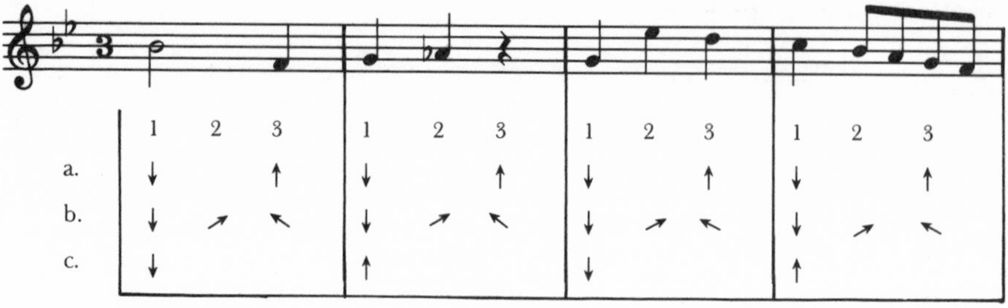

method of beating."[15] This method, which is the one adopted for use in this book, appears in Fig. V-4a; there is one beat per measure, with the downward motion of the arm occupying two counts and the upward motion occupying the third one.[16] Thus, one measure corresponds to the *tactus inaequalis* of Renaissance music.

Another, newer method of beating time in the minuet is described by Saint-Lambert (Fig. V-4b).[17] The arm moves three times per measure—down, to the side, and up. There is a problem because the word "temps" is used in two different ways. If the first system of beating time is used one may speak of one true beat per measure, with three quarter-note pulses. But when the second system is used theorists such as Saint-Lambert spoke of there being "three beats per measure," thinking of each arm movement as a beat; the pulses would be eighth notes under this system. The advantage of the second system is that the sixteenth notes constitute a significant level of rhythm. However, sixteenth notes are rarely used in French or German minuets of the first part of the eighteenth century or earlier, not even in Bach's minuets, except in an ornamental fashion. Thus we count the eighth notes as taps, the quarter notes as pulses, and the measure as one beat.[18]

A third method of beating the minuet (Fig. V-4c) was used by dancing masters of the period,[19] who made a downward motion of the arm for one measure (known as the "good" measure) and an upward one for the following measure (known as the "bad" or "false" measure). This does not contradict what the musicians did, but simply underscores what the dancers were thinking—*their* measures were twice as long as those in the music. The concept of beat, however, was the same as that of the first method of beating in the sense that one measure is considered equal to one beat. As the theorist Loulié wrote, "The only reason for using $\frac{6}{4}$ instead of twice $\frac{3}{4}$ [in barring the minuet] is because in $\frac{3}{4}$ the good beat is not distinguished from the false beat; and it is for this reason that dancers beat the Minuet in $\frac{6}{4}$ although it is notated in $\frac{3}{4}$."[20]

It is easy to see that a discrepancy in the use of the word "temps" would lead to different descriptions of the tempo of the minuet. If one thinks of three beats per measure, the beats seem to move quite quickly; but if one down-and-up movement of the arm per measure equals one beat, the beat seems to move rather slowly. It moves even more leisurely if one thinks as the dancing masters did, with one measure for the "down" and one measure for the "up" movement of the arm.

Many music theorists of the late seventeenth and early eighteenth centuries describe minuet music as fast; for example, Bacilly ("rapid, skipping style"[21]); Georg Muffat ("very brisk"[22]); Kuhnau ("quick, speedy"[23]); Brossard ("very gay and very fast," quoted above). What is fast about minuet music is the movement of the three quarter notes within the measure, which is a way of thinking of the second method of beating the minuet (Fig. V-4b). The minuet is indeed fast in relation to most of the other dances in triple meter. The courante is slowest, according to the English dancing master Kellom Tomlinson, because it has three very slow half-note beats per measure. Next, and in order of quickness, come the sarabande, the passacaille, and the chaconne, all moving by three quarter-note beats per measure. The minuet follows, and finally, fastest of all, is the passepied, which moves by three eighth notes to the measure.[24] The music theorist Borin states the same idea in his 1722 treatise, with the dances in a slightly different order.[25] He describes the five degrees of movement possible for a measure with three beats ("la mesure à trois temps"):

1. Fort Grave
2. Grave (Sarabande, Passacaille, Courante)
3. Léger (Chaconne)
4. Vîte (Menuet)
5. Tres-vîte (Passepied)

Probably the safest way for modern performers to determine the tempo of a minuet is first to consider the tempo of the dance music in relation to that of the other dances in triple meter, as Tomlinson and Saurin have stated. Next, consider the tempo of the social dance itself.[26] Finally, consider whether the minuet may sound well performed faster or slower. A tempo faster than $\downarrow$. = 42–46 MM will not permit clear projection of the frequent harmonic changes (which reflect the counter-rhythms of the harmonic changes and the steps) or of hemiolias and syncopations in the music; the risk is that of trivializing this dance. Lecointe writes in mid-century, "I know nothing in the whole Art of Dancing more noble, more expressive, nor more elegant than the Minuet."[27] A further word of advice comes from the French theorist Saint-Lambert, who stated in 1701 that minuets for listening alone are performed in a *slower* tempo than those which accompany dancing.[28] This may confuse rather than clarify the tempo problem, but at least it extends an already wide variety of opinion on this controversial issue.

The minuet dance rhythm (Fig. V-5) consists of a harmonic-rhythmic

Fig. V-5: Model for the Minuet Dance Rhythm
I–3–2, $\frac{3}{4}$

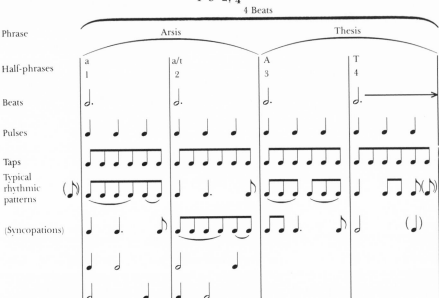

phrase four beats (measures) in length, with a thesis on beat 4 and an internal subgrouping of 2 + 2 beats. The metric structure is thus I–3–2; if sixteenth notes appear they are ornamental. Occasionally an upbeat is present. *Notes inégales*, when appropriate, are on the tap, or eighth-note, level. A frequent device for holding together the four-measure phrase is the use of hemiolia in measures 2 and 3. Syncopation also appears frequently on the pulse level; it occur in thetic as well as arsic measures.

The four-measure phrase is normally balanced or answered by a second four-measure phrase with an even greater sense of arrival (thesis) on measure 8. Almost all phrases in minuets of the early eighteenth century are constructed of multiples of four measures; odd numbers of measures are rare, though they were not uncommon in the mid-seventeenth-century minuets of Jean-Baptiste Lully.[29] As in most of the other French dances, the melodies of the minuet normally have a narrow range of pitch and tend to move stepwise rather than in large intervallic leaps. This kind of melodic discipline, combined with the regularity and balance in the phrase structure, would quickly become tedious were it not for the syncopations, hemiolias, and other rhythmic nuances inherent in the style.

The first strain of a minuet song by L'Affilard illustrates many of the minuet's characteristics (Ex. V-1). The punctuation of the poetry clearly demonstrates the four-measure phrases and their balanced, "question and answer" construction. The poetry in the first half of each eight-

Ex. V-1: Minuet air, **L'Affilard:Principes** (1705), p. 98.

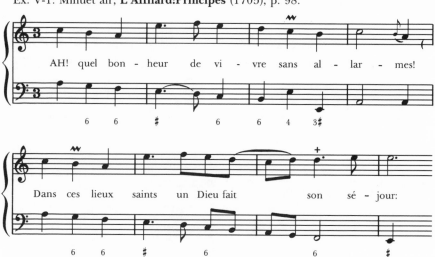

measure section closes with a feminine ending, and the answering half closes with a masculine ending. The composer, leaving nothing to chance, writes breath marks for the singer after each four-measure segment of the eight-measure phrase. The harmony reinforces the poetry by a strong cadence on every eighth measure (e.g., the phrygian cadence on measure 8) and a less strong one at the halfway point of each phrase. The melody has a single-octave range and moves either stepwise or (occasionally) by small, chordal intervals. The composer has avoided any possibility of two-measure phrases by utilizing text holdovers (e.g., "vivre" in measures 2–3 and hemiolias in measures 6–7).

Numerous hints for the performance of minuets in this period exist in the bowings, fingerings, and phrasings written in by composers. Ex. V-2 gives the first strain of a menuet by Dandrieu with written-in fingerings. The syncopations in measures 1 and 3 have to be articulated (that is, one must leave a small space between the two notes) because of the indicated fingerings. In addition, in the even-numbered measures all three pulses are bound together, so that an alternation of arsis and thesis occurs continually, reinforcing the dance pattern and giving an ebb and flow to the music.[30]

Notes inégales on the eighth-note level are characteristic of minuets in the French style. In Ex. V-3 the long-short type is appropriate for the stepwise notes in the upper voice of measure 4; immediately preceding this, the composer has indicated the short-long type of inequality in the last two pulses of the measure.

French minuets of the seventeenth century did not always use four-measure phrases. The so-called Menuet de Poitou featured phrases of 3 +

Ex. V-2: Keyboard fingerings in a menuet by Jean-François Dandrieu (early eighteenth century).

Ex. V-3: Opening of "Menuet," **Couperin:Pièces** (1713), IIIe. Ordre.

3 measures, which would have created very interesting cross-rhythms with the dance whether the steps in use at the time covered two measures or three. (Scholars have not yet discovered what kind of minuet steps were in use in the seventeenth century, but it is certainly possible that they were more complicated and subtle than those employed in the eighteenth century.) The "Menuet de Poitou" appears in the dance music of Lully, and also in the works of other composers such as Louis Couperin (Ex. V-4), whose minuet illustrates not only the use of 3 + 3 phrase structure but also a *double*. Minuet *doubles* also appear in the keyboard works of Gaspard Le Roux, and one of his minuets has two *doubles*.[31] This shows an interest by French composers in the type of elaboration which would soon inspire Bach. Minuet elaborations might originally have been improvisations arising from the need for more music to accompany the long social dance. Bach makes abundant use of such elaborations to expand the expressive possibilities of the minuet, while still retaining the poise of the ballroom dance.

Ex. V-4: Excerpts from "Menuet de Poitou," showing *double,* by Louis Couperin (mid-seventeenth century).

BACH'S MINUETS

Bach composed twenty-eight titled minuets, most of which actually consist of two minuets to be played in sequence plus a return to the first one. The two minuets usually contrast sharply in style, texture, instrumentation, and mode or key. Four sets label the second minuet a "trio," and in these four, as well as in several other sets, the texture consists of two or three voices over a bass part, in contrast to a single voice over a bass in the first minuet. The metric and phrase structures are identical to those of the French minuets discussed above, and many of the same compositional procedures appear as well. All except one of Bach's titled minuets are made up of four-measure units, but the first strain typically contains eight or more measures, not four, as in many of the French compositions mentioned earlier. The only exception is the first minuet of the keyboard Overture in F major (BWV 820), which is in the 3 + 3 phrase structure of the "Menuet de Poitou." Bach's minuets generally retain the calm nobility, serenity, melodic simplicity, and rhythmic subtlety of their French predecessors. They appear in a variety of instrumentations, including some for flute, violin, cello, lute, or keyboard solo, and several for orchestra. We have included two pieces marked only "tempo di menuetto" (BWV 173a, No. 4 and BWV 829) since their style and phrase structure are based on four- and eight-measure groupings similar to that of Bach's titled minuets.

The Early Minuets

BWV 1033 is an undated flute sonata with almost constant eighth-note movement, originally for unaccompanied flute but now featuring a continuo part, which was probably a later realization by a student of Bach's.[32] BWV 822, a keyboard suite consists of three undated minuets which are probably arrangements of another composer's work. They illustrate the practice of putting two or more minuets together to make a piece long enough to accompany a dance. Minuet I is repeated after both Minuet II and Minuet III, resulting in a rondeau form (ABACA). Ornamentation or other elaboration might enhance the repeats of Minuet I, especially if one also repeats both strains each time. Minuet II is a mirror of Minuet I—the treble of Minuet I becomes the bass of Minuet II, and vice versa.

The Overture in F major for keyboard (BWV 820) is full of charm and begins to sound like the mature Bach. It is entitled Overture because its first movements are a French overture and an entrée. It contains Bach's only extant "*Menuet de Poitou*," constructed in tertiary groups of measures with an alternation of feminine and masculine cadences. The contrasting trio uses the familiar 4 + 4 phrase structure but with two additional features of balance: the last four measures of the first strain are almost an exact repeat of the first four measures, and the last eight measures of the second strain are a literal repeat of the whole of the first strain. Since both minuets are in F major, some performers may choose to play the trio slightly slower than the first minuet.

The minuet from the Sinfonia in F major (BWV 1071) is an early version of the familiar First Brandenburg Concerto. Pairs of horns, a trio of oboes, strings, and bassoon create a six-part texture with a rather startling opening. The I_{b5}^{6} announces right away that the harmony is going to create a long phrase; as promised, there is no rest until the dominant chord at the end of the strain, in measure 12. Bach marks the slurs in this long, elegant line to reinforce the two-measure unit derived from minuet steps, creating a flowing alternation of arsis and thesis measures within the phrase. The grouping of measures in the trio, scored for two oboes and bassoon, contrasts nicely in the relative minor because of its clearly defined four-measure phrases and simpler melody and harmonies. Balance is enhanced by the return of most of the first strain as the final eight measures of the second strain. The simplicity of melody, harmony, and texture in this trio invites the soloists to add ornamentation in the French style.

The English suites contain only one set of minuets, those in BWV 809 in F major. Even though Minuets I and II are in different keys, both have the same two-voice texture and melodic style, requiring the performer to use careful articulations to contrast the two pieces. Bach has incorporated the minuet syncopation in opposite ways in the two minuets. In Minuet I it appears in measure 1 (and sometimes in measure 3) of the four-measure phrase; in Minuet II it regularly appears in measure 2 (sometimes in measure 4) of the phrase. With a long *agrément* on the second pulse of the measure with syncopation, and a prominent articulation before it, the rhythms will come to life and also contrast well from one minuet to the other. *Notes inégales* are appropriate for the stepwise eighth notes of Minuet I, but they must be performed with subtlety. In Minuet II, they are not appropriate for the broken-chord-style eighths in the lower voice (e.g., measures 1, 2, and 5) but sound well elsewhere; the short-long variety would add interest to the eighths of the upper voice in Minuet II, measures 11 and 18 and other analogous situations.

Minuets from Köthen

Bach's compositions written in Köthen include minuets for solo violin, cello, lute, and keyboard, as well as for orchestra. The eight French suites will be discussed separately because scholars are still unsure whether they were written in Köthen or in Leipzig.

The secular Cantata BWV 173a, *Durchlaucht'ser Leopold*, was written for the Köthen prince's birthday in 1717. It contains a duet for soprano and bass, marked "Al tempo di minuetto," and accompanied by strings and a pair of flutes. Portions of the cantata, including this duet, were later adapted as *Erhöhtes Fleisch und Blut* (BWV 173) for the second Sunday in Pentecost (Leipzig, 1724), with the "tempo di minuetto" indication deleted. Although this duet is not a minuet structurally—it is in three sections but has no trio or contrasting second minuet—it is a minuet rhythmically. The measures are grouped mainly in twos and fours, with frequent hemiolias preceding cadences; the movement is largely conjunct; and balance and serenity shine from every line of the text.

The only minuets among the solo violin works are in Partita III (BWV 1006). Their elegant simplicity is beloved by violinists but also by lutenists, since Bach wrote a lute version as well (BWV 1006a). Performers on either instrument will profit from studying both versions, since ornamentation, voice leading, and phrasing are slightly different. Minuet I contains a six-measure phrase (measures 13–18), which is unusual in Bach's minuets. Slurs given in measures 19–26 of both versions of Minuet I offer an opportunity for varied and interesting grouping of the eighth notes. The bowings in the Bach-Gesellschaft edition are different from those in the P 967 manuscript of the violin Partitas (see Exx. V-5a and c), and the lute version presents yet another possibility (Ex. V-5b). Minuet II begins with a suggestion of musette style with the note *B* held for three measures. Several measures in which the eighth notes are slurred in twos while moving by thirds or in conjunct motion (e.g., measures 5–6 and 8) suggest performance in *notes inégales*. Bach puts a slur across the bar line (which was unusual in dance music), possibly to hint at a hemiolia in measures 22–23, which is appropriate to the lute version as well.

Ex. V-5: J. S. Bach, measures 19–26 from a minuet. a. for solo violin, BWV
1006, Bach-Gesellschaft edition; b. for lute, BWV 1006a, Bach-Gesellschaft
edition; c. for solo violin, BWV 1006, Bach Ms. P 976.

Arpeggio and broken-chord figures outline the harmonies in both minuets
of Suite I for solo cello (BWV 1007). The bowings in Minuet I again appear
differently in the Bach-Gesellschaft edition than in the P 26 manuscript. As
Ex. V-6a shows, the P 26 manuscript is more lively and more closely articulated, emphasizing the individual pulses rather than larger units, as in the
Bach-Gesellschaft edition. Further variety in the grouping of eighths occurs

in Minuet II, which is in the parallel minor. Three eighths are frequently slurred together to create a mordent (e.g., measures 1 and 3), forming a strong contrast with the slurs of Minuet I. In the second strain trochaic groupings in measures 10, 12, and 18 are suggested by slurs over the first four eighth notes of the measure (Ex. V-6b); while measures 13, 14, and 22 are bowed $2 + 3 + 1$ (Ex. V-6c).

There are so many inaccurate bowings in the Bach-Gesellschaft edition of both minuets from Suite II for solo cello (BWV 1008) that the performer needs to consult a manuscript facsimile or authoritative edition for the actual bowings written in by Bach. Minuet I has a charming alternation of arsic and thetic measures in the style of this dance, normally with two or three harmonies in arsic measures (e.g., measures 1 and 3) and only one harmony for the thetic measures (e.g., measures 2 and 4). Minuet II lacks this regularity and further contrasts with its predecessor by an almost continually moving line of eighth notes. *Notes inégales,* at least on repeats, could enhance both dances.

BWV 841, 842, and 843 are three minuets from the W. F. Bach *Notebook* of 1720. They are in the keys of G major, G minor, and G major and may be played in numerous ways, for example as separate pieces or in rondeau fashion (BWV 841, 842, 841, 843, 841). According to Karl Geiringer, the first one was written by W. F. Bach, the third by J. S. Bach, and the second jointly by father and son.[33] The original copy has carefully marked slurs.[34] The first minuet is straightforward, simple, and balanced, if a little repetitious. The second is somewhat more angular melodically and more interesting harmonically, yet still perfectly balanced, and enhanced by occasional use of a little

Ex. V-6: Selected bowings from Bach Ms. P 26, Minuet for solo cello, BWV 1007. a. Minuet I, measures 1, 5, 9, 17, and 19; b. Minuet II, measures 10, 12, and 18; c. Minuet II, measures 13, 14, and 22.

tremoletto figure of two sixteenth notes, beginning in measure 1. The third minuet is the longest and most unusual. It is the only one of Bach's minuets that exploits the Italian tremoletto figures from beginning to end. An interesting mix of French and Italian compositional practices, the dance begins with a musette-like pedal that extends through the first five measures with the Italianate figures continuing in both voices. Bach's use of the keyboard's lower register at the end of the second strain is unprecedented for dance music, but satisfying as an instrumental excursion. This minuet, perhaps more than the others, demonstrates that the structure of the minuet can be disguised underneath skillful figurations.

The little trio, BWV 929, occurs in a Partita by G. A. Stölzel in the W. F. Bach *Notebook* and was published as Prelude No. 10 in *Various Short Preludes and Fugues,* edited by Hans Bischoff. It is not only a perfect little minuet in rhythm and structure, but a flawless example of three-part counterpoint, employing syncopations and suspensions in which each voice has an equal role.

The minuet from the First Brandenburg Concerto (BWV 1046) is essentially the same as the earlier version, BWV 1071, except that there are now two additional pieces which serve as "trios," with the first minuet returning da capo (by verbal instruction) after each one. Minuet I is set for the full orchestra, consisting of two horns, three oboes, bassoon, strings, and continuo. The overall form is: Minuet I, a second minuet (for two oboes and bassoon), Minuet I, Polonaise (in $\frac{3}{8}$ meter, for strings and continuo), Minuet I, Trio (in $\frac{2}{4}$, for the two horns, with the oboes playing a "bass" part), Minuet I. The whole makes a festive conclusion to the Concerto. Several small alterations appear in the second minuet—the bass of measures 12 and 13 becomes an extended pedal on C, and one additional harmony change occurs in measure 15.

The elegant minuets from the orchestral Suite in C major (BWV 1066) contrast well because of the eight-measure phrases in Minuet I and the four-measure phrases with numerous feminine cadences in Minuet II. The instrumentation enhances this contrast—the pair of oboes and a bassoon of Minuet I drop out in Minuet II. It could be further strengthened by the use of several strings on a part in Minuet I and only one instrument to a part in Minuet II. Syncopations occur in both dances and should be strongly articulated; e.g., in measures 2 and 7 of Minuet I and measures 1 and 9 of Minuet II.

Minuets in the French Suites

It is not clear from the sources of the eight French Suites whether Bach originally intended to include minuets at all. Only the first suite (BWV 812) contains a minuet and trio in all the eighteenth-century sources, and scholars are not certain about the position of the minuets in these suites. In the B minor, C minor, and E major suites the minuet appears after the gigue in some manuscripts (as if it had been added later) and before the gigue in others. Modern editions of the suites generally do not mention this matter of placement. The Neue Bach-Ausgabe is not helpful because it is based on the Altnikol manuscript of about 1750, in which minuets always precede gigues.[35]

On this evidence it is reasonable for modern performers to put the minuets last if they so desire. However, the placement of the minuet may affect the tempo of the gigue. A gigue in the final position will generally sound better in a faster, gayer tempo, while in another position it may be taken somewhat more slowly so as to contrast with the minuet coming last. Although one would not alter the minuet tempo similarly, one might consider adding a trio when the minuet is in last place and a trio is lacking; this would create a more substantial ending to the suite. A suitable trio could be chosen from among the other works of Bach, or one could use other dances as trios, such as the Polonaise in the E major suite. Precedents for this occur in the First Brandenburg Concerto (BWV 1046), discussed above. To carry this idea even further, a performer might remember *La Bourée d'Achille,* in which the form is bourée-minuet, bourée (Fig. III-1), and choose to end the suite BWV 819 with a *da capo* of the Bourée.[36]

Bach shows himself a master of imitative counterpoint in both minuets of the D minor French Suite (BWV 812). In Minuet I the opening melodic material of the soprano voice is woven through all three parts, appearing in the second strain in the bass (measures 9–12), then in the tenor (measures 13–14), and again in the bass (measures 21–22). A syncopation is also present with various ornamentations: in measures 3 and 11 with a long trill; in measures 6, 9, and 21 with a short trill; and in measures 10, 17, and 18 with a written-out mordent. Resting on several pedal points, the harmonic rhythm changes rapidly. The syncopation becomes a kind of motto theme in Minuet II, beginning in measures 1, 3, and 5 of both phrases of the first strain, and continuing with ever more frequency in the second strain. Some performers will enjoy varying the amount of space left before the second pulse in each of these measures, as well as the ornamentation on the second pulse itself. Stepwise eighth notes offer countless opportunities for *notes inégales.* In addition Bach offers ambiguous moments when, as in measures 10, 12, 34, and 36, the lower voice seems to be in $^6_8$ (♩. ♩.) and the upper voice in $^3_4$ (♩ ♩ ♩).

The minuet in the C minor French Suite (BWV 813) is in a simple, two-voice texture without imitation. Slurs over six-note groups imply a somewhat faster tempo than would be the case if more articulations were written in. Sequences extend the second strain. In performance, a regular alternation of arsic and thetic measures is easy to project, giving a sense of flow to this artless gem. A second minuet, found only in the P 420 manuscript (c. 1725), is also in two voices but it has a good deal of interspersed broken-chord texture.[37] Measure 11 suggests a $3 + 3$ articulation of eighth notes.

The continuous broken-chord style of Minuet I of French Suite III (BWV 814) again implies a somewhat faster tempo than usual; its strict two-voice texture projects an instrumental excursion more than a direct reflection of the dance music. The second eight measures of the first strain are an almost literal repeat of the first eight measures. But even in a faster tempo interesting articulation possibilities occur, such as in measure 18, where the two voices can have contrasting patterns (discussed above for BWV 812, Minuet II, measure 10ff.). The stately trio offers a complete contrast. Its harmonic and textural complexity suggests a slower tempo and stronger articulations. Each of the three voices is distinctive and will come alive with imaginative ornamentation, some of which is offered in the Bischoff edition. For example, one might ornament the upper voice by a *coulé* on the first note of measure 14, a short trill to the initial eighth note in measure 20, and a *port de voix* at the beginning of measure 22. Measures 5, 13, 17, and 21 invite counter-articulations, since they contain the ambiguous figure that appears in BWV 812 and 814. *Notes inégales,* though inappropriate in Minuet I, may enhance the stepwise passages in Minuet II.

The simple, short minuet in French Suite IV (BWV 815a) does not occur in most sources of the French suites and is found in manuscripts P 418 (c. 1723) and P 420 (c. 1725) only, as if it were an afterthought to a suite written earlier; it now appears in an appendix in the Neue Bach-Ausgabe.[38] Slurs group many of the eighths by twos, and syncopations on the second pulse occur twice in the second strain (measures 10 and 12).

The single minuet from the E major French Suite (BWV 817) is a model of elegance and clarity, with a "question-and-answer" phrase structure, which is always enjoyed as an expression of a Classical affect. Even the little excursion in measures 11–16 does not disturb the tranquility. The mordent figure in the bass might be slurred as a group of three eighth notes; the stepwise eighths of the upper voice invite a lilting inequality. As mentioned previously, some performers will elect to perform the Polonaise as a "trio" to this minuet, as Bach did in the Minuet of the First Brandenburg Concerto.

Bach's only minuet notated in $\frac{3}{8}$ meter, in the keyboard suite in A minor (BWV 818a), is highly figured in a Germanic style. Duplet and triplet figures alternate on the tap level—could this have been an experiment which was later brought to fruition in the D major minuet of BWV 828 in the *Clavier-Übung?*

The two minuets from the keyboard suite in Eb major (BWV 819) are French in their underlying phrase structure, which matches that of the danced minuet, but German in their continuous figuration. Minuet I begins with a pedal on Eb, in musette style, but never returns to it after the first four measures. Sequences extend the second strain, and ornamentation of most of the quarter-note pulses helps to give shape to the four- and eight-measure phrases. The key relationship of the two minuets is unusual, for Bach rarely used the tonic minor in the second of two minuets. Even more unusual is the key of Eb minor—rarely found in Baroque music. Minuet II has an upbeat, which is also unusual but not unheard of in minuets. A pedal is simulated by hovering around Eb in the bass for the first few measures, and *notes inégales* would make these figures more interesting. The last eight measures of the second strain are an almost literal repeat of the first one.

Minuets from Leipzig

The minuets from Bach's Leipzig period are the most suave, effortless, and imaginative of all. The two in the B♭ major keyboard Partita (BWV 825) contrast sharply with each other. Minuet I is in broken-chord style throughout, with few internal cadences, and manifests the same elegance and suavity of Minuet I from the B minor French Suite (BWV 814). The groupings of notes suggested for the latter would work beautifully in this dance as well. Minuet II is in four-part texture, using strict counterpoint, pedal points, suspensions, tight voice leading, and perfectly balanced phrases; in addition, its rhythms beautifully reflect French minuet steps, especially the step-unit illustrated in Fig. V-3a. The syncopations (measures 2, 6, 10, and 14) may be emphasized by separating pulses 1 and 2 and adding an ornament to pulse 2; alternatively they could be de-emphasized as they are in the dance step-unit of Fig. V-3a.

The single minuet from the D major keyboard Partita (BWV 828) is based on the rhythmic phrases of the dance but embellishes these with flourishes (e.g., measures 1 and 5) and several syncopations (measures 2, 6, 22, and 26). Distinctive of this minuet are the alternating and sometimes simultaneous duplet and triplet figures on the tap level. This feature is not unique in Bach's music; it also occurs in the minuet of BWV 818a, described above, and in the corrente of the D minor solo violin Partita (BWV 1004). Most performers will choose to resolve the dotted-eighth-and-sixteenth-note figures of measures 7 and 23–24 so that they fit with the triplets. A moderate tempo will best project an affect of elegant gaiety.

The "Tempo di Minuetto" of the keyboard Partita in G major (BWV 829) is another testament to the breadth of Bach's imagination in expanding on the dance "idea." Retaining the four-measure dance structure within the phrases, this prelude-like piece is written almost entirely in arpeggio figuration, with five feminine cadences (measures 4, 12, 16, 20, and 52), longer harmonic sequences than in any of Bach's other titled minuets (measures 5–10, 25–28, and 45–50), and at least two opportunities for echo effects (measures 33–36 and 37–40). Most curious of all is the notational implication of ternary groups of eighth notes broken only at cadence points and at measures 41–44. Bach also uses this idea, though not as consistently, in the Little Prelude in D minor, No. 5 in Bischoff's *Twelve Little Preludes for Beginners.*[39]

Bach's last two minuets are in the orchestral suites BWV 1069 and 1067, which were written about ten years apart. BWV 1069 has two minuets, both of which stress syncopation in imaginative ways. In Minuet I—scored for oboes, bassoon, strings, and continuo—a trill decorates the second note of the syncopation, emphasizing the arsic quality of measures 1, 5, and 7. In the second strain syncopation appears in almost every measure, in one voice or another, with a hemiolia leading to a major cadence in measure 16. Both minuets have a four-part texture, but Minuet II greatly reduces the forces to two violins, one viola, and continuo. The simple, four-measure phrases contrast with the longer ones of Minuet I, though the second strain has some surprises, as in measure 16. Continuo eighth notes are slurred 2 + 2 in most cases, precluding too fast a tempo.

The single minuet of BWV 1067 is also in four-part texture, with a flute used coloristically to double the upper line of the strings. Taken at a minuet dance tempo, and with the varied groups of slurred eighth notes clearly projected, this piece exudes grace and charm. Its Classic proportions are perfect for dancing the minuet, and there is no reason to doubt that it could easily have served as dance accompaniment, as could many of the other minuets discussed here.

BWV 831/I

CHAPTER 6
The Passepied

The passepied is a delicate, rhythmically exciting dance, though it has never been given much attention by scholars. It was very popular in French Court dancing of the early eighteenth century, but it appears much less often in suites of the period than do the minuet, the gavotte, and the bourée. The list of composers who used it at least once (e.g., Gaspard Le Roux, Montéclair, Dieupart, François Couperin, J. K. F. Fischer, Telemann, Kuhnau, J. E. Pestel) is much shorter than the list of those who did not use it at all. Bach composed only four passepieds, three pairs and a single dance.

The passepied is dismissed by most writers simply as a "fast minuet." This idea probably derives from Sébastien de Brossard, who wrote in his *Dictionaire de Musique* (1703): "It [the passepied] is a minuet whose movement is quite fast and gay."[1] His comment was widely quoted by writers throughout the eighteenth century and is still repeated today. In reality the passepied is quite a different type of piece. Though their musical phrase structure is identical to that of the minuet, passepieds are not only faster but contain unusual rhythms—offbeat accents which occur at surprising times to delight (or possibly upset) the listener. Passepieds also have longer phrases with fewer points of arrival and may be accented in a more vigorous manner than do minuets.

The origin of these offbeat accents probably lies in the early history of the passepied, before the music was reworked by French dancers and musicians of the late seventeenth century to become one of the graceful, characteristic, official dances of the French Court. Ex. VI-1 shows one of the few surviving musical examples entitled passepied which derive from these earlier times. It features a 3 + 3 phrase structure in a quick duple meter, with rapid harmonic changes to complement the bold rhythms. This piece may be compared with even earlier passepieds in Praetorius' *Terpsichore* (1612) and Mersenne's *Harmonie Universelle;* though of a somewhat different structure, they also feature vigorous harmonies and rhythms.[2] These early examples are important because they help to characterize a dance which has been little

Ex. VI-1: *Les passe-pieds d'Artus,* opening of orchestral dance, **Ecorcheville:Suites,** Suite V (c. 1650–68).

studied by musicologists and for which relatively few sources of information have survived.

The character of most passepieds in the early eighteenth century is that of a fast and lively dance, as Brossard stated. Writers as late as Türk use words such as "gay" and "cheerful" in connection with the passepied,[3] probably because of Brossard's influence. Passepied music is often associated with the pastoral tradition, as were the gavotte, bourée, and minuet, although eighteenth-century writers do not mention this. Among German writers, Walther called it "playful" or "flirtatious,"[4] and Johann Mattheson described it as frivolous, fickle, and less passionate than the gigue:

> Its nature is quite close to *frivolity:* for with all its disquiet and inconstancy, such a passepied has by no means the zeal, passion or ardor which one comes across with a volatile gigue. Meanwhile it is still a kind of frivolity which does not have anything detestable or unpleasant about it, but rather something pleasant: just as many a female who, though she is a little inconstant, nevertheless does not therewith lose her charm.[5]

Thus, though it is not as passionate as the sarabande or as intense as the gigue, it is also not "moderate," like the minuet and gavotte. "Lightly fickle" might describe it, as well as the already mentioned "playful," cheerful, and gay.

The tempo is fast, but, as in the minuet, only a comparison with other dance types will help the performer to determine what this means.[6] Of the triple-meter dances, according to Borin, the passepied is the fastest, coming after the courante, sarabande, passacaille, chaconne, and minuet. Thus, Brossard actually gives good advice when he compares the tempi of minuet and passepied—performers should consider how fast a minuet goes and play passepieds slightly faster. Freillon-Poncein,[7] Quantz,[8] and Rousseau[9] all state the same idea. A good tempo for dancing many passepieds, which agrees with that of L'Affilard, is ♪ = MM 129, which is about MM 42–44 per measure.[10] The present authors often prefer a slightly faster tempo in the minuet, and we also suggest a slightly faster tempo for the passepied, about MM 46–48 per measure.

The "remodeled" form of the passepied probably originated later than that of the minuet; the earliest minuets in the theatrical works of Jean-Baptiste Lully are from the 1660s, but the six passepieds appear only in the 1680s.[11] While the dance steps of the passepied were, in fact, minuet steps taken at a slightly faster tempo,[12] their effect was quite different. Instead of the elegance of carefully prepared *demi-coupés* and the few, prearranged figures of the minuet, the passepied dancers moved with smaller, quicker steps through a long series of evolving figures forming varied geometrical floor patterns. These included various types of circles around one another, parallel circles holding hands, and angular moves toward and away from one

another in many different directions. The patterns became even more interesting in the contredanse because two to four couples participated at once,
not just one.

Passepied dance music is in $\frac{3}{8}$, with phrases in a length divisible by four
measures in order to accompany the units of four tiny steps set to each two
measures of music.[13] The many figures required several pieces of music, not
just one, and most passepieds are set to at least two bipartite pieces, with one
or both repeated several times according to various schemes. Table IV shows
the repeat structure in four of the most popular passepieds which have survived in notation.[14] Passepieds were also popular in the theater, appearing in
works by Campra, Destouches, Desmarets, Lalande, Mouret, and J.-Ph.
Rameau, but no theatrical choreographies survive in notation.

TABLE IV

Repeat Structure of Musical Accompaniment in Several Passepied
Choreographies

Numerals refer to the number of measures in a strain.

Le Passepied (1700)

A	A	B	B	C	C	D	D		A	A	B	B	C	C	D	D
8	8	8	8	8	8	8	8		8	8	8	8	8	8	8	8

La Bretagne (1704)

A	A	B	B
8	8	16	16

La Gouastalla (1709)
(in $\frac{6}{8}$ time)

A	A	B	B	A	A	C	C	A	A
4	4	4	4	4	4	4	4	4	4

La Nouvelle Bourgogne (1707)

A	A	B
8	8	16

The passepied dance rhythm (Fig. VI-1) is the same as that of the minuet
except for the $\frac{3}{8}$ time signature and the upbeat. The dance rhythm consists of
a rhythmic-harmonic phrase four beats (measures) long with a thesis on measure 4. The typical rhythmic patterns shown in Fig. VI-1 first appear in the
passepieds of Lully.

Ex. VI-2 shows part of the lively passepied with which Gaspard Le Roux
ends his Suite in F. In the second of these two eight-measure phrases he uses
hemiolias (measures 10–11 and possibly 14–15) as well as syncopations (measures 12–13) to create excitement. Ex. VI-3 shows a passepied with an extension in measures 12–13. The listener is surprised because the expected thesis

Fig. VI-1: Model for the Passepied Dance Rhythm
I–3–2, $\frac{3}{8}$

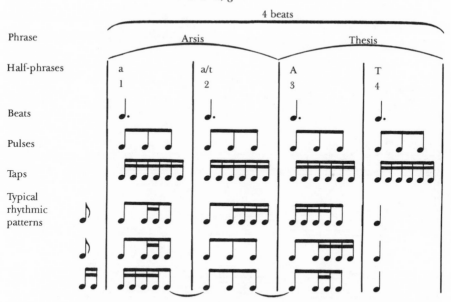

in measure 12 is avoided and the sense of balance temporarily disappears, followed by a hemiolia before the thesis in measure 16. It seems likely that Mattheson was referring to these characteristic devices when he termed the passepied "fickle." The Dieupart example is in the style of an elaboration on a simpler, now lost melody. *Notes inégales* will enliven the eighth notes.

Some composers called attention to the passepied hemiolia by making it a "double measure" ($\frac{3}{4}$ measure within a piece in $\frac{3}{8}$), as the reprise of François Couperin's keyboard piece shows (Ex. VI-4, measure 14). This Passe-pied, first published in 1713, is full of performance indications such as elaborate *agréments* and strong articulations (e.g., measure 9, pulse 3). Formally, it embraces the minuet trait of phrase repetition: measures 5–8 are essentially a repeat of 1–4, and the last eight measures of the reprise are their duplicate (not shown).

Interesting performance suggestions are also available in the implied articulations of bowings by Montéclair and Dupont (not shown).[15] The latter further comments: "Regarding the bowing of the passepied—it should be played like the minuet except one should play the eighths of the Passepied like the quarters of the minuets and the sixteenths like the eighths of the minuet."[16] Thus, sixteenth notes are to be articulated with care and may move with inequality, even as the eighth notes do in a minuet. Other writers who discuss performance in the passepied mention that it should be played "lightly."[17] Bach inherited all of these passepied characterstics and, as we

Ex. VI-2: Opening of Passepied by Gaspard Le Roux, from Suite in F major, *Pièces de Clavecin* (1705).

shall see, did not hesitate to carry the process even farther than did his predecessors.

BACH'S PASSEPIEDS

Bach's few dances in this form are masterpieces of the genre. Though Bach did not employ the notational device of the "double measure," he used hemiola and other vacillating groupings of eighth notes to create long, elegant phrases replete with the slightly off-balance rhythmic effects so charac-

Ex. VI-3: Opening of second strain, measures 9–16, of Passepied from Suite in D major by Charles Dieupart (early eighteenth century).

Ex. VI-4: Opening of second strain, measures 9–15, of Passe-pied, **Couperin:Pièces,** II. Ordre (1713).

teristic of the passepied. His seven passepieds include a set of two for orchestra, and two sets of two plus a single dance for keyboard. The keyboard pieces are in $\frac{3}{8}$, the orchestral ones in $\frac{3}{4}$.

The passepieds of BWV 1066 form the final movement of the C major orchestral suite. It was not unusual to end a suite with passepieds, as some

scholars have suggested.[18] This suite consists simply of an overture, a courante, and five French dances popular in the early eighteenth century (gavotte, forlane, minuet, bourée and passepied). Besides, Gaspard Le Roux
had already used the passepied to end his F major harpsichord suite (Ex. VI-
2). In BWV 1066 the second passepied is an elaboration of the first one. It
uses the same melody as the first passepied but with different orchestration
(e.g., violins an octave lower) and different harmonies, and it adds an obbligato part for the oboes reminiscent of Dieupart's in Ex. VI-3.

Bach shows his virtuosity by creating long lines with a subtle use of hemiolia: In Passepied I a syncopation on the third pulse of a measure is tied
across the bar line (e.g., measures 2–3 and 6–7), suspiciously like a hemiolia
but not strongly reinforced by the harmony. In the same place in Passepied
II, the syncopation is deliberately denied by the harmony. This type of syncopation reappears in the second strain: in measures 18–19 it occurs two measures before the end of the phrase, but in measures 25–26 it comes,
unexpectedly, three measures before the end. The ending is further enhanced by a surprising harmonic twist in the penultimate two measures. Both
passepieds are scored for two oboes, bassoon, strings, and continuo.

The first passepied of the E minor English Suite (BWV 810) is in rondeau
form with two couplets, each sixteen measures long. The Rondeau section
also consists of sixteen measures, with the second half an elaborated version
of the first half, again reminiscent of Dieupart (Ex. VI-3). The first couplet
has melodic syncopations in measures 20–22 (tying together the fourth, fifth,
and sixth measures of the phrase) and a weak harmonic cadence on D at
measure 24; this propels the movement onward and negates any sense of
closure until measure 32, which is preceded by a typical hemiolia. *Notes inégales* are appropriate for this couplet, as well as for the rondeau. The second
couplet features interesting groupings that could be phrased to group two $\frac{3}{8}$
measures into a "double measure"; i.e., measures 49–50, 53–54, and at least
the upper voice of 56–61.

With Passepied II we turn from elaborations to the charm of the French
pastorale, or musette, with a duet over a drone bass and the typical passepied
rhythms deriving from the time of Lully. Bach moves to a higher register on
the keyboard and does not neglect rhythmic surprises (measures 12–15 and
20–23).

The single passepied from Partita V for keyboard (BWV 829) has us continually off balance. When examined, the dance phrases are actually regular
groups of four and eight beats, but cadences are avoided or cleverly elided in
such a way that the dance acquires a breathless quality. Strong accents, beginning with a real separation between the upbeat and measure 1, will enhance the rhythmic life of this piece. There are three possible hemiolias,
measures 6–7, 25–26, and 42–43. A pair of distinctive melodic patterns
emerge. One is in measures 1–2 and the other is the pattern of sixteenth
notes in measure 21, which appears in all the voices of the second strain. It

ends the dance as a descending sequence in the soprano over 7–6 suspensions between tenor and bass.

The two passepieds from Overture in the French Style (BWV 831) fully express Bach's genius. Passepied I explodes with energy with a virtuosic trill on the opening dissonant harmony in measure 1, propelling it into the rest of the dance phrase. Again, a large articulation between upbeat and downbeat will help project this energy to the listener. The hemiolia in measures 5–6 (an unusual part of the phrase for a hemiolia) rises over a chromatic bass, which leads to the cadence. The last eight measures of the second strain are an almost literal repeat of the first.

Passepied II is quieter in mood: the upbeat is on the same harmony as the downbeat of measure 1, implying a much smaller articulation than was the case in Passepied I; a drone bass imitates the musette much of the time; and the balanced four-measure phrase structure is more clearly evident. In the second strain Bach explores changing groups of eighths and sixteenths that fluctuate between two rhythmic patterns familiar from Lully. But listeners may not tarry, for they must return to the turmoil and excitement of Passepied I.

BWV 817

CHAPTER 7

The Sarabande

     The sarabande had had a long, illustrious, even tawdry history by the early eighteenth century.[1] From its probable origins in Spanish and New World folk arts—it was a dance accompanied by singing and instruments—the sarabande appeared in Italy in the early seventeenth century as a colorful, tempestuous, exotic dance. It was accompanied by castanets and by a guitar or guitars playing continuous variations on a series of harmonies, the chords punctuated by the fiery *rasqueado* strums and rhythms so loved by the passionate. Its opponents called the sarabande "lascivious" and wrote tracts against it.

    The French tamed the sarabande, at least in theory. In its noble form at the French Court, the extant choreographies reveal a dance that seems calm, serious, and sometimes tender, but ordered, balanced, and sustained. The step-units are generally the same as those used in most other dances—*tems de courante, pas de bourée,* various forms of the *coupé* (Fig. VII-1). There is no step-unit particularly associated with the sarabande, though many choreographies incorporate elegant leg gestures—*battements* and *pirouettes*—which can be impressive at a slow tempo.

    Hints of a passionate performance, however, appear in numerous pieces which incorporate teasing hesitations before an expected movement and double-time steps on the repeat of a strain of music.[2] These hints become

Fig. VII-1: Music and dance in the opening of "La Royalle," Pécour, *Nouveau Recueil* (c. 1713), p. 1.

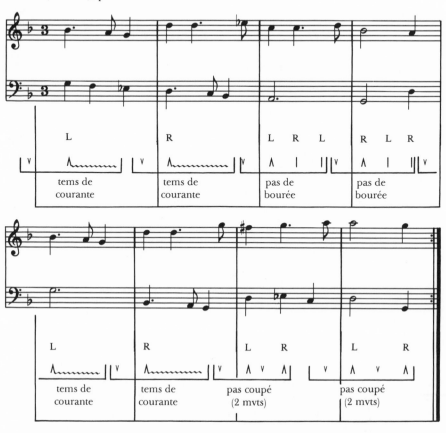

more plausible in light of Patricia Ranum's stunning recent discovery, in the appendix of Pomey's long-forgotten French and Latin dictionary published in Lyons in 1671, of the following description of a solo sarabande:

> At first he danced with a totally charming grace, with a serious and circumspect air, with an equal and slow rhythm [*cadence*], and with such a noble, beautiful, free and easy carriage that he had all the majesty of a king, and inspired as much respect as he gave pleasure.
> Then, standing taller and more assertively, and raising his arms to half-height and keeping them partly extended, he performed the most beautiful steps ever invented for the dance.
> Sometimes he would glide imperceptibly, with no apparent movement of his feet and legs, and seemed to slide rather than step. Sometimes, with the most beautiful timing in the world, he would remain suspended, immobile, and half leaning to the side with one foot in the air; and then, compensating for the

rhythmic unit [*cadence*] that had gone by, with another more precipitous unit he would almost fly, so rapid was his motion.

Sometimes he would advance with little skips, sometimes he would drop back with long steps that, although carefully planned, seemed to be done spontaneously, so well had he cloaked his art in skillful nonchalance.

Sometimes, for the pleasure of everyone present, he would turn to the right, and sometimes he would turn to the left; and when he reached the very middle of the empty floor, he would pirouette so quickly that the eye could not follow.

Now and then he would let a whole rhythmic unit [*cadence*] go by, moving no more than a statue, and then, setting off like an arrow, he would be at the other end of the room before anyone had time to realize that he had departed.

But all this was nothing compared to what was observed when this gallant began to express the emotions of his soul through the motions of his body, and reveal them in his face, his eyes, his steps and all his actions.

Sometimes he would cast languid and passionate glances throughout a slow and languid rhythmic unit [*cadence*]; and then, as though weary of being obliging, he would avert his eyes, as if he wished to hide his passion; and, with a more precipitous motion, would snatch away the gift he had tendered.

Now and then he would express anger and spite with an impetuous and turbulent rhythmic unit; and then, evoking a sweeter passion by more moderate motions, he would sigh, swoon, let his eyes wander languidly; and certain sinuous movements of the arms and body, nonchalant, disjointed and passionate, made him appear so admirable and so charming that throughout this enchanting dance he won as many hearts as he attracted spectators.[3]

We have quoted this passage in full because of its implications for an understanding of both the music and the dance of French sarabandes, with a possible carry-over to Bach's music. The passage includes verification of the idea of nonchalance along with a noble carriage (paragraph 1) and describes the use of several contrasting moods within a single piece (paragraph 9). In paragraphs 3 and 4 it mentions a variety of step-units—springs, *glissés*, pirouettes, leg gestures, and "long steps" (*grands pas*, which may have been a reference to *tems de courante*). The allusions to rhythm are perhaps most fascinating of all. Paragraph 3 speaks of holding up the rhythm for a moment, then making up for the time lost, which seems to describe *tempo rubato*. Paragraph 8 may refer to fluctuation of the beat (subtle ritards and accelerandos), though the text does not say so explicitly. Also interesting is the performer's use of pantomime, by face, steps, and "all his actions" (paragraph 7). The pantomime begins after the dance is well under way, after the audience is already paying close attention to the presentation.

Writers of Bach's time used a wide variety of terms to describe the sarabande but consistently alluded to an intensity of expression. Some spoke of it as "grave" or "ceremonious."[4] Others called it "majestic"[5] or "serious."[6] Rémond de Saint-Mard believed that it was "always melancholy, and exudes a delicate yet serious tenderness."[7] Johann Mattheson insisted that the sarabande "has no other emotion to express but ambition."[8] James Talbot, as quoted by Robert Donington, writes in 1690: "Sarabande a soft passionate Movement . . . apt to move the Passions and to disturb the tranquillity of the Mind."[9]

The music to "La Royalle" (Fig. VII-1) shows many of the sarabande's characteristics in the early 18th century. The metric structure (III–2–2) consists of three quarter-note beats per measure in a time signature of 3. Sarabandes generally had 3 or $\frac{3}{4}$ as time signatures; some had $\frac{3}{2}$, in which case the piece moved by three half-note beats per measure. The harmonic change is primarily on the level of the beat, and the phrases are consistently four or eight measures long.

A good tempo for dancing is ♩ = approximately MM 69,[10] although some dancers will not be able to sustain the difficult, slow gestures of the choreograhies at that tempo, or they may conceive of the sarabande as a faster dance. The reasons for performing sarabandes slowly are aesthetic not technical, since it is actually easier to dance them at a faster tempo. Obviously the time-word "slow" does not require or imply a specific tempo for all sarabandes or all performers. Music theorists of the late seventeenth and the eighteenth century who mention sarabande tempo agree that it was slow or very slow.

Nevertheless, several composers use time-words which imply variety in sarabande tempi. François Couperin, for example, marks some pieces "sarabande" and some "sarabande grave."[11] Montéclair gives examples of two types in his *Principes de Musique,* a "sarabande grave" in $\frac{3}{4}$ and a "sarabande légère" also in $\frac{3}{4}$ but marked "Gay. Mouvement de Chacone,"[12] implying that the latter is in the faster tempo of the chaconne. The French harpsichordist Gaspard Le Roux also wrote sarabandes in at least two tempi.[13]

Variation techniques are important to the soloistic style of the sarabande by the late seventeenth century. Many composers included *doubles,* or ornamented repeats, for sarabandes. Gaspard Le Roux wrote a twenty-four-measure sarabande, in bipartite form, followed by eleven more couplets, which are different *doubles* on the same piece. Among the German composers who wrote *doubles* to their sarabandes are Froberger, Pachelbel, Erlebach, Kuhnau, and Johann Mattheson. In some manuscript sources of French Court dancing one finds variations written into the dance music.[14] One may conclude that improvisation was an important element in this type of dance music. Mattheson refers in a somewhat derogatory manner to the use of variations:

> For playing [sarabandes] on the clavier and on the lute one lowers oneself somewhat with this category of melody, uses more liberties, indeed, even makes doubles or arpeggiated works of it, which are commonly called variations, though *Double* by the French. Lambert, the father-in-law of Lully, tended to use such diminutions, if I may say so, even in vocal sarabandes. Each to his own taste; but such would not be mine.[15]

The sarabande dance rhythm (Fig. VII-2) consists of a harmonic-rhythmic phrase of 12 beats (four measures). The thesis, or release from tension, occurs on beat 10 (beginning of measure 4) and diminishes further (becomes more thetic) going into beat 12. A preliminary thesis is often heard in measure 2 (beats 4, 5, and 6), beginning on beat 4 and continuing into beat 6, but is often "spoiled" by harmonies and rhythms which keep the movement going forward. Thus the common patterns of motion and repose in the sarabande are almost always (counting measures) aTAT or aaAT, unless the composer creates an eight-measure phrase by using unrestful harmonies and rhythms in measure 4.

Fig. VII-2: Model for the Sarabande Dance Rhythm
III–2–2, $\frac{3}{4}$

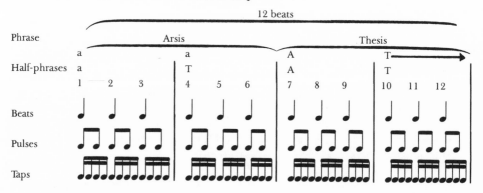

Balance is an important sarabande characteristic, and one seldom encounters phrases which are not four or eight measures long; phrases of five, six, or nine measures occur only rarely. This extreme simplicity of phrase structure, with its anticipated rhymes (question and answer, or statement and counterstatement), appears also in the gavotte and the minuet. But the sarabande was much older, both as a dance and as dance music, and the very simplicity of the phrase structure led composers writing for a soloist to experiment with various techniques and styles. By the early eighteenth century there is no one sarabande type or form, but an invariable phrase length and shape which appears in seemingly endless modifications. These varieties have never been systematically listed and studied by scholars; some of the compositional styles exploited by Bach are the classic French sarabande (Ex. VII-1 and Fig. VII-3), variation techniques (Exx. VII-4 and 5), and the use of an upbeat (Ex. VII-6).

The classic French sarabande, typical rhythms of which are shown in Fig. VII-3, is undoubtedly the most widespread sarabande style in this period, not only in French music but also in Italian, German, and English works. The

Fig. VII-3: Typical rhythmic patterns in the sarabande.

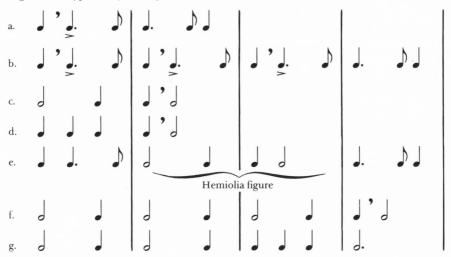

rhythm in Fig. VII-3a shows the typical "sarabande syncopation." In this six-beat phrase, the second beat is the high point and is more strongly accented than the first; beat 4 is the thesis, or release from tension, and beat 6 is even more thetic.

A keyboard sarabande by Dieupart (Ex. VII-1) shows a four-measure phrase consisting of two of these patterns in a row, followed by another four-measure phrase made up of two more such patterns. In measures 1 and 3 the composer emphasizes beat 2 by a dissonant harmony and an *agrément* (which begins with a dissonance). Beats 4, 5, and 6 are thetic and all on the same harmony; the *agrément* on beat 4 (thetic) would be performed with less emphasis than the one on beat 2 (arsic).

Performers who wish to emphasize the passion of the sarabande in this characteristic phrase may articulate strongly before beat 2, articulate again (but with less strength) before beat 4, and shorten the eighth note preceding beat 4 to a sixteenth note (see Ex. VII-2). The composer has emphasized the climactic nature of beat 2 by using a dissonant harmony. In a sarabande syncopation with a consonant harmony on beat 2, especially if it is the resolution of a feminine cadence, the performer may choose not to articulate before it, or to articulate only slightly. Since four of these patterns make up the first strain of Dieupart's piece, the performer will need to use ingenuity to shape the whole eight-measure phrase. Some suggestions are: 1. Shape the succession of two-measure patterns by making each "beat 2" more arsic than the one before, with the high point in measure 5. 2. Articulate ties across the bar line to create two-measure segments (measures 2–3 and 4–5). 3. Use *notes inégales* with the eighth notes in the bass, measures 6–7, to create move-

Ex. VII-1: First strain of the Sarabande from Suite in F minor by Charles
Dieupart (early eighteenth century).

Ex. VII-2: Sarabande syncopation.

ment toward the thesis. 4. Vary the types of trills (e.g., in measure 7 add a
vorschlag on beat 2, approaching the trill from below, and a turn between
beats 1 and 2).

Another typical sarabande rhythm (Fig. VII-3b) consists of a four-measure
phrase with the thesis on beat 10, preceded by three measures of the syncopation module (short-long). Here beats 2, 5, and 8 are all emphasized, and
the performer identifies one of them as the high point, using the techniques
just described.

In Fig. VII-3c and d the syncopation module is not in the arsic measure
but in the thetic measure. In this case the articulation of the syncopation
would be more restrained (less emphasized or dramatic) than when the syncopation is in an arsic measure. Often the composer will contribute toward a
restful quality by using the same harmony on a syncopation in a thetic measure, or by a feminine cadence.

Fig. VII-3e shows the characteristic hemiolia figure in measures 2–3 of the
four-measure phrase, preceded by an arsic syncopation module. Sometimes
the hemiolia figure will be ambiguous, so that one may choose to articulate it
or not, or even to perform it differently on the repeat of the passage.

Fig. VII-3f shows a sarabande phrase with the syncopation module only in the thetic measure 4. In Fig. VII-3g the rhythmic pattern has no syncopation module at all. Ex. VII-3 shows a twenty-measure keyboard sarabande by Louis Couperin with no syncopations, yet it is clearly in the classic French style in other respects. The consistently trochaic rhythms terminate in feminine cadences every fourth measure. The composer himself has "altered" some of the eighth notes preceding a thesis to sixteenth notes (e.g., measures 9 and 11).

Other styles of sarabande writing leave even more to the imagination of the performer. Böhm's sarabande (Ex. VII-4) is without figuration, but the "bare bones" of the harmonic structure invite performers to add their own elaborations. Even though no syncopation modules are explicitly written, some performers will be able to incorporate them by interpolating rhythms presented in Fig. VII-3 onto the chord. On the other hand, some sarabandes seem to be a written-out variation for which the simple version is missing or not included. Reinken's sarabande (Ex. VII-5) uses several different figurations in a piece which seems neither serious nor grave nor melancholy nor lyrical, but merely a series of harmonies in balanced, four-measure phrases in slow triple meter; the performer is left with great freedom to determine the mood of the piece!

An upbeat in the sarabande is unusual but not unheard of, but its use presents an interesting problem for the composer. An upbeat alters the rhythm and the sense of balance by introducing iambs across the bar line. The only other dance type that consistently exploits the idea of rhythms across a bar line is the gavotte. Muffat's Sarabanda (Ex. VII-6) uses the strongest dissonances on beat 1 of the first measure of each of the four-measure phrases. If this use of dissonance is perceived as a rhythmic climax at the beginning of the first full measure, the movement of the phrase begins with a jolt and progresses downward from there—a forceful effect which Bach used as well. Several of his sarabandes show Bach experimenting with various kinds of upbeats and harmonic dissonances.

The "Sarabande L'Unique" by François Couperin (not shown) is another example of a sarabande which exceeds convention without actually breaking all the norms.[16] Two affects are juxtaposed in this piece; after firmly establishing the slow, noble gestures of the classic French sarabande, the piece is suddenly interrupted twice, by two measures marked "vivement" in which very fast, lively rhythms rudely intrude upon the grave affect. Even though this interruption occurs in the arsic part of the phrase, it profoundly disturbs the mood of the piece; one is reminded again of Pomey's description of the sarabande.[17]

The freedoms and possibilities in sarabande composition must have intrigued Bach, and one easily imagines him rising to meet such challenges.

Ex. VII-3: Sarabande in B minor by Louis Couperin (mid-seventeenth century).

Ex. VII-4: First strain of Sarabande by Georg Böhm (1690s).

Ex. VII-5: Opening of Sarabande by Johann Adam Reinken (1680s).

Ex. VII-6: Opening of orchestral Sarabanda by Georg Muffat, Concerto IV, "Dulce Somnium."

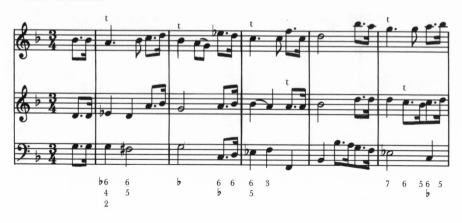

BACH'S SARABANDES

Bach wrote more sarabandes than any other dance type, if we include the *doubles,* which are essentially variations rather than ornamentations of a dance. Sarabandes appear in five early keyboard and lute works and in all six English suites between the Weimar and early Leipzig years; in all the French Suites, the Suites in E♭ major and A minor for keyboard, Partitas I and II for solo violin, the six solo cello suites and a lute version of the sarabande of the Fifth Suite, and the Partita for solo flute, which come from the Köthen years; and in all six keyboard Partitas, the Overture in the French Style, the Suite in B minor for orchestra, and the C minor Partita for lute, which probably come from the years in Leipzig.

Over a period of approximately thirty-three years Bach experimented with and refined a wide variety of sarabandes. He wrote them with and without upbeats, and no two upbeat figures are the same; he wrote short sarabandes (BWV 832, 965, and 1007 each consist of only two eight-measure strains) and very long ones (BWV 1013 has two strains of sixteen and thirty measures respectively); he wrote a sarabande in which the first strain is repeated *da capo* (BWV 823), one with a written-out petite reprise in the *double* (BWV 818), stately sarabandes, lyrical sarabandes, sarabandes with constant dotted rhythms and a marchlike character which recall the French overture and *entrée grave,* and many which present elaborate and harmonically complex dance stylizations. Only one ensemble piece contains a sarabande, the B minor suite for orchestra. Thus, in Bach's hands the sarabande is essentially a virtuoso piece for a soloist, who has the freedom to use subtle performance techniques not available to larger groups.[18]

Early Sarabandes

The sarabande in the Suite in B♭ major (BWV 821), for keyboard, begins imitatively and may well have been conceived as having one beat per measure (the dotted half note) in a metric structure 1–3–2; the harmonic rhythm is slow, with one or two changes per measure. Bach uses modal interchange in measures 14 and 16–17. This piece is probably in the tradition of the French sarabandes marked "légère."

The sarabande in the Suite in F minor for keyboard (BWV 823) is unusual in that it is in ABA form; a *da capo* sign appears at the end of the second strain. In addition, measures 9–12 essentially repeat measures 1–4. This is not an original idea of Bach's, for, as Richard Hudson has pointed out, Italian composers such as Buoni in 1693 "sometimes repeated the opening melody at the end of the second section, creating a rounded binary form.[19] BWV 823 is very chromatic; the performer can add to this intensity by overdotting the quarter notes in measures 7, 8, 15, 19, 26, and 27, and by clearly articulating the hemiolia in the penultimate two measures (26–27).

The sarabande from the keyboard Partie in A major (BWV 832) is stylistically similar to the *entrée grave,* or French overture style, with its preponderance of sharply dotted rhythms and heavy chords. Almost every measure has a syncopation module, which challenges the performer in shaping the phrases, since each syncopation plays a different role in the total effect. In arsic measures the dotted note could be lengthened. The last four measures contain an interesting harmonic twist, with a Neapolitan sixth in measures 14–15.

BWV 965 is an arrangement of the sarabande from Johann Adam Reinken's Sonata No. 1 in A minor from the *Hortus Musicus* (1687).[20] Reinken's work is a trio sonata with two eight-measure strains, a simple piece which might well have been improvised upon by performers of the day. Bach's version for keyboard follows the original fairly closely as to phrase structure but improves the part-writing here and there, keeping strictly to three voices, which contain much more individual interest than does their model. Ornaments on the second beat of the syncopation module (e.g., in measures 1 and 2) will help bring out the sarabande character of this piece.

The sarabande from the Suite in E minor (BWV 996), for lute, is notated in $\frac{3}{2}$, so that the half note, not the quarter note, is the beat. The piece is elaborately ornamented with French *agréments*, Italian *tiratas* (measure 13), and other flourishes filling in the melodic intervals. Trochaic rhythms greatly outnumber the few syncopation modules, though careful articulation of the latter will help bring clarity to a vast array of ornamentation.

The Six English Suites for Keyboard

In the English Suites Bach elaborates extensively upon the basic sarabande rhythms of Fig. VII-3. Now one finds interesting harmonic adventures (particularly in Suites I, III, and IV); the introduction of sequences, pedal points, new textures, and written-out elaborations (Suites II, III, VI); and longer, more-complex forms. None of the sarabandes has an upbeat, but in all six the sarabande rhythms from Fig. VII-3 are exploited and embellished with both French and Italian ornamentation.

The sarabande in English Suite I in A major (BWV 806) has what might be termed a motto theme: the rhythm of the upper voice in the first two measures is repeated almost continuously throughout the piece. This motto theme has the syncopation module in the second, or thesis measure, as in Fig. VII-3d. The motto appears in sequences (measures 21–23) and is also used imitatively (measures 25–end), all of which contributes to the cohesiveness of this dance. The emphatic second beat of the syncopation module is sometimes consonant, as in measure 8 (albeit with a 4–3 suspension in the inner voice), but sometimes quite dissonant (measure 10); as pointed out earlier, one may emphasize the arsic quality of these dissonances by a large space or an articulation before them. In the second strain the thetic measures 16, 20, and 24 contain wonderful Italianate flourishes leading inexorably toward the next sarabande phrase. As in BWV 832 (above), Bach digresses to the Neapolitan sixth of iv in the relative minor (measure 13) and to the iv of iv of the relative minor (measure 14), which makes for splendid harmonic surprises. It is interesting to note that the opening melody (measure 1) is reminiscent of "Quia respexit," an aria from Bach's *Magnificat* (BWV 243), and "Schlafe mein Liebster," from the *Christmas Oratorio* (BWV 248).

In the sarabande from English Suite II (BWV 807) the syncopation module appears most often in a thetic measure, which gives a quiet affect to the piece. Bach's agréments, which may be used on the repeat of each strain, are reasonably elaborate and consist chiefly of diminutions—the filling in of melodic intervals and the embellishing of chords. If the tempo is not too slow the use of rhythmic freedom will greatly enhance the performance of the sixteenth notes of these repeats.

Even more elaborate ornamentation and harmonies greet us in the sarabande in G minor of English Suite III (BWV 808). Yet the piece is harmonically rooted by the many drone notes, or pedal points, in the bass. Dissonant harmonies propel us toward cadences that in turn release the tension. For example, the harmonic adventures of measures 13–16 move from a diminished-seventh chord in measure 13 to vii° in measure 15, and VI in measure 16, with a double appoggiatura figure in the middle voice. For a regal, majestic quality, the performer may enhance the syncopation modules by changing the even eighth notes to dotted eighths and sixteenths and by highlighting beat 2, either by arpeggiating the chord or by ornamenting it. Bach offers his own suggestions in the diminutions.

After the varied repeats of the sarabandes in BWV 807 and 808 Bach lets performers use their own imaginations in English Suite IV, BWV 809. However, many ideas can be gleaned from the previous ornamentations (e.g., for arpeggiating and decorating the chords of measures 1–2). Again Bach uses a motto theme in the opening figure; one way to intensify it is to overdot the first dotted eighth note and shorten the subsequent thirty-second notes. Interesting harmonies conclude the piece (measures 21–23), moving from the dominant on the second beat of measure 21 through V_3^4 of the dominant and V_5^6 of the dominant to the dominant again in measure 23.

The sarabande of English Suite V (BWV 810) also begins with a motto theme. It is a lyrical, tender piece, extraordinary in the fluidity of its phrases. Usual cadence points are often avoided or weakened (e.g., measure 4), and the final eight measures of the piece (17–24) are a *tour de force* of simplicity in motion. The syncopation module consistently appears in thetic measures, with feminine cadences in which the second chord is consonant. Bach incorporates ornamentation into the texture—turn-like figures (sixteenth notes in measures 8, 9, and 12), *coulé* (measure 14), mordents (measures 5–6 and 13–14, upper voice), and even short-long *notes inégales* (measure 13, upper voice).

Bach may have intended the sarabande of English Suite VI (BWV 811) as a rather slow piece, since it has a signature of $\frac{3}{2}$, with the beat being the half note. If this is the case, the original sarabande will require many arpeggiated chords, ornaments, and imaginative elaborations even before the *double* is played. In the opening phrase, for example, the syncopation modules in measures 1 and 2 can take a long trill on the second beat of the measure, with the climax of the phrase coming in the second module. In measure 7, beat 2, the notated mordent should also be a long trill. Chromatic harmonies and cadential suspensions create an air of seriousness and gravity in this sarabande, but in the *double* Bach suggests a contrasting affect. The figurations in the *double* are those of the "stile brisé," or arpeggiated style, popularized in the seventeenth century by lutenists. These figurations do not emphasize the straightforward patterns with many dotted rhythms, which characterize the original sarabande, but consist of a constant movement of eighth notes, suggesting a freer, more *rubato*, sensitive, and intimate style of performance. Sometimes ornaments are notated, as in the written-in approach to the *agrément* in the upper voice of measure 7, beat 1.

The Two Sarabandes for Solo Violin

Bach wrote his two sarabandes for solo violin in Köthen. Partita I (BWV 1002) begins with a sarabande using triple and quadruple stops to make heavy, widely spaced chords which may be arpeggiated in various ways and which lend themselves to occasional rhythmic freedom. The melody comes and goes, but the syncopation module is hardly evident here. Rather, a series of rich harmonies in phrases of 2 + 2 measures flow on inexorably, with thetic points almost always on beat 1 of the even-numbered measures. The *double* offers a striking contrast. It is in the straightforward Italian virtuosic, rather angular concerto style. Even though the *double* is in $\frac{9}{8}$ it may have the same tempo as its model in $\frac{3}{4}$, according to Kirnberger.[21] No bowings for the *double* appear in Bach's autograph manuscript.

The sarabande in Partita II (BWV 1004) is far more complex than its predecessor; syncopation modules abound, with rich French and Italian ornamentation superimposed on the basic sarabande rhythms of Fig. VII-3. The performer needs to add even more, however; for example, measures 1, 2, and 6 cry out for a trill on the dissonant beat 2. The Italian-style diminutions are spectacular and will delight an audience, especially if the familiar sarabande rhythms are clearly projected as well. A great variety of bowings is evident in the notation, with notes grouped by twos, threes, fours, sixes, sevens, and even tens. Bach has extended the form of this sarabande by providing extra measures, in an even more virtuosic style, after the end of the second strain.

Sarabandes for Solo Cello

All six of Bach's solo cello suites contain sarabandes, and each is a unique contribution to the literature for that instrument. The first one, in Suite I (BWV 1007), announces the sarabande rhythm clearly in the first four measures. It then moves to what some cellists consider a melody but which actually consists of figurations on the sarabande dance phrase, leading neatly to the thesis on a feminine cadence at the beginning of measure 8. Further feminine cadences appear in thesis measures 12 and 16. The P 26 manuscript, in the hand of Anna Magdalena Bach, indicates groupings of two and four notes except for the six-note grouping of the *tirata* figure at the end of measure 6.

The sarabande from Suite II (BWV 1008) is somewhat longer in both its strains. The familiar sarabande rhythmic pattern of Fig. VII-3a is clearly Bach's starting point in forming the phrases, and the syncopation module is always active and arsic except in the final measure of both strains. To intensify the rhythmic patterns in Fig. VII-3a, for example, in measures 1–2 one may either put a mordent on beat 1 and leave a space before the following sixteenth note, or articulate with a space before the sixteenths preceding beat 4, shortening them to compensate. These articulations may also be used in other analogous places. The key of D minor and the intensity of this piece suggest a grave character and a slow tempo.

A somewhat brighter quality and perhaps a slightly faster tempo seem appropriate for the C major sarabande in Suite III (BWV 1009). The rhythm of Fig. VII-3f, which features four-measure phrases without division into two subsections, underlies at least the first strain. Hefty chords strengthen the first beat of many arsic measures, and the rhythmic pattern ♩ ♪♩♩ dominates the action until the extension beginning in measure 13, which culminates on a strong cadence on the supertonic (measure 15). From there to the end the figuration changes, with written-in turns and melodic sequences which lead to an emphatic final cadence accented by a syncopation module. The bowings in the Bach-Gesellschaft edition, which are grouped by twos and fours, are almost identical (a few are missing) with those in the Bach manuscript P 26.

In Suite IV (BWV 1010), the sarabande is a stately, majestic piece whose dotted rhythms are reminiscent of the *entrée grave* style. According to Quantz, the character of this style is best achieved by lengthening the dotted note, detaching the bow during the dot, and shortening the following quick note or notes. In addition, he says the bow should be detached at each quarter note whether it is dotted or not.[22] The four- and eight-measure phrases are clear and eloquent, with frequent use of the rhythm of Fig. VII-3d (e.g., measures 1–2). No slurs are present in the P 26 manuscript.

In the last two sarabandes for solo cello Bach experiments even further. The scordatura tuning of Suite V (BWV 1011)[23] is used to project a sarabande with an angular melodic line in almost constant eighth-note movement. The underlying rhythms are that of Fig. VII-3g, which omits the syncopation module. Bowings of the P 26 manuscript are in twos and fours, as they appear in most editions. (See also the lute arrangement of this piece, BWV 995, below.)

As for Suite VI (BWV 1012), scholars are not certain whether it was intended for the "viola pomposo," the violoncello piccolo, or some other similar instrument.[24] Today this sarabande is, of course, performed by cellists even with its stringent technical demands. The $\frac{3}{2}$ meter again suggests a slow, majestic performance. The idea of the written-in appoggiaturas in measures 6–8 is revived dramatically in the second strain but this time in the interval of the sixth (measures 17, 21–22, etc.), and sometimes in sequential movement. Although Bach writes in numerous ornamented passages for the upper voice, some performers will want to embellish syncopation modules, such as in measures 1–3, with an *agrément* or an arpeggio on beat 2. The modal interchange in measures 25–28 provides a refreshing harmonic contrast and heightens the dramatic buildup in the second strain.

A Sarabande for Solo Flute

The Partita in A minor for solo flute, (BWV 1013) was probably written during Bach's last year or two at Köthen and is the longest one he wrote (16 + 30 measures). At first glance it seems unlike a sarabande because of the consistent eighth- and sixteenth-note movement. It is probably a *double* based on a simpler structure, a technique used by Reinken and other composers before Bach (Ex. VII-5). The harmonic movement follows sarabande rhythms and is actually rather slow; often a single measure will have only one harmony throughout. Flutists wonder where to breathe—there is only one internal cadence in the first strain (measure 4) and three in the second (measures 20,

26, and 34), and the eighth or sixteenth notes usually continue in spite of the cadences. A significant caesura may occur after the cadence on the dominant in measure 34; it is here that the opening material of the first strain reappears. Bach writes in some turns (e.g., measures 11 and 14) and *tiratas* (measures 10 and 12); they sound best when they are clearly articulated and when a sarabande dance tempo is chosen for the piece.

Sarabandes in the French Suites

The D minor sarabande in French Suite I (BWV 812) strikes one as a lament, with its descending bass, plaintive melody, sustained dissonance, and cadential suspensions embellished by appoggiaturas (measures 8 and 24). Some performers will stress the second beat of syncopation modules (as in measures 2, 4, 10, etc.) with an articulation before it (♪♪) and/or add a mordent or a *port de voix*. Others will consider Bach's use of the same harmony in these places to indicate that the stress is on the beginning of the measure, not the second beat. In the second strain Bach quotes the opening melody (from the first strain) in the bass voice, for five measures. With great élan he uses fresh harmonies this time, beginning on the dominant and turning toward the subdominant. Snatches of this exquisite melody recur from time to time, to the delight of the listener.

The sarabande of French Suite II (BWV 813), in C minor, again features an elegant melody. *Double* techniques and chordal figurations embellish the harmonies, which are more complex and chromatic than those in the sarabande from the flute partita. The opening rhythm is that of Fig. VII-3c, with the syncopation module in the thetic position, and this rhythm recurs frequently throughout the piece. The artless melody actually contains many written-out ornaments, such as single and double appoggiaturas (measures 12–13) and quasi-turns (measure 16). In studying the melody one notes the ornamental and nonharmonic tones in order to separate them from the rest of the texture, thus exposing the underlying sarabande harmonies and rhythms. This might also have been the point of departure for Bach in the Prelude in C major from the *Well-Tempered Clavier*, Book I (BWV 846). In the second strain sequential movement leads to a climax, starting in measure 20 and rising finally to the high C to produce a dramatic ending.

Syncopation modules are almost entirely lacking in the quiet sarabande in B minor from French Suite III (BWV 814). It is based on the rhythm of Fig. VII-3g; Louis Couperin (Ex. VII-3) offered an example of this technique. A harmonic reduction of Bach's piece reveals a sarabande with perfectly balanced phrases woven into a three-voice texture with ornamented suspensions. The melody line is passed from one voice to the other, dissolving into large, angular intervals and dissonant harmonies which lead to the final cadence of each strain. The sarabande from French Suite IV (BWV 815) has a motto theme (used earlier in the A major English Suite, BWV 806), which persists throughout the piece and embodies the syncopation module nicely. Bach's ornamentation in the first five measures suggests similar additions to analogous passages. The harmonic movement of this sarabande is unique: the opening I_7 (which is really IV_7 of the dominant) creates tonal ambiguity that keeps the listener in a constant search for the tonic until the very end of the piece, where the steady, lyrical movement of eighth notes resolves itself in an arpeggiated cadence on E♭.

The G major sarabande from the French Suite V (BWV 816) is almost twice as long as any other sarabande in the French Suites. Using a strict 4 + 4–measure framework, Bach writes a lyrical, diverse melodic line, supported by two lower voices that create a varied contrapuntal duet below it, complete with ornamentated suspension cadences. The liberally decorated melody will sometimes bear additional ornaments (e.g., a mordent on the F♯ opening the second strain, and on the G in the measure following; a *port de voix* on the E in measure 30). Notes following a dotted-quarter or eighth note may be shortened, suspending the movement "in air," for an enhanced thetic quality in the following measure.

The majestic sarabande in E major, in French Suite VI (BWV 817), again shows Bach to be a master at ornamentation of the simple harmonic rhythms of this dance. As in the preceding sarabande, performers may enhance the arsic moments by altering groupings of dotted quarter and eighth notes to double dotted quarters and sixteenth notes. The arsic syncopation modules are dissonant on the second beat and lend themselves to long trills, which elongate the opening appoggiatura. Arpeggiated chords challenge the performer to play them in a variety of ways, not necessarily bottom to top; for example, in measures 10 and 12 the voice leading suggests a top to bottom rendition; one might also begin in the middle.

Other Keyboard Sarabandes from Köthen

In the keyboard Suite in A minor (BWV 818) Bach writes a *simple* and a *double* sarabande, with interesting figurations in both. The *simple* is an elegiac piece with a persistent, falling arpeggio figure and frequent appoggiaturas leading from beat 1 to beat 2 of the measure. Shortening the final eighth note of the measure will heighten this rhythmic gesture. The *double* consists of constant eighth-and-sixteenth-note movement. One may add excitement by stressing the second beat of some measures (e.g., measure 1) by overdotting the first note and leaving a tiny separation or space before the ensuing sixteenth note. *Notes inégales* may also enhance the stepwise sixteenth-note passages. Bach ends this *double* by notating a *petite reprise*.

BWV 818a, from a later manuscript, is probably a copy of BWV 818 by Bach's student H. N Gerber; there is no *double*, as in BWV 818. The sarabande in BWV 818a is in the *entrée grave* style, in which eighth and sixteenth notes may be shortened to emphasize the syncopation module that occurs in both arsic and thetic measures. Although the extensive ornamentation is interestingly varied, more might be added (e.g., trills on beat 2 of measure 13 and beat 3 of measure 15). Harmonically, this sarabande holds interest continually—notice the exciting dissonant chromaticism in measures 14 and 18!

The sarabande in the keyboard Suite in E♭ major (BWV 819) again uses the noble style of the French *entrée grave* (see BWV 832 for an earlier example). The techniques suggested above (for BWV 018) also apply here, especially *notes inégales*, which enhance the character of the French style.

The Leipzig Sarabandes

The Leipzig sarabandes, which include those from the six keyboard Partitas, represent Bach's crowning achievement in this genre. The Partita sarabandes are the ultimate examples of dance stylization in all of Bach's works, in which a virtuoso soloist can take the listener to heights of perception found nowhere else in dance music. Each Partita sarabande stands alone as a piece, quite apart from the others in the suite. The Partitas make up Bach's third and last collection of six keyboard suites; they were published separately, in 1726–31, and together as Opus 1 of the *Clavier-Übung* (1731).

The Sarabande in the B♭ Partita (BWV 825) is a majestic, stately piece in which the sarabande rhythms are clear throughout, although they are embellished with Italianate melodic diminutions sprinkled with occasional *agréments;* in measure 19 the written-out mordents are themselves decorated by trills. For an especially dramatic presentation, the opening measures (and analogous places) of both strains could be arpeggiated and the following sixteenth note shortened.

Although not so titled, the sarabande in Partita II (BWV 826), appears to be another written-out *double* (see BWV 1013). The best approach to such a piece is to make a harmonic reduction to reveal the simple version; such a reduction will enable the performer to separate ornamental from non-ornamental tones in the *double* and essential dissonances from nonessential dissonances (see Ex. VII-7). Such a procedure is especially important in this sarabande because the upper line actually embraces two voices, soprano and alto, which have become one line.[25]

The sarabande in Partita III (BWV 827) combines several features which lift it out of the ordinary: a very simple harmonic structure, virtuoso keyboard techniques used as a *double* of some forgotten *simple*, an upbeat, and contrapuntal texture. The underlying harmonies are uncomplicated in order to enable the fantasies of the composer to soar. Indeed, the change and return of the different figurations continually delight the attentive listener, who may hear the same idea come back in different form, in a different voice, or upside down. The simple harmonies hold it all together, with the use of predictable sequences in the second strain.

The piece begins imitatively, and all three voices have interesting material

Ex. VII-7: J. S. Bach, opening of Sarabande, BWV 826 (harmonic reduction).

at one time or another and sometimes at the same time. The upbeat adds another twist. As we have seen in Ex. VII-6, it alters the rhythm and the sense of balance by introducing iambs across the bar line. Only a few composers used an upbeat in the sarabande, but, given the challenges, it is understandable that Bach would want to try his hand at it. The iamb becomes the dominant rhythmic module, with the thesis still in measure 4 but with neither syncopations nor hemiolias, which are very common in sarabandes.

Careful articulations help to project these atypical rhythms and to clarify the contrapuntal texture. For example, a space before the beginning of measure 1 tells the listener that there is, indeed, an upbeat. Triplet figures need their own identity and should not be slurred to one another or to a following eighth note. The second note of the upbeat has a mordent indicated, but it could be played with a carefully articulated trill instead, each time it occurs.

The sarabande from the D major Partita (BWV 828) combines still other unusual features to create a unique *tour de force* in the genre. The dramatic gesture of the opening two measures seems to signal the familiar sarabande syncopation module, but the dissonant second beat is weakened by a melodic suspension so that one is not aware of a syncopation but listens carefully to the written-in arpeggio of measure 2. A long, exuberant, embellished melody follows, juxtaposed to the opening gesture but never recalling it. Careful performers will articulate before each turn, slide, *tirata,* and *passaggio* which Bach notates into the melody. *Rückungen* appear, in which syncopations on the eighth-note level anticipate chordal tones.[26]

In the second strain the opening gesture returns, for two measures only, followed by a much more elaborate melody and accompaniment. This section of the piece almost seems like the development section of a condensed sonata form![27] The gesture of the first strain finally returns in the tonic (measures 29–30), and the key of D major is clearly confirmed by conventional harmonic patterns (though overlaid with an ever more exuberant melody).

In the G major sarabande of Partita V (BWV 829) Bach combines the crisply dotted rhythms of the French *entrée grave* style[28] with the "iambs across the bar line" of an upbeat, resulting in a piece with strong forward motion and an equally strong sense of arrival at the end of the four- and eight-measure phrases. Few syncopation modules or hemiolias are present to remind the listener of other sarabandes; rather, one is led by Bach to a more-rarified atmosphere. The trio-sonata texture (two upper voices accompanied by a bass) adds another dimension, and the use of appoggiaturas in the dotted-note figures puts icing on the cake. Again, the wise performer will carefully articulate beat 1 of the first full measure so that the listener can more easily sort out the complexities of this highly stylized dance.

Another upbeat and more dotted rhythms confront us in the rhapsodic, majestic sarabande from the E minor Partita (BWV 830). It is rhapsodic because of the elaborate *passaggi, agréments,* arpeggiations, and restlessly changing harmonies; majestic by means of the dotted rhythms and the harmonic richness. Bach may have used Muffat (Ex. VII-6) as his model when he moved from the upbeat to a strong dissonance on beat 1 of the first full measure. The effect is stunning, throwing listeners off balance and holding them in suspense until the resolution in the third beat of measure 2. If one arpeggiates the first two chords the rhythms will be even harder to distinguish, leading listeners to *terra incognita.* The toccata offers useful clues for appropriate types of arpeggiation.

Some performers give up the sarabande idea altogether, resulting in a piece which sounds as though it is in compound duple meter. This works, but one need not sacrifice the triple meter so characteristic of sarabandes; with effort, the "tripleness" may be retained by accenting the first beat of each measure and by choosing a sarabande tempo that allows the piece to move by quarter-note beats, not eighth-note beats.

Bach's last known keyboard sarabande, in the Overture in the French Style (BWV 831), is far different from the sometimes flamboyant and experimental ones just described. The sarabande rhythmic pattern of Fig. VII-3a is clearly projected throughout. The elaborations are simple and clearly French, with counterpoint and chromatic harmonies which are just as clearly German. The three- and often four-part counterpoint is seamless, moving fluidly from the beginning to the end of each strain. Bach uses avoided cadences (measure 8 in the first strain and measure 16 in the second one) to enhance the forward movement. Performers may add *agréments* (e.g., a mordent on beat 2 of measure 1, upper voice) where they are needed, and play the sixteenth notes *inégales,* to complement Bach's use of the French style in this piece.

The other surviving Leipzig sarabandes include two for lute and one for orchestra. The lute sarabande in BWV 997 is an elaboration *(double)* over a bass line. The bass keeps to a pedal point on C for the first seven measures, finally coming to the dominant in measure 8. The piece uses the rhythms of Fig. VII-3f and g, and the syncopation module is present only in subtle ways (e.g., measure 8). This grave but eloquent piece features an Italianate melodic line of haunting beauty, with an opening figure reminiscent of the sarabande in BWV 806.

Another sarabande for lute, BWV 995, is simply a transcription of the fifth cello suite (BWV 1011). It is transposed from C minor to G minor but is otherwise quite faithful to the original.

The sarabande from the orchestral Suite in B minor (BWV 1067) is the only one for an ensemble group. It is scored for flute, two violins, viola, and continuo but is in four-part texture, since the flute doubles Violin I. This piece is another remarkable example of avoided cadences; there are only two cadences, one at the end of each strain. The counterpoint is also unusual; Bach employs canon at the twelfth between the melody and bass lines, a difficult feat he (or any other composer) rarely attempted! The slurs, which group eighth notes mainly by twos in the flute and violin parts, may be applied to the other parts as well, especially the bass when it is in canon with the upper parts.

BWV 807

CHAPTER 8

The Courante

"The [musical] transformations of the courante might be compared to the frolicking of a fish who plunges, disappears and returns again to the surface of the water."[1] With this vivid and charming metaphor Jules Ecorcheville portrays the elusive surprises and nuanced change which are so much a part of the French courante, certainly the most ambiguous of all the court dances but also the grandest in style and the noblest in character. The courante of Bach's day derives from early seventeenth-century dance and music at the French Court of Louis XIII. Its extraordinary popularity among aristocrats is reflected in the fact that it occurred more often in seventeenth-century French harpsichord and lute music than did any other dance. Bach inherited a courante tradition deriving from a number of mid-seventeenth-century geniuses, among them the French lutenists Denis and Ennemond Gaultier; the French harpsichord composers d'Anglebert, Louis Couperin and Chambonnières; and such leading German keyboard composers as Froberger, Reinken, Buxtehude, Böhm, Pachelbel, J. P. Krieger, and Kuhnau. Thus he drew not only on the rhythms of French courantes as they had long been danced in Germany (see chapter 1) but also on courantes in the rich, fruitful heritage of baroque keyboard and lute music.

The French courante was variously described as serious and solemn (Dupont,[2] Masson,[3] Walther[4]), noble and grand (P. Rameau,[5] Compan[6]), hopeful (Mattheson[7]), majestic (Quantz[8]), and earnest (Türk[9]). All these qualities imply a slow tempo. In fact, the courante is the slowest of all dances with three "temps" (beats) to the measure, followed in order of increasing speed by the sarabande, passacaille, chaconne, minuet, and passepied.[10] However, some courantes are faster than others, according to evidence from several early eighteenth-century French composers. François Couperin's *Les Nations* (1726) contains pieces marked as follows: "Premier Courante. Noblement"; "Seconde Courante. Un peu plus viste"; "Courante. [no tempo indication]"; "Seconde Courante. Un peu plus gayement."[11] Nicholas-Antoine Lebègue wrote a "Courante grave" followed by a "Courante gaye," both in the French style.[12] This may reflect a performance practice in which the second of two succesive courantes is played a little faster than the first. Some writers referred to the courante as "fast," but what they undoubtedly meant is that the notes move quickly. An example is Georg Muffat's instructions on bowing in the Lullian style. The English translation commonly appears as, "Because of the rapid tempo of courantes . . . ," but the literal meaning of both the German and the French text is "Because of the speed of the movement of the notes. . . . "[13]

As a dance the courante originated earlier than most other French Baroque dances. It was already flourishing in the early and mid-seventeenth century under the reign of Louis XIII, and it was also danced with unbridled enthusiasm at the English Court of Charles II (reigned 1660–85). According to Pierre Rameau, court balls under Louis XIV began, after the branles, with His Majesty dancing the courante. The king was said to have practiced this dance daily for all the twenty-two years that the eminent dancing master Pierre Beauchamps could be his teacher. Rameau also states that Louis XIV danced the courante better than did any other member of his Court and with a "quite unusual grace," suggesting that the king wanted his reign, his kingdom, and his person to be identified with this dance.[14]

Though by the early eighteenth century in France other dances were more popular than the courante it was one of the three most important French social dances practiced in Germany at that time, according to *Rechtschaffener Tanzmeister,* a 1717 encyclopedic treatise by Gottfried Taubert.[15] This dance contained all the principles of a basic French dance technique, according to Taubert, and it also served as the opening dance at formal court balls, making its perfection an important goal for all Germans who might participate in these ceremonious occasions.

The dance has several unique features: it moves in $\frac{3}{2}$ meter in a very slow tempo, which makes it the slowest of all baroque dances; its characteristic step-units all cross bar lines; and the characteristic step-units are used only in this dance. Taubert discusses these step-units and calls them the "short" and the "long" *pas de courante.*[16] The short *pas de courante* is simply the *tems de courante,* a step which rises on an *élevé* and then continues slowly gliding,[17] preceded by a *pas tendu,* a leg gesture ending in a step ("pied en l'air et le poser ensuite"; Fig. VIII-1a). The immense dignity of this step in a slow tempo made it appropriate to inaugurate the whole dance (Fig. VIII-2, measure 1). All the older French courante choreographies (those which probably predate 1700) begin with a *tems de courante,* though without notation of the *pas tendu.*[18]

Fig. VIII-1: Two step-units for the courantes, as described in **Taubert:Rechtschaffener** (1717), pp. 576–77, 581–86. a. Short *pas de courante;* b. Long *pas de courante.*

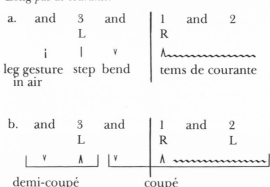

Figure VIII-1b illustrates Taubert's long *pas de courante,* which Pierre Rameau calls simply the *pas de courante;* it is made up of a demi-coupé and a coupé, straddling the bar line and taking up beat 3 of a measure and beats 1 and 2 of the following measure. It emphasizes a rhythm of $\frac{3}{2}$ ♩ | ♩. in which a single arsic beat is followed by a thesis twice as long. This step-unit in itself embodies the courante: the performers must sustain the long thesis in a noble, compelling manner, with dignity and composure—still a challenge to dancers of our own day.

Taubert describes several forms of the dance and presents three choreographies, but unfortunately the music is lacking. In the simplest form the gentleman holds the lady's left hand throughout the dance. They begin at the foot of the hall, move up the hall, turn widely leftward, and come back, forming an oval or an ellipse. The lady moves on the outside of the turns with larger steps, the gentleman inside. The lady performs a short *pas de courante* and seven long *pas de courante* during this figure; the gentleman does the same except that he uses the short *pas* on the corners of the turns.

Fig. VIII-2 shows a choreography with music, using more-varied step-units in a through-composed piece with different step-units and rhythms on the repeat. The dancers move in opposition to each other, not together as in the simple form of the dance just described. *La Bourgogne* was first published in Paris in 1700. It was published again in Leipzig in 1705 in a somewhat

Fig. VIII-2: Music and dance in the first strain of *La Bourgogne,* **Pécour:1700 Recueil,** pp. 43–44.

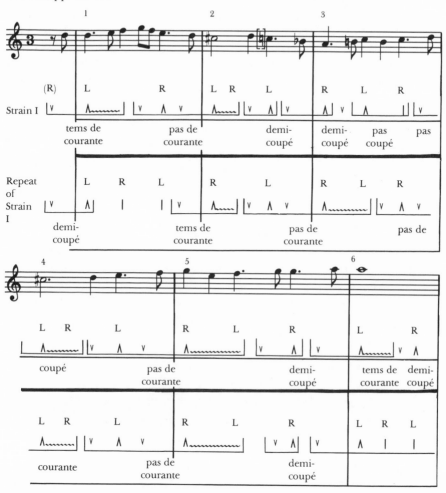

different choreographic notation and with description in German; obviously this piece was known in Bach's Germany.[19] A rather slow tempo is appropriate, possibly $\downarrow$ = MM 56.[20] Almost all the dance measures have the $\frac{3}{2}$ $\downarrow$ | $\circ$ rhythm, which is arsic on the last beat of the measure and thetic for the first one and a half or two beats of the following measure; the only exceptions are measure 3 in the first phrase and measures 1 and 6 in the repeat.

This emphasis on beat 3 and beat 1 of the following measure may be what Georg Muffat meant when he discussed courante bowings. He said that the odd-numbered beats of a measure (i.e., 1 and 3) are always played down-bow, whereas each even-numbered beat (i. e., beat 2) does not necessarily have to be down-bow; in his words, "those that begin the odd beats and thus *emphasize the dance rhythm all the more* are always played down-bow [italics ours].[21]

The music, moving in shorter note values (quarter and eighth notes), actually forms a kind of obbligato melody to these slow, dignified steps. One might well think of the step-units of Taubert's simplest form of the courante (a short *pas* followed by seven long *pas*) as a stabilizing force for the play of the ambiguities and ever-changing rhythms of the music. In Ecorcheville's metaphor, the music is an elusive, frolicking fish, far from the repetition, balance, and order so characteristic of most French Baroque dances.

Several aspects of the courante combine to create this elusive quality, chief among them the use of mixed meters. Ex. VIII-1 illustrates some of the ways composers use meter change to avoid repetition and balance. Although the time signature is $\frac{3}{2}$, and the first two measures are in this meter, measures 3 and 4 appear to be in $\frac{6}{4}$, at least in the upper voice. (Measures 5 and 6 end the strain in $\frac{3}{2}$ and $\frac{6}{4}$ respectively, which is a common way to end a courante strain. To add to the imbalance, measure 3 or 4, or both 3 and 4, could be read as simultaneous mixed meters, with $\frac{6}{4}$ in the upper voice and $\frac{3}{2}$ in the lower.

What keeps all this from being chaotic? Fig. VIII-3 shows a model for the courante dance rhythm, in $\frac{3}{2}$ (and occasionally in $\frac{6}{4}$), with a thesis at the beginning of every measure. Each strain in the courante usually has at least one internal cadence, often at the beginning of measure 3 or 4. The arsic high point of a phrase typically is in the beat just before the thesis of a

Ex. VIII-1: First strain of Courante by Gaspard Le Roux (1705).

Fig. VIII-3: Model for the Courante Dance Rhythm

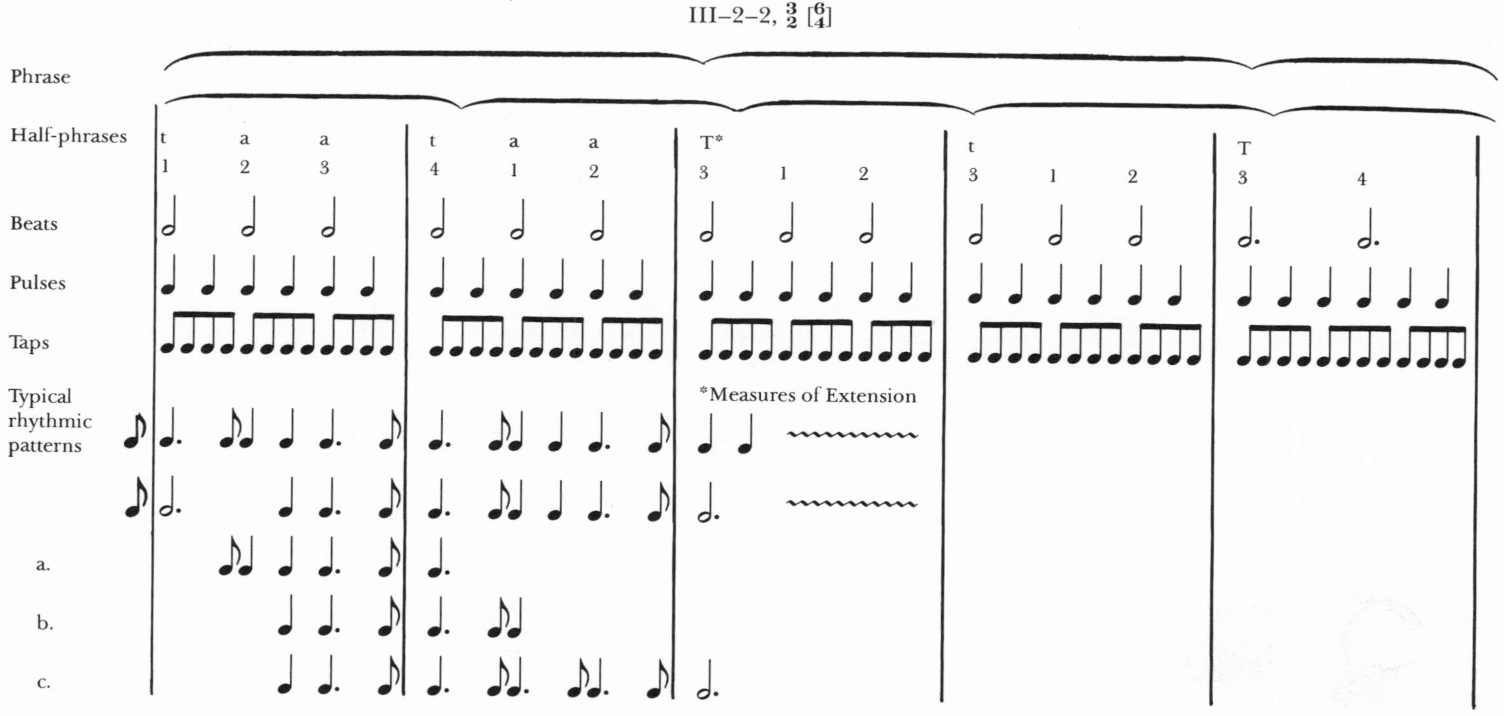

III–2–2, $\frac{3}{2}$ [$\frac{6}{4}$]
Phrase
Half-phrases
t a a
1 2 3
t a a
4 1 2
T*
3 1 2
t
3 1 2
T
3 4
Beats
Pulses
Taps
Typical rhythmic patterns
*Measures of Extension
a.
b.
c.

cadence. The unifying factors are: a thesis or point of arrival at the beginning of every measure; certain recurring rhythmic patterns, marked (a–c); clearly defined cadences every few measures; and an opening "gesture" (the upbeat and beat 1 of measure 1), which clearly announces the beginning of the piece. Most of these features occur in the music to *La Bourgogne*.

Ex. VIII-2 is unusual in that it begins in $\frac{6}{4}$; measures 2 and 6 are in $\frac{3}{2}$, measures 3 and 5 are in $\frac{6}{4}$, and measure 4 has features of both meters. The performer may choose which meters to emphasize in these ambiguous measures, and might even render the voices differently on the repeat. This courante by François Couperin was cited as an example of mixed meters by Kirnberger:

> Because of the different weights of their beats, $\frac{3}{2}$ meter has no other similarity with $\frac{6}{4}$ meter except that both contain six quarter notes [in a measure]. Yet it is to be noted as something special that good composers of old have treated the courante, which is generally written in $\frac{3}{2}$, in such a way that both meters were

Ex. VIII-2: First strain of Courante, **Couperin:Pièces** (1713), I. Ordre.

often combined in it. Consider, for example, the first part of a courante for keyboard by Couperin in example [VIII-2].

The second and sixth measures and the bass melody of the seventh measure of this courante are in $\frac{3}{2}$ meter, but the other measures are written in $\frac{6}{4}$. In the works of J. S. Bach there are a number of courantes treated in this same way.[22]

Kirnberger believes measure 4 to be in $\frac{6}{4}$ meter, though some might disagree. He implies that such measures can be performed either way.

Other aspects of the "elusive quality" of courantes include the "nonfunctional" harmony, which was common in seventeenth-century courantes, and phrases of variable length. The organization of beats into a phrase is always a surprise to the listener, although the first cadence frequently falls at the beginning of measure 3 or 4, and subsequent cadences occur every two to four measures after that. Deceptive and avoided cadences are common, and consecutive phrases or phrase segments always have different lengths and different rhythms. Furthermore the length of each strain is variable, and it is common for the two strains to be of contrasting lengths. For example, the number of measures per strain in the five titled courantes by Jean-Baptiste Lully, dating from the mid-seventeenth century, is as follows: 4 + 6, 6 + 7, 7 + 8, 6 + 7, and 6 + 11.

Performance style grows out of the structure of each courante. *Notes inégales,* when appropriate, are on the eighth-note level. Cadences should be highlighted. Whatever meter the performer chooses to project in a given measure, or given melodic part, should be projected clearly. Single eighth notes can be shortened so as to intensify certain beats, for example, the upbeat of a strain or the last eighth note before a cadence or a thesis. This is clearly implied by Quantz: "The quavers that follow the dotted crotchets in the loure, sarabande, courante and chaconne must not be played with their literal value, but must be executed in a very short and sharp manner."[23]

He also wrote that stringed instruments must "detach the bow during the dot" of a dotted quarter note. This would leave a little space and, coupled with a shortening of the eighth, greatly intensify the rhythmic pattern. Later he adds, "The *entré,* the *loure,* and the *courante* are played majestically, and the bow is detached at each crotchet [quarter note] whether it is dotted or not."[24] Though the intent of this statement is less clear, it probably indicates that each quarter must be bowed separately and not slurred. Dupont had said the same thing about the courante in his 1718 *Principes de Musique.*[25] Muffat, explaining the Lullian style of bowing, directed that every quarter note, and almost every eighth, should be bowed separately.[26]

Keyboard fingering, slurs, and ornamentation appear in a courante by Dandrieu (Ex. VIII-3), providing more instruction in articulation. The opening flourish of both strains is enhanced by the upward arpeggiation

Ex. VIII-3: First strain of Courante by Jean-François Dandrieu, Suite IV, with fingering added by the composer (early eighteenth century).

of the first chord and the slurred quarter notes in the bass. Shortening the upbeat will strengthen this effect. The use of *agréments* on pulses 4 and 5 of the first measure of each strain effectively forces a small articulation between the two and subtly accents beat 3 of the measure. *Agréments* help to accent the beginning of most of the other measures. Dandrieu uses a deceptive cadence in the middle of the first strain, but a much more substantial cadence in measure 8 of the second strain (not shown), enhanced by arpeggiation and a slur in the bass. Also valuable are François Couperin's elaborations on the courante of Ex. VIII-2, which appear in his first *Ordre* (not shown); they include soprano-line dotted rhythms, elaborate flourishes, and intricate ornaments along with articulation indications for the repeat of each strain. As we shall see, the courantes of Bach are different in several ways from those of his French predecessors, but he guards well the majesty and nobility of this seventeenth-century Court dance.

BACH'S COURANTES

It is unlikely that Ecorcheville's "frolicking fish" metaphor influenced Bach, for there is much less ambiguity in his courantes than in those of the French composers just discussed. Bach uses mixed meters often, but their elusive effect is softened because his clear harmonic progressions establish a particular meter even when the rhythms do not. Marpurg commented on the meter of the courante in 1763, advising the performer to play even the $^6_4$ sections in $^3_2$:

> [$^6_4$ is] the proper rhythm of the Courantes in the French style, which indeed belong strictly to $^3_2$ time, yet it approaches in various places very near to the $^6_4$ time, in respect of the external form of the measure; the difference is generally to be marked by playing the $^6_4$ passages with a $^3_2$ accent. The late Herr Capellmeister Bach has left us a sufficiency of genuine models of the proper Courante time.[27]

It could be that German performers played "the $^6_4$ passages with a $^3_2$ accent," although we have not found other statements to this effect. It could also be the case that the ambiguity so enjoyed in the seventeenth-century was no longer pleasurable by 1760.

Another feature of Bach's courantes, in contrast to those of the French composers, is that all the individual strains have an even number of measures, frequently divisible by four, and often both strains have the same number of measures. Balance and order seem to be more important for Bach than they were for his predecessors, and in all but five courantes (those in BWV 806 [Courante II], 814, 819, 828, and 831) the meter is quite solidly $^3_2$.

All of Bach's eighteen French courantes are marked $^3_2$ except for the one in French Suite III (BWV 814), which has a time signature of $^6_4$. Courante II in English Suite I (BWV 806) is followed by two *doubles*, which are essentially variations, not merely different ornamentations. The courante is not used as a basis for works apart from the dance genre; one finds no courante arias or choruses in the cantatas, for example. Most of Bach's courantes are for keyboard; there are also two for lute, one for orchestra, and one for solo cello.

The courante for lute in the Suite in E minor (BWV 996), though dating from the middle of the Weimar years, shows a composer who fully understands the genre. The harmony is consistently clear. The first cadence is on the dominant, at the beginning of measure 3, where the upper voices appear to be in $^6_4$ while the bass is in $^3_2$. The next major cadence is on the dominant at the end of the strain, where in typical courante style the penultimate measure is in $^3_2$ and the final one is in $^6_4$. The second strain features two relatively weak internal cadences, in measure 16 on the subdominant and in measure 18 on the relative major, before the strong E major ending. The use of $^6_4$ in measures 18–19 intensifies the movement toward the final cadence, as does the rising chromatic line of measures 20–21. The lower-level rhythmic patterns of Fig. VIII-3a,b,c appear regularly; the eighth notes may be crisply shortened.

Courantes in the English Suites

All the English suites contain French courantes. All are comparatively lacking in ambiguities, especially in comparison with some of the later courantes, and their very clarity makes them good pieces to study. An almost continual eighth-note movement adorns the slow $\frac{3}{2}$ meter, beamed in groups of four (not six), perhaps vindicating Marpurg's ideas about the courante strictly in $\frac{3}{2}$ time.

The A major English Suite (BWV 806) is the only work that contains two courantes, and the second one has two *doubles*. Courante I has two ten-measure strains, each in $\frac{3}{2}$ except for its final measure, and each with a deceptive cadence in its penultimate measure. The numerous stepwise eighth notes suggest *notes inégales,* at least on repeats. Courante II reveals Bach the pedagogue, ever willing to show performers how to embellish keyboard dances. The sarabandes of English Suites II and III contain similar *doubles.* Some discretion may be assumed here: performers may play all four courantes or make a selection among them; one or both *doubles* may be used for repeats of Courante II. Four courantes in a row might be too much for a modern audience, though it is hard to know about audience preference in Bach's day. Bach sets the *doubles* in contrasting styles. The first has mostly Italian ornamentation, with *tremoletti* and *tiratas* as well as the usual trills and other *agréments;* the second is quite French in style, and *notes inégales* are appropriate here.

Metrically, Courante II shifts around and contains several measures where $\frac{6}{4}$ or even ambiguity temporarily confounds the listener (e.g., measures 1, 3, 9, 11, 15, and 19). These measures are partially clarified in the second *double* by barring; in the voice with eighth notes there are groupings of six in measures 1 and 3, for example, and groupings of four in measures 2 and 4–7. François Couperin also used this technique (Ex. VIII-2). The $\frac{6}{4}$ meter is used in all the internal cadences (measures 3, 11, 15, and 19), as well as in the final measure of each strain. The lower-level rhythmic pattern ♩ ♩ ♪ | ♩ is quite common in this courante because there are so many $\frac{6}{4}$ measures. In the original version of Courante II, the rhythm ♩. ♫♫ occurs often in the lower voice right after a cadence. One might clarify these measures by articulating after the fourth pulse of the upper voice and by shortening the final eighth note. Sparse internal cadences—except for measure 4, only a brief touching on the vi chord in measure 7, and the cadence on the subdominant in measure 18—ensure forward movement.

The A minor courante in English Suite II (BWV 807) has only one measure in which the $\frac{6}{4}$–$\frac{3}{2}$ conflict unequivocally occurs: measure 18, where the upper voice is slurred in $\frac{6}{4}$ and the lower voice in $\frac{3}{2}$. Bach has chosen to smooth out the dotted rhythms in this dance by almost continual groups of four eighth notes. He uses imitation in the opening four measures, after which sequential melodic material carries the harmony to touch on the VI chord. The first real cadence, however, does not occur until the end of the strain. The second strain begins with the opening melodic material inverted, has one cadence in its sixth measure (iv), and does not rest again until the final cadence. The strains are balanced: 12 + 12 measures. Bach's handling of the melodic material is ingenious, as the opening idea recurs in many guises throughout the piece. Performers should observe carefully the four-note slurs; *notes iné-gales* are appropriate.

The courante in English Suite III (BWV 808) is another seamless master-piece of melodic writing, the voices coming and going at will. The meter is $\frac{3}{2}$ except for the final measure of each strain, leaving the listener free to follow the voices without fear of complexity, as in a vocal duet or trio. Clear dotted rhythms remind one of the courante as a dance, however, in the penultimate moments of most phrases (measures 15, 19, 23, and 31). The strains are perfectly balanced with 16 + 16 measures.

In English Suite IV (BWV 809) Bach again uses two and three voices imitatively, pitting the familiar courante lower-level rhythmic patterns (Fig. VIII-3a,b,c) against groups of eighth notes. The characteristic pattern ♩ ♪♩. ♩. ♪ always occurs in the measure before a cadence (measures 7, 12, and 19). As in BWV 808, the piece is entirely in $\frac{3}{2}$ except for the ending of each strain; clearly articulating the final two measures of the strain to show the contrasting meters will emphasize the style of the courante. Other appropriate courante techniques include *notes inégales* on stepwise eighth-note passages and the lengthening of dotted notes and shortening of suc-ceeding eighth notes, especially on beat 3 of a measure.

The courante in BWV 810 is unique among those in the English Suites. Using the contrapuntal techniques of the previous courantes, Bach incorpo-rates the delayed or tied appoggiatura (e.g., measures 1, 3, and 4), the nor-mal appoggiatura (e.g., measures 7 and 3), pedal points (measures 6–8 and 24–26), and long trills (measures 18–19). In this *tour de force* he never ob-scures the various courante patterns, which culminate on beat 1 of most measures and often on a harmony of repose. An articulation before such measures is necessary, and an *agrément* of some kind may be added to beat 1 even when it is not indicated. *Notes inégales* will intensify the eighth-note movement against the stately dotted rhythms.

The two strains of the courante in English Suite VI (BWV 811) are 16 + 16 measures long, made up of 10 + 6 and 5 + 5 + 6 measure groupings. The lower-level courante patterns are given exclusively to the soprano voice. This piece is a study in avoided cadences and driving sequential harmonies, which must be carefully articulated so that the listener does not lose the "feel" or affect of the courante. For example, one may articulate the opening measure as in Ex. VIII-4. Only with this kind of precision will the sometimes wandering harmonic patterns be held in check.

Ex. VIII-4: Opening measure of J. S. Bach, Courante, BWV 811.

Courantes from Köthen

The only courantes for solo cello and for orchestra are from Köthen. The courante in C minor from the fifth cello suite (BWV 1011, which is in scordatura tuning[28]) is a very serious and difficult piece. It has double, triple, and quadruple stops; few internal cadences; and harmony which can best be termed "adventuresome." All the bowings indicate $\frac{3}{2}$ meter, though $\frac{6}{4}$, with its ambiguity, might be a possibility in places such as measure 3. Shortening the eighth note after a dotted quarter, as Quantz advised, is imperative to sharpening the rhythms in this piece; the affect will quickly become abstract and heavy without such definition.

About a decade later, in Leipzig, Bach made a lute arrangement in G minor of this courante (BWV 995). It is particularly valuable to compare this version with its model, for BWV 995 is preserved in the composer's autograph, with additional ornaments and with bass notes to fill out the harmony.

The courante in French Suite I (BWV 812) continues with compositional techniques already described. It is entirely in $\frac{3}{2}$, except for the final measure of each strain, though the soprano voice of measures 2 and 4 might conceivably be thought of in $\frac{6}{4}$. The two strains are unequal—10 + 14 measures— with 7 + 3 and 6 + 8 measures for phrases within each strain. The lower-level courante patterns (Fig. VIII-3a,b,c) are freely interspersed throughout the three or more voices. Since there is much repetition of certain figures, as well as imitation, the performer can help create unity by plotting a desired articulation pattern and repeating it with recurrences of the same figure. For example, the opening soprano line might be played as in Ex. VIII-5, with the final Bb of measure 1 coming after the C♯ in the alto voice. The same articulation pattern would fit in the soprano part in measures 6 and 11. The two pairs of eighth notes which make up beat 2, forming melodic intervals of a second and a third respectively, might be articulated similarly throughout the courante. Elaborate ornaments such as the *double cadence* would beautify this piece, e.g., on beat 2 of measures 8, 15, and 23.

The courante in French Suite III (BWV 814) is Bach's only courante with the $\frac{6}{4}$ time signature. Even so, the measures preceding several important cadences appear to be in $\frac{3}{2}$ (i.e., measures 4, 11, 17–18, and possibly 24–27),

Ex. VIII-5: Opening soprano line of J. S. Bach, Courante, BWV 812.

at least in one of the voices. The initial melodic material permeates the piece and lends itself to more than one interpretation; for example, ♪|♩. ♪♫♫♩. ♪|♩ or ♪|♩. ♪♫♫♩. ♪|♩, the latter conceived with an implied mordent.

According to Alfred Dürr, the keyboard suites in A minor and E♭ major (BWV 818 and 819) may well have been youthful works by Bach that were copied at a later date.[29] The courantes in BWV 818 and 818a are irregular simply by being so regular: two strains of 4 + 4 measures each. The original version (in BWV 818) is a comparatively uncomplicated piece, in $\frac{3}{2}$ except for the final measure of each strain, with clear harmonies and simple rhythms. BWV 818a is a later, more interesting version, an elaboration on BWV 818 with a stronger opening (the arpeggiated chord), a few changes in the bass line, and some written-out ornamentation of the soprano line. The courante in BWV 819 is also structurally regular but metrically irregular. The time signature is $\frac{3}{2}$ but most of the piece is in $\frac{6}{4}$. Measures 11, 16, and 19 are in $\frac{3}{2}$, and the penultimate measure of the second strain can be played in either $\frac{6}{4}$ or $\frac{3}{2}$. Bach has smoothed out almost every characteristic lower-level dotted courante rhythm (those from Fig. VIII-3a,b,c) and set these rhythms in a series of uncomplicated harmonies.

The courante from the C major orchestral suite (BWV 1066) is in four-part texture, since oboes and bassoon double the first violins and the bass. This beautiful dance, the only courante for orchestra, glides along effortlessly in the most regal fashion, with its characteristic dotted rhythm courante patterns, lush harmonies, and long, sweeping phrases that have few clear cadences. A suggestion of a *da capo* comes in measure 21, where Bach returns briefly to the opening material, only to extend it from measure 24 to the end with sequence-like figures. This glorious suite must have thrilled its Köthen and Leipzig audiences of the 1720s.

The Leipzig Courantes

These last three surviving French courantes are the ultimate in dance stylization. All are from late keyboard works and feature three-part texture; extensive embellishment, which includes written-out ornaments; and enough ambiguity to intrigue. All require attention to the characteristic courante dotted rhythms in order to project the stately nature of the dance. In Partita II (BWV 826) the courante falls into a 6 + 6 and 4 + 3 + 5 measure structure. The motive using four sixteenth notes is found in every measure, as either a *tirata* figure or a turn. The meter is $\frac{3}{2}$ throughout except for the final measure of each strain, but with the constantly changing melodic elaborations there is no chance for ennui.

The courante in Partita IV (BWV 828) is more problematic than any of its predecessors. Bach uses the internal shift of $\frac{3}{2}$ and $\frac{6}{4}$ meters in a subtler and more enigmatic fashion than he did in BWV 806, 814, and 819. Almost every measure is ambiguous and can be performed in several different ways, metrically. It is precisely because the performer must make a specific decision in every measure that this courante is so fascinating. It would be appropriate to give the courante "signature" by clearly playing the penultimate measure of each strain in $\frac{3}{2}$ to contrast with the final $\frac{6}{4}$ measure. Some performers will enjoy experimenting with shortening certain notes, such as the last note of the soprano part in measures 1–3, though the piece is already quite intense without tampering with these spots. Perhaps Kirnberger had this noble masterpiece in mind when he referred to meter shifts in Bach's courantes.

The courante in the Overture in the French Style (BWV 831) is fairly balanced in phrase structure, cast in strains of equal length (12 + 12), internally organized as 4 + 8 and 6 + 6. But at the same time it is a magnificent example of Bach's complete understanding of the French courante style, embellished with touches unique to his own genius. The opening measures have a pedal point on B with figuration which reaches to the low register of the harpsichord. The bass-line rhythms here accentuate arsic places in the courante rhythmic pattern, an idea which returns in measures 20–21. Shortening of eighth notes (or sixteenths) preceding beats 1 and 3 of the measure will lend a courante "feeling" in this piece. Arpeggiation, where indicated, is usually most successful from the top note down in order to preserve proper voice-leading. Bach's final statement on the courante is unsurpassed.

BWV 816

CHAPTER 9
The Corrente

The early eighteenth-century Italian corrente is a virtuoso piece for violin or keyboard soloist. It usually consists of a continuous elaboration in eighth or sixteenth notes over a bass line in fast triple meter, with simple texture, slow harmonic rhythm, and phrases of varying lengths. Metrically speaking, most correntes have one beat to the measure and are in a I–3–2 metric structure (Fig. IX-1), though some very ornate ones with continual sixteenth notes actually move with three beats to the measure in a III–2–2 structure (Fig. IX-2). Normally, the time signature is $\frac{3}{4}$ and there is an upbeat. The tempo is moderate to fast, depending on the level of the beat and the amount of rhythmic interest at the tap level.

Techniques of elaboration include arpeggiation, sequential repetition, two melodic parts combined into a single line, figures resembling an Alberti bass, and passage-work covering several octaves. Most performance techniques derive from Italian string practices, which often grouped many more than two or three notes in a facile, fluid manner of execution. Harmonic change, which is usually on the first and third beats of a measure in III–2–2 metric structure, or the first and third pulses in I–3–2, offers the performer the most reliable guide to articulation. Ornamentation is sparse, and French *notes inégales* are outside the style.

Correntes and corontos were danced in Italy, England, and many other

Fig. IX-1: Model for the Corrente Dance Rhythm

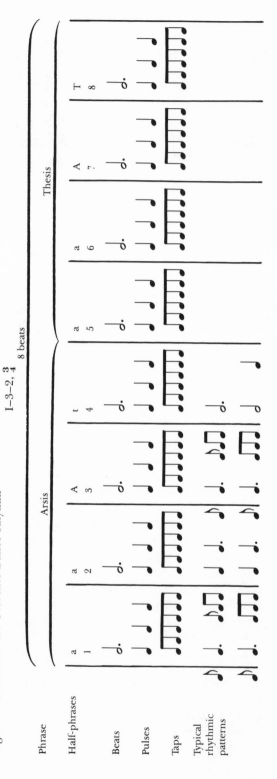

Fig. IX-2: Alternate Model for the Corrente Dance Rhythm

parts of Europe in the late sixteenth and early seventeenth centuries. References abound in literature of that period. For example, in Sir John Davies's poem *Orchestra* (c. 1594), verse 69:

> What shall I name those current traverses,
> That on a triple dactyl foot do run
> Close by the ground with sliding passages?
> Wherein that dancer greatest praise hath won
> Which with best order can all orders shun;
> For everywhere he wantonly must range
> And turn and wind with unexpected change.[1]

This passage implies floor patterns of an erratic or irregular nature, danced close to the ground with sliding and running steps in some form of a "triple dactyl foot" (probably a dactyl [♩ ♪] in triple meter). Michael Praetorius mentions the dance in *Syntagma Musicum*, referring to "certain measured up and down skips, as if [one were] running while dancing."[2] This adds the idea of skips or hops to that of running. The Italian dancing master Cesare Negri gives more-technical information in his important dance manual, *Nuove Inventioni di Balli* (1604), since several pieces of music entitled "corrente" have a specific choreography.[3] Although the step-units vary from piece to piece, it is useful to consider two dance patterns commonly used in these correntes since they contain rhythms also present in the music.[4]

One pattern is the *Seguito ordinario con saltino* (ordinary sequence with little hop), a succession of hops and steps, which has been reconstructed by Putnam Aldrich as follows:

Stand with the left foot forward.
  1. Hop on the right foot.
  2. Step forward on the left toe.
  3. Hop on the left foot.
  4. Step forward on the right toe.
  5. Hop on the right foot.
  6. Advance the left foot forward, flat.
  7. Touch the ground with the right foot.
  8. Step forward flat on the left foot.

This pattern is simply an "ordinary sequence" (a step-unit previously described by Negri) with little hops preceding each step.[5] Ex. IX-1a shows how it may be set to music. The rhythmic shape of the pattern is that of two active beats (1–2) followed by a point of arrival on beat 3 and part of 4 (AATT). Below it is an elaboration of the music in early seventeenth-century Italian style. The rhythm ♩. ♫♩ probably corresponds to Sir John Davies's "triple dactyl foot" mentioned above.

A second pattern of beats common in correntes (Ex. IX-1b) is the use of

Ex. IX-1: Music and dance in two early seventeenth-century correntes; dance steps interpolated from Cesare Negri, *Nuove Inventioni di Balli* (Milan, 1604). a. Vincenzo Calestani, *Madrigali et Arie* (Venice, 1617), p. 30; b. Antonio Brunelli, *Scherzi, Arie, Canzonette, e Madrigali, Libro Terzo* (Venice, 1616), p. 28.

several *sottopiedi* ("underfoot"), each occurring to one beat of the music. For one *sottopiede:*

1. Spring sideways to the left, raising the right foot backwards.
2. Thrust the right toe behind the left heel, projecting the left foot forward.

In this pattern each beat corresponds to the arrival from a sideways leap (more energetic than a little hop) with the "underfoot" thrust coming between the beats. The rhythmic shape of the pattern is ATAT, with a point of arrival on beat 4, not beat 3. Below the music are more elaborations, mostly using the ♩♪ ♩♪ rhythm on each beat.

Thus, corrente dance accompaniment is made up of phrases four triple beats in length (or multiples of four beats). The beats are grouped in various ways, including ATAT and AATT. Below the metric level of the beats a trochaic unit (♩ ♩ or ♩♪) is very common. This is a characteristic feature of corrente music and represents the "skipping" quality of the dance. In performance one may incorporate a skipping affect by special attention to the short, or last, part of the trochaic unit, using techniques such as an articulation before and after it, or just before, or just after. Carefully varying the strength of these articulations will do more than any other technique to shape the phrase and instill "corrente character" into the performance. Upbeats should be detached.

The four triple beats form a point of departure for longer phrases in stylized dance music, and composers freely used phrases not divisible by four measures. They also mixed the patterns within the same dance, so that the emphases of active and passive beats would change as the piece progressed.

Ex. IX-2 illustrates these points. The first strain of Corrente Prima is seven measures long in the shape ATAT–hemiolia–T. In other words, this seven-measure strain consists of the four-measure phrase of Ex. IX-1b followed by a hemiolia and a thesis measure. Corrente Seconda, which has two beats to the measure, begins with the rhythm of Ex. IX-1a; the shape of this strain is AATT AATT AAAT, a thirteen-measure phrase in which the final five-measure segment could be thought of as an extension of the original shape, AATT. Notice that the trochaic nature of the beat is different in each dance; Frescobaldi emphasizes the "short" foot of the trochaic subdivision more in Corrente Prima than in Corrente Seconda. The performer could capitalize on this observation to contrast the two pieces. Notice also that the trochaic beats are predominantly arsic, and that in thetic places the beat is undivided (e.g., Ex. IX-1a, beats 3–4 and 7–8; Ex. IX-1b, beats 4 and 8; Ex. IX-2a, beats 2, 4, and 7; Ex. IX-2b, measure 7).

The French courante probably developed about the same time but went in the direction of rhythmic ambiguity in a very slow tempo in soloist music (see chapter 8). It was generally more influential in stylized dance music of the Baroque period, becoming the standard second dance of the solo instrumental suite as established by Froberger.[6] Italian correntes, by contrast, went in the direction of elaborations over the less-complex rhythms of the early-seventeenth-century corrente.

In the works of Froberger, nine courantes are in $\frac{3}{2}$ with the ambiguities of the French courante and seven are in $\frac{3}{4}$ time, with few hemiolias, and resemble correntes. By the late seventeenth century Italian composers used both styles, while French and German composers specialized almost entirely in the French courante. Ex. IX-3 shows the beginning of a corrente by Arcangelo Corelli; it is actually a French courante except for the barring and despite the tempo marking "allegro." By contrast, Ex. IX-4 shows an Italian corrente by the same composer. The titles are identical but the music is quite different. This cavalier attitude toward titles is carried over into the music of Bach and Handel, who wrote both courantes and correntes which appear wrongly titled in modern editions; i.e., Italian correntes may be titled "Courante" and French courantes may be titled "Corrente," for no apparent reason. However, it is not difficult to distinguish the two dance types once one is familiar

Ex. IX-2: First strain of two correntes from Girolamo Frescobaldi, *Il Secondo Libro di Toccate, Canzone, Versi D'Hinni, Magnificat, Gagliarde, Correnti et Altre Partite* (Rome, 1637). a. Corrente Prima; b. Corrente Seconda.

with them. By the late Baroque both French and German composers wrote Italian correntes in instrumental music.

The affect of the corrente is one of "Sprightfulness, and Vigour, Lively, Brisk and Cheerful," according to Mace.[7] The early dance refer-

Ex. IX-3: Opening of Corrente by Arcangelo Corelli, Op. 2, No. 1 (1685).

ences and descriptions cited above reveal that it was gay and cheerful, in comparison with other, more-serious dances. The use of a floor pattern which ran unpredictably in various directions also indicates a more informal, entertaining type of dance. Writers often failed to distinguish between corrente and courante; e.g., Grassineau, in his *Dictionary* of 1746, said "Corrente, a sort of quick-running French dance. See Courante." Most theorists had little or nothing to say about the corrente, but Bach was attracted to it and added his own stamp of genius to this dance form from the Renaissance.

BACH'S CORRENTES

Bach continued with the idea that a corrente is a piece for keyboard or violin soloist. The eighteen pieces which survive are for keyboard or string solo (violin or cello), except for BWV 1013, which is for solo flute; there are no correntes in his orchestral music or concertos. All are in $\frac{3}{4}$ meter except the last two, which are in $\frac{3}{8}$, and all begin with an upbeat of some sort. All feature "running" notes, but only one has a *double*, probably because the corrente is already harmonically an elaboration. Sometimes the running notes create a lilting, skipping type of movement with

Ex. IX-4: Opening of Corrente by Arcangelo Corelli, Op. 2, No. 10 (1685).

duplet or triplet eighths on the tap level, but other times an extremely dynamic, virtuosic corrente results, dominated by sixteenth and even thirty-second notes.

The Early Correntes

Two pieces date from Bach's Weimar years. The corrente in the keyboard suite in B♭ major (BWV 821) has the metric structure I–3–2, moves by eighth notes, and is short, consisting of 6 + 6 measures in each strain plus an additional four measures for the ending. Sequences and broken-chord texture, those staples of corrente writing, dominate this little dance. A fast tempo seems appropriate since the harmonic rhythm is slow. In the keyboard sonata in A minor (BWV 965) the corrente is a much more ambitious effort. It was rewritten from the Sonata in A minor of Reinken's 1687 *Hortus Musicus*. It has the metric structure III–2–2. Though it is a long piece with rambling harmonies, it does reach a climax in measures 25–31 and again, using chromaticism, in measures 40–47. The texture is more imitative than soloistic.

Correntes for Solo Instruments: Violin, Cello, Flute

Most of Bach's surviving correntes are from his Köthen years, including all those for an unaccompanied instrument. The First Partita for solo violin (BWV 1002) contains Bach's only corrente with a *double*, possibly because all the other dances in the Partita have *doubles*. The metric structure is I–3–2 (III–2–2 in the *double*), and the pace is relentless in both correntes, with unbroken eighth notes in the first one and a steady stream of sixteenths in the second. The performer has two guides to interpretation—the bowing indications in the first corrente, taken from the P 967 manuscript,[8] and the harmony.

Bowings often indicate a slurring of the first three eighth notes in the measure, particularly when they represent a widely spaced, arpeggiated harmony. Notable exceptions are in measures 72–75, where the sequences are slurred ♩♩♩♩♩♩ | ♩♩♩♩♩♩ and measures 76 and 78, slurred ♩♩♩♩♩♩ | ♩♩♩♩♩♩, which creates an exciting rhythmic imbalance just before the two-measure final cadence. In general, bowings form the shape of the phrases. For example, measures 1–6 are grouped by bowing and harmony in pairs, alternating a measure in a single harmony and a measure with a harmonic change on the third pulse, which is hinted at by the bowing. One might imagine a hemiolia in measures 8–9, preceding the first cadence at measure 10, since the last portion of a possible hemiolia is indicated in the bowing in measure 9. An intensely careful study of the harmonies underlying the figuration will enable the performer to give the listener more than a long line of single notes in these correntes. Cadences at measures 10, 18, 48, 60, and possibly 72 need articulation and will provide welcome rests from the constant flow of energy.

The other corrente for solo violin is in Partita II (BWV 1004). Bach plays with the tap-level rhythms by alternating triplet figures with skipping, jaunty dotted rhythms, effectively inhibiting any sense of "relentless drive" which may result when a single tap-level movement dominates, as it does in BMV 1002. The triplets are slurred in several different ways; compare, for example, measures 1, 5, 11, and 22–23. The vexing question of whether to perform the dotted rhythms as ♩. ♪ or ♪. ♪ (triplet) must be resolved by each performer, but there is some freedom here since they do not occur simultaneously with the written triplet figures, as they do in the correntes of BWV 815 and 825. It was not unusual for early seventeenth-century Italian composers to use mixed duple and triple groupings on the tap level.[9] Suffice it to say that playing ♪. ♪ (triplet) will result in a quieter, more-coherent piece with a single mood, while ♩. ♪ will create more energy by emphasizing the contrast between the two types of tap-level movement. Since there are no strong internal cadences in this piece, the articulation of these rhythms assumes great importance.

Five of the six suites for solo cello contain correntes and gigas, while the Fifth Suite has a French courante and a French gigue. It seems to have been Bach's intention in these five suites to exploit the virtuosic possibilities of the cello as a solo instrument by incorporating two fast, technically demanding Italian dances.

The corrente in Suite I, in G major (BWV 1007), has the metric structure III–2–2. It begins with a clear eight-measure opening phrase but subsequently falls into irregular groupings. In this corrente, as in many of Bach's other dances, virtuosic writing and a high degree of stylization and embellishment may tempt the performer to think more in terms of the quarter-note pulse level than of the measure level. However, the ornamented single harmonies that fill many measures and the long, flowing pedal points (e.g., measures 14–15) serve to remind one of the overall "running" character of the corrente and the necessity of thinking simultaneously on at least two levels. A variety of slurs from the P 26 manuscript offer suggestions for bowing.[10] For example, the sixteenth notes in measure 1 are in groups of six, but in measure 3 they are 2 + 4. All mordent figures are grouped by threes (e.g., measure 5); six-note groups occur in measures 8, 17, 19, 20, 21, and 28; and there is a seven-note group in measure 38.

The corrente from the Second Suite for cello (BWV 1008) has the structure III–2–2. It is even more relentless than that of the First Suite and also incorporates a few double and triple stops. Again the performer will need to be aware of both the measure level, moving by very slow dotted half notes, and the underlying harmonic-rhythmic pattern, ♩ ♩ | ♩ ♩ . This trochaic rhythm should be felt and projected by the performer, even though there are a plethora of notes to confound one. That is the challenge. In order to highlight the third beat of a measure one could group the sixteenth notes in twos, or detach the last two sixteenths of the measure.

Continuous eighth notes present another exercise in harmonic analysis for the performer of the corrente in the Third Suite (BWV 1009). Slow harmonic changes reveal the underlying corrente rhythms of Fig. IX-1 and indicate a metric structure of I–3–2, with each measure as one beat. Again an opening eight-beat pattern is followed by practically no internal cadences except for measures 56–57, in the second strain. Sequences, figures in Alberti bass style, and arpeggios make up the elaboration techniques of this majestic, flowing corrente.

Varied tap-level rhythms characterize the Fourth Suite (BWV 1010), with metric structure III–2–2, as they did in the Violin Partita, BWV 1004. Bach uses duple eighth notes, triplet eighths, and sixteenths to make this a joyous, sparkling dance, full of variety and contrast, enhanced by the security of several important internal cadences (measures 8, 23, 26, 42, 56, 61, and 64).

Bach's last extravagant gesture for the cello correntes is the one in the Sixth Suite (BWV 1012), which is arguably the most intriguing of the five here described. It was written for an instrument with five strings, not four,[11] making possible a new kind of instrumental color in the high range of the countertenor. The metric structure is III–2–2, and the bold melodic patterns flow effortlessly up, down, and around over a range of almost three octaves. The piece has charm, elegance, rhythmic variety, and even the joy of familiar sections returning at the end of each strain. There are few internal cadences except for measure 8, but sequential harmonic movement, primarily by measures, ensures the clear sense of direction for which Bach is so justly famous. The *coulés de tierce* in the first and succeeding measures are always slurred together, and the other sixteenth notes are often grouped by fours to articulate the quarter-note beats.

Bach's only work for unaccompanied flute, Partita in A minor (BWV 1013), also includes a corrente, with the structure III–2–2. This piece is not as idiomatic for its instrument as the analagous works just described for the violin and the cello. There are many long passages in which the line must be interrupted for a breath, and it will help preserve the integrity of the beat if the breath does not occur just before a bar line except in sequential passages. The last two sixteenth notes of selected measures might also be detached to enhance the "swing" of the corrente dance rhythm.

Correntes in the French Suites

Four of the French Suites contain correntes. They are all masterpieces, but on a much smaller scale, with much more balance and with a more-obvious sense of continuity (due to the presence of a bass line) than the expansive correntes in the solo violin and cello suites. The corrente in French Suite II (BWV 813) begins with a clearly defined four-measure phrase and continues with simple sequences to other cadences in measures 8, 16, and 24 to end the first strain. A fairly rapid tempo will project whole measures as beats in a metric structure of I–3–2. The texture is two-part throughout, though interesting imitative writing in two and three voices occurs in the middle of the second strain. Figures resembling Alberti basses and arpeggios flesh out the harmonies, which include sequences and the trochaic corrente pattern ♩ ♩. When this pattern is embodied in the harmony, as in measures 9–13, the performer may clarify groupings by phrasing the bass line ♪♪ ♩ or the upper voice ♫♫♫ . Hemiolias are also part of the harmony and may be phrased across bar lines accordingly (measures 14–15, 36–37, and possibly 22–23).

The corrente from French Suite IV (BWV 815) has the metric structure I–3–3. The piece is reminiscent of the corrente in BWV 1004, for solo violin, but this time the tap-level triplet and dotted rhythms occur simultaneously rather than consecutively. Most performers will choose to resolve the ♪.♪ figures to triplets ♪♪♪ throughout the piece; at a fast tempo it is practically impossible to do otherwise. This is a gay, rollicking dance in which internal cadential points are avoided in the headlong forward motion. There are generally only one or two harmonies in a measure, implying a fast tempo.

Cascading *tiratas* and rapid broken-chord figures form the basis of Bach's elaborations in the corrente of French Suite V (BWV 816) with a III–2–2 metric structure. However, the piece will lose some of its sparkle if it is played "as fast as possible," for the trochaic corrente rhythms will disappear and only a blur of sound will remain. Bach often writes two harmonies on the third beat of the measure (e.g., measure 2) and these should be articulated to bring out the trochaic rhythm, possibly as 2 + 2 or simply with an articulation before beat 3. This is a cheerful, lighthearted dance in balanced phrase structure, mainly a two-voiced dialogue; it sounds well with a light touch as the constantly moving sixteenth notes ornament the harmony.

The E major corrente, in French Suite VI (BWV 817), has the structure III–2–2. It is much like the dance just described, and the same comments apply. There will be an even greater temptation to go "as fast as possible" because the passage-work is tossed from hand to hand in a lighthearted fashion as the bass line temporarily disappears.

Correntes in the Keyboard Partitas

There are four correntes among the six partitas of Clavier-Übung I. They also emphasize the virtuoso character of Bach's late works in the dance medium and are among the finest and most imaginative correntes ever composed.

The corrente from the First Partita (BWV 825) has the metric structure I–3–3. It recalls in its skipping rhythms and running qualities the figurations of two earlier ones, in BWV 1004 for cello and in the French Suite BWV 815. Like these earlier pieces the corrente in BWV 825 has few places to rest within each strain; the only interior cadence is in measure 45. Bach often seems about to make a cadence but instead veers off into some new area of activity. The most exciting instances of this are the rising ornamented lines on a pedal point beginning at measure 13 in the first strain and at measure 50 in the second. Several dynamic trills are notated in each strain, and more could be added for extra interest; for example, on the long note of measures 5–10 and 13. As in BWV 815, most performers will find it easier to resolve the dotted-eighth-and-sixteenth figures to triplets, though, if the tempo is slow enough, a contrast of the two figures could be used to create a less lilting but more serious, intense, abstract piece. In fact, the next corrente to be discussed, in Partita III (BWV 827), uses these jagged rhythms throughout.

BWV 827 presents Bach's most driving, abstract expression of the corrente idea, far from the rollicking, joyous motions of dancers skipping around the room. In III–2–2 metric structure, its tap level features no triplets, but four sixteenths or dotted-eighth and sixteenth-note figures. Its only rival for intensity is the corrente in BWV 1008, for solo cello. Like the corrente in BWV 825, just discussed, it avoids interior cadences (except for measure 42 in the second strain) and features sequences, pedal points, arpeggios, broken chords, and much variety in the harmonic rhythm. The challenge in this piece is to discover if there is some lightheartedness left to temper its seriousness.

In the corrente in Partita V (BWV 829), Bach returns to the lilting simplicity of BWV 813 but takes the idea much further than before. Both pieces are in the metric structure 1–3–2, both have a three-note upbeat leading to a two-voice texture, and both work out the harmonies with sequences and arpeggio figures. However, in place of the balanced phrasing of the earlier piece, Bach avoids cadences and keeps moving until the end of each strain. For example, the first strain begins by passing through a "token" dominant on measure 8 and continues through another avoided cadence in measure 24 to the end, in measure 32. In the second strain, with the soprano and bass roles interchanged, the cadence avoided at measure 40 would have balanced the opening pattern of 4 + 4 beats. The performer can capitalize on this by retarding slightly before measure 40 and then surprising the listener by surging on through! A cadence on the relative minor at measure 48 comes exactly at the mid-point of the second strain. Of course the performer does not actually stop at any of these points, but makes sure the listener hears them—they articulate the form. Why did Bach write this corrente in $\frac{3}{8}$ instead of $\frac{3}{4}$? Perhaps to ensure that the sixteenth notes would be played in a truly sparkling, effervescent manner.

The last Bach corrente, from the E minor Partita (BWV 830), is the most unusual and problematic of all. By far the longest (54 + 62 measures in length), it is an extremely ornate piece with extensive Italian ornamentation such as *passaggi, tiratas*, and other decorative filling in of melodic intervals. It is in $\frac{3}{8}$, implying a metric structure of 1–3–2 in a fast tempo. It is a good idea to articulate the bass line ♩♩♩ in order to clarify the corrente "swing" and ensure that this crucial feature of the dance does not get lost amidst Bach's extensive elaboration. Another word of advice: be careful not to let this elaboration/ornamentation assume a melodic function, which will slow down the movement of one beat per measure; rather, let rhythmic considerations dominate.

This corrente employs an interesting contrapuntal device known as *Rückungen*.[12] These are harmonically syncopated notes in which one tone anticipates the next harmony. They are used in this corrente to introduce new articulation and add variety; examples are measures 13–15 in the first strain and 15–17 in the second one. A simple legato articulation will highlight these measures and provide a break in the complexity. Although the first two measures of both strains also have *Rückungen*, it is better there to use the "swing" articulation mentioned above, in order to define the corrente dance pattern at once. This highly elaborated dance shows, perhaps more than any of the others, the wealth of imagination that Bach brought to the corrente.

CHAPTER 10
The Gigue

A dizzying variety of styles, metric structures, textures, types of upbeat, affects, and time signatures confronts the one who would understand Bach's gigues. Forty-two dances have survived, under titles as diverse as "gigue," "giga," "jig," "jigg," and "gique," and in time signatures such as $\frac{3}{8}$, $\frac{6}{8}$, $\frac{12}{8}$, $\frac{12}{16}$, $\frac{9}{16}$, C, and ₵. What do these pieces have in common beyond the fact that they bring to a close a suite of dances?

We divide Bach's gigues into three types—the French gigue, giga I, and giga II—based on an analysis of metric structure. Ex. X-1 shows the beginnings of three gigues from Bach's French Suites, each illustrating one of these three types. Giga I (I–3–2) is different from the other types in that its tripleness is on the tap, or lowest, rhythmic level. It also has the slowest harmonic rhythm, giving it an illusion of great speed and a very fast tempo. The French gigue (II–2–3) and giga II (II–3–2) share a similar metric structure but are different because the French gigue has numerous dotted rhythms (as opposed to the predominantly even eighth notes in giga II), a simpler texture, and slightly faster tempo (as opposed to the more-complex textures and slightly slower tempo in giga II).

Table V summarizes these and other differences, all of which will be discussed in more detail as this chapter proceeds. Separate sections are devoted to the French gigue, giga I, giga II, and "Gigues Notated in Duple Meter." (The loure, a metrically related dance sometimes referred to as a "slow gigue," has its own chapter.)

Ex. X-1: Three types of gigue in the music of J. S. Bach. a. French gigue
(I–3–2), from French Suite II, BWV 813; b. Giga I (II–2–3), from French
Suite V, BWV 816; c. Giga II (II–3–2), from French Suite VI, BWV 817.

TABLE V

A Comparison of Gigue Types

Characteristic	French gigue	Giga I	Giga II
Unpredictable phrase length	X	X	X
Balanced phrasing in some pieces, especially at the beginning of strains	X	X	X
Beats organized differently in each piece	X	X	X
Lively or joyful affect	X	X	X
Imitative texture in most pieces	X	X	X
Either one or two beats per measure	X	X	X
Moderate tempo	X		X
Slower tempo (with "illusion of fast")		X	
Some ornamentation	X		X
Little ornamentation		X	
Tripleness on pulse level	X		X
Tripleness on tap level		X	
Harmonic change within triple groups (2 + 1)	X		X
No harmonic change within triple groups		X	
Varied groupings by slurs	X		X
Almost all slurs over three-note groupings		X	
Large variety of time signatures		X	X
Few or no internal cadences		X	X
Occasional internal cadences	X		
Some fugues or quasi-fugues		X	X
No fugues or quasi-fugues	X		
Little or no use of "sautillant" figure		X	X
"Sautillant" figure used almost constantly	X		

BWV 813

THE FRENCH GIGUE

The most distinctive feature of this characteristically French dance is its graceful lilt, produced by the almost constant use of the "sautillant" figure,

♩♫ in ⁶⁄₈, ♩. ♪♪ in ⁶⁄₄. The lilt is produced when groups of two or four of these figures are used in a balanced fashion, as in the first four measures of Fig. X-1. It is true that canaries also use the "sautillant" figure almost constantly, but the canarie has a slightly faster tempo, a consistently balanced phrase structure, and a simpler texture without much counterpoint.

The French gigue is "lively and spritely," according to theorists Furetière,[1] Richelet,[2] Lacombe,[3] and Compan.[4] Others attribute a happy quality to the French gigue; e.g., Christoph and Stössel[5] and Türk.[6] Brossard says that it has "a skipping quality."[7]

The first strain of the *Gigue de Roland* (Fig. X-1), a popular dance in the early eighteenth century as well as a favorite in current revivals of French Court social dancing, serves as an excellent introduction to the French gigue. The "sautillant" rhythm occurs almost continuously, in one voice or the other. The metric structure (II–3–2) is triple on the pulse level but otherwise duple, and the beat is the dotted half note in ⁶⁄₄ time. Harmonic changes always occur on the first pulse of a beat and very frequently on the third pulse as well, giving an uneven, skipping quality to the piece. The dance steps underline this rhythm since they move in the same way as the harmonic changes, that is, on the first pulse of a beat and often on the third (as in beat 1 of measures 3, 6, 7, and 8). Most of the dance steps are lively leaps or hops. The strain is made up of a four-measure phrase with a weak cadence in both dance and music, followed by a five-measure phrase. Thus the whole nine-measure phrase is interesting, because unpredictable, and not balanced, as in the gavotte or minuet. The two voices of the music enter imitatively, adding another textural variety.

Although most French gigues have a time signature of ⁶⁄₈ or ⁶⁄₄, it is not unusual to find a signature of 3, especially in the seventeenth century. Whatever the signature, or the title, one must examine the metric structure to determine if the piece is, in fact, a French gigue. The characteristics mentioned at the beginning of this section serve as a guide in this determination.

The tempo of the French gigue is described by most theorists as fast.[8] However, it is important to keep in mind that these writers are comparing the gigue with other French dances, and even the fastest of them is in a moderate tempo by modern standards. For example, dance historian Wendy Hilton stated that a comfortable tempo for dancing some French gigues is ♩. = MM 88 in ⁶⁄₄ time, possibly a little faster when the time signature is ⁶⁄₈ with the dotted quarter note as the beat.[9] Montéclair describes the beating of ⁶⁄₄ and ⁶⁄₈ as follows: "The ⁶⁄₄ is beat to two *tems*. It has the value of three quarter notes for each *tems*. The ⁶⁄₈ is beat to two very light *tems*. . . . It contains two measures of minor triple [³⁄₈] in which one

Fig. X-1: Music and dance in the first strain of *Gigue de Roland*, **Feuillet:1700Recueil,** p. 8.

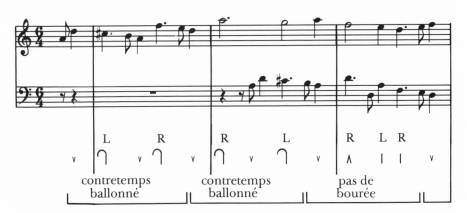

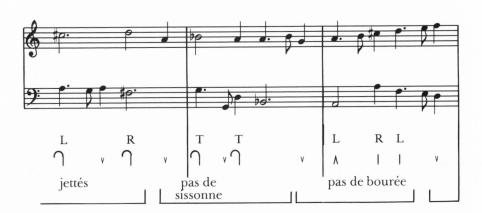

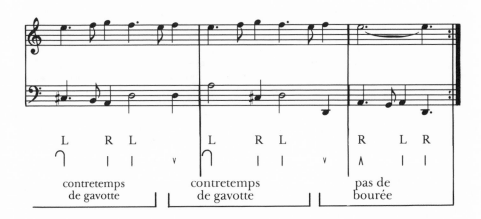

beat is down and the other up.''[10] He also states that the gigue is more properly notated by $\frac{6}{8}$ than by $\frac{6}{4}$.[11]

Another way to view the tempo is offered by Masson, who states that the gigue beats are about the same tempo as beats in the bourée and the rigaudon.[12] Thus the two beats per measure of the *Gigue de Roland* (Fig. X-1) would be in the same tempo as the two beats per measure of *La Bourée d'Achille* (Fig. III-1). Neither the bourée nor the gigue sounds well in a very fast tempo, which may easily convey an atmosphere of frenzy or anxiety.

Fig. X-2 shows a model of the dance rhythm of the French gigue. Some French gigues have phrases of irregular, unpredictable length, as in the *Gigue de Roland*, while others make occasional use of the balanced effect produced by two- and four-measure phrases. The opening four measures of the *Gigue de Roland* have the same balance and pattern of arsis and thesis often found in the bourée—ATAT. In the eight beats of a four-measure phrase, the thesis occurs on beat 7 or 8, and there may be a secondary thesis on beat 3 or 4.

French gigues often use the rhythmic devices of syncopation and hemiolia. In Ex. X-2 the upper voice forms a syncopation against the bass in measure 2; and in measures 3 and 8 the reverse occurs. Hemiolia appears in the penultimate measure. The entire gigue conveys a capricious, jaunty manner, which is possibly the intention of the composer, since the name "Brus-

Fig. X-2: Model for the Gigue Dance Rhythm
II–3–2, $\frac{6}{8}$; I–3–2, $\frac{3}{8}$

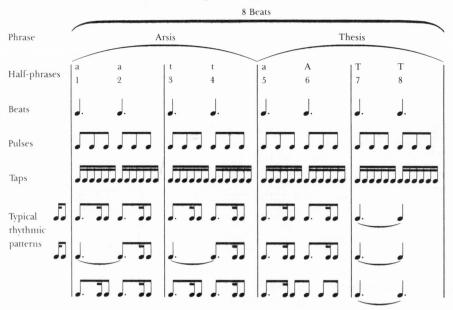

canbille" was the pseudonym of Deslauriers, a notorious seventeenth-century French comedian.

Several French theorists provide bowings which underline the rhythmic concepts just described. In Ex. X-3a Muffat's bowings bring out a lilt in the gigue by using down-bow at the beginning of the first beat of the measure and up-bow at the beginning of the second beat. In addition the three pulses of the beat are articulated with separate bow strokes. The syncopations in measures 2 and 6 are also delineated with separate bowing.

Another theorist who gives bowings (not shown) is Dupont, who adds that one emphasizes the dotted-eighth note and passes the sixteenth note quickly.[13] This apparently means that one should intensify the dotted note and shorten the shortest note. Dupont's bowings agree in general with Muffat's. Quantz is also in agreement, stating "the gigue is played with a short and light bow-stroke, and the canarie, which is always in dotted notes, with a short and sharp one."[14] It is difficult to know without experimentation exactly what differences Quantz intended between gigue and canarie bowings, but he does specify that there is a difference.

Montéclair (Ex. X-3b) provides two different sets of bowings for the gigue,

Ex. X-2: First strain of "Gigue Bruscanbille" by Jacques Chambonnières (mid-seventeenth century).

Ex. X-3: Bowing patterns in the gigue. a. **Muffat:FP** (1695); b. **Montéclair: Violon** (1711–12), p. 18.

showing further possibilities. He does not attempt to follow the Lullian "rule of the down-bow," which, as described by Muffat, decrees that a down-bow occur on the first note of each measure. However, he does specify separate bow strokes for all notes, whatever their value.

In a French gigue by Dandrieu (Ex. X-4), the keyboard fingerings and the ornamentation appear to articulate the beat rather than individual pulses and taps. Using Dandrieu's fingerings no two beats would be slurred together, though the dynamic markings "doux" and "fort" nicely set off one group of two beats against another group of two and lend a sense of balance to the piece.

Ex. X-4: Opening of a gigue by Jean-François Dandrieu, with fingerings by the composer (early eighteenth century).

Ex. X-5: Opening of gigue air, **L'Affilard:Principes** (1705), p. 105 [♩. = MM 116].

L'Affilard's dance song (Ex. X-5) seems to have balanced phrases of 8 + 8 measures in the first strain, but the composer subtly avoids such balance. In the first strain both phrases have an upbeat and are actually composed of 3 + 5 measures, as delineated by the text, the harmonic cadences, and the breath marks of the song. A feminine cadence in measure 3 keeps the phrase moving forward. Articulations analogous to those required by the violin bowings (Ex. X-3) are specified by L'Afflilard—the singer must articulate each note with a syllable, no matter how short the note is.

BACH'S FRENCH GIGUES

Only six of Bach's dances qualify as French gigues. They are in the metric structure I-3-2 or II-3-2, exploit the "sautillant" figure almost continuously, and have a comparatively simple texture. All of them are in a minor key, begin with an upbeat, and contain balanced phrasing at least at the beginning of the two strains. All but two early works and a piece for solo cello begin imitatively.

We pass quickly over Bach's two early French gigues: In the keyboard suite in F minor (BWV 823) the gigue is a contrapuntal *tour de force* but it is only a fragment, albeit with some interesting echo passages. There is also a gigue in the keyboard suite in G minor (BWV 822), but that may be the work of another composer.

The often-performed "gigue" from French Suite II (BWV 813) is the longest of Bach's French gigues. It begins with a strong sense of balance, created by groups of 2 + 2 beats but truncating the phrase at measure 8. The charm of this piece is created by a subtle manipulation of balance. The first strain, which gives the impression of being one long phrase with only a slight pause at the cadence on E♭ in measure 24, is actually made up of three segments, each preceded by an upbeat: 7 or 8 measures, 15 or 16 measures, 8 measures. So skillfully are the segments joined that the listener loses track of the design until the cadence at the double bar; Bach hints at balance but avoids it. The constant "sautillant" rhythm is relieved only in the second strain by interspersed four- and six-note groups of sixteenth notes. The secret of this piece lies in teasing the listener by appearing to come to a resting place but avoiding it and veering into material which propels the piece ever forward. Frequent points of imitation add to the pleasant confusion.

Karl Geiringer refers to the use of the "skipping rhythm of the French *canarie*" in this piece and in the later French gigue in the Overture in the French Style (BWV 831).[15] His comments underline the fact that the "sautillant" rhythm and a simple texture were characteristics of both the French gigue and the canarie. However, these two gigues by Bach are not true canaries. The one in BWV 813 lacks the balanced phrasing of the canarie, and BWV 831 concludes with the other one—it seems unlikely that Bach would have ended his public statement on the French style with such an uncommon dance as the canarie, charming though it is. Rather, these pieces, though similar to canaries, actually illustrate yet another ramification of the "gigue idea."

The gigue from the Fifth Suite for solo cello (BWV 1011) and the one from BWV 813 come from the Köthen years, and both are in the key of C minor. Scordatura tuning[16] is used in the cello piece. The harmonic and color possibilities offered by unusual tuning helps explain why this gigue is more refined and more harmonically interesting than those in Bach's four previous suites for cello.

Bach continues his exploration of balance and imbalance in the gigue segment shown in Ex. X-6. In measure 15 he begins a set of two triple "mega-measures" in which the "sautillant" figure seems transported to the measure level, but at the end of the strain, measures 21–24 restore the duple balance inherent in the metric structure of the French gigue. In the second strain, sequences in measures 41–52 lead to an extension in measures 55 and 56 created by trills on E♭ and E♮; these take on the function of a deceptive cadence and in turn lead to a climax on measure 57. The two triple mega-measures return in measures 61–63 and 64–66; this time they include an exciting syncopation in measure 61 followed by six balanced measures (not four as at the end of the first strain). In spite of the imbalances introduced in this piece, the underlying harmony is that of eight-measure phrases.

BWV 995 is an embellished transcription of BWV 1011 for lute. Although many of his dance transcriptions are almost literal copies of their original model, Bach adds new material here by introducing a second voice, often in

Ex. X-6: Gigue by J.S. Bach for solo cello, BWV 1011, measures 13–24.

imitation of the soprano, which supplies an interesting bass line and fills in the harmonies.

One of the most interesting French gigues of all is from the Overture in the French Style (BWV 831). It is almost entirely in two-part texture. The bass voice takes a subservient, non-imitative role until almost the end, when it finally asserts its authority in measure 36. In spite of writing balanced phrases for almost the entire piece, Bach creates a superb French gigue by clear harmonic organization using sequences and suspensions and writes surprising *tiratas* to fill in the "sautillant" figure. The *tiratas* are particularly effective in the exciting drive to the final cadence.

BWV 816

GIGA I

The Baroque love of complexity is nowhere more joyously and enthusiastically expressed than in the dance types we designate "giga I" and "giga II," each with its own metric structure, tempo, and overall character.

"Giga I" refers to Baroque pieces entitled "gigue" or "giga" (or related terms) in whose metric structure tripleness appears on the lowest level of rhythm. In fact, giga I is the only Baroque dance type which consistently has triple groupings at the lowest metric level. Portions of pieces by Buxtehude and Handel (Exs. X-7, X-8) clearly illustrate the tripleness of giga I in two different notations, even though the Buxtehude gigue has two beats per measure and the Handel gigue has four. Another characteristic of giga I is

Ex. X-7: Opening of Gigue by Dietrich Buxtehude (c. 1680).

Ex. X-8: Opening of Jigg by George Frideric Handel, from Suite in E minor (1733).

that the texture is normally contrapuntal, imitative, and sometimes fugal (Ex. X-7), though Ex. X-8 shows that it can also be homophonic.

The cadential structure of giga I is sharply different from that of most other Baroque dances. Important cadences appear only at the end of each strain, with interior cadences either avoided or run through in a relentless sense of forward motion. This results in long pieces which can accumulate great energy and which are aesthetically far removed from Baroque dances with predictable cadences. In the Buxtehude gigue no intermediate thetic points hinder the effort toward the only cadence, at the end of measure 11. In the Handel piece suspensions and sequences negate any possible resting places until the end of the strain in measure 6.

Still another characteristic of giga I is that most phrases are of an unpredictable length. In Exx. X-11 and X-12 the opening phrases give no hint of their eventual resolutions. Even so, some gigas have more balance and interior cadences than others. Ex. X-9 shows the beginning of a well-loved piece

Ex. X-9: Opening of Giga by Arcangelo Corelli, Op. 5, No. 9.

by Corelli, which is a giga I by virtue of its tripleness on the lower metric level. But it begins with a strong sense of balance, has two interior cadences (measures 4 and 13), and is homophonic except for a few imitative moments toward the end of the strain (not shown). Another giga I characteristic is the use of jagged or uneven rhythms (upper voice of measure 1). Although this distinctive rhythm, which seems to "hop" rather than "walk," causes the music to flow unevenly, that very unevenness actually propels the music forward. Corelli's giga probably reflects the balanced phrasing of the earlier seventeenth-century jigs as found, for example, in the *Fitzwilliam Virginal Book;*[17] by Bach's time gigas normally use unbalanced phrasing except, occasionally, in the opening few measures of a piece.

In the model rhythm for a giga I in $\frac{12}{8}$ time (Fig. X-3), there are two beats per measure, and the metric structure is II–2–3. One may often assume this underlying structure even when the piece is not so notated. For example, if a giga I is notated in $\frac{6}{8}$ (Fig. X-4), which would result in the metric structure I–2–3, one might still think of two measures as one. In gigas the grouping of beats into measures is generally less important than it is in most other Baroque dances, since balance and the repetition of rhythms of a definite length and shape are seldom present. From this point of view it often does not matter whether the notation contains one, two, or four beats per measure. This may explain why there are so many different meter signs in gigas: one finds them notated in 3, $\frac{3}{4}$, $\frac{6}{4}$, $\frac{3}{8}$, $\frac{6}{8}$, $\frac{9}{8}$, $\frac{12}{8}$, $\frac{12}{16}$, $\frac{24}{16}$, and even ₵ in the works of composers other than Bach, who, alone, also uses $\frac{9}{16}$. These time signatures do not necessarily give information about metric structure; often they are a

Fig. X-3: Model for the Giga I Dance Rhythm
II–2–3, $\frac{12}{8}$

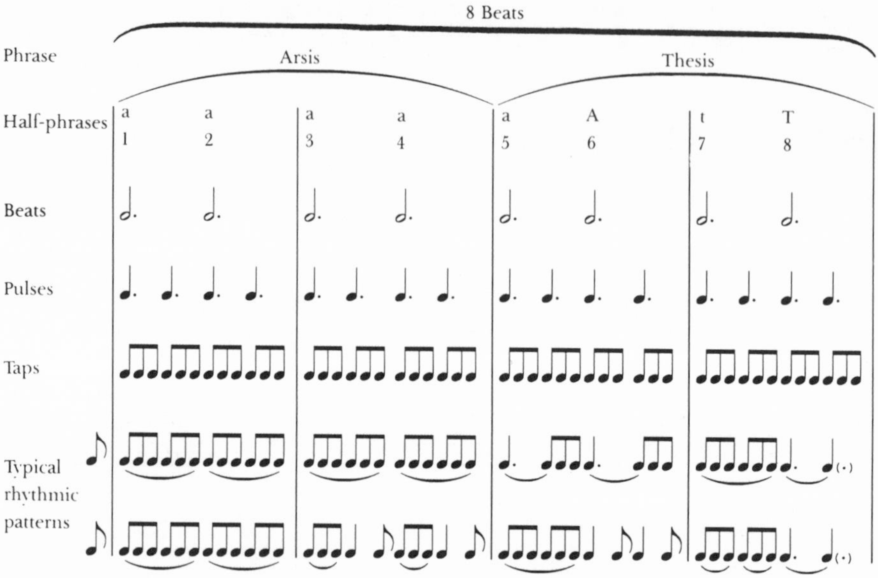

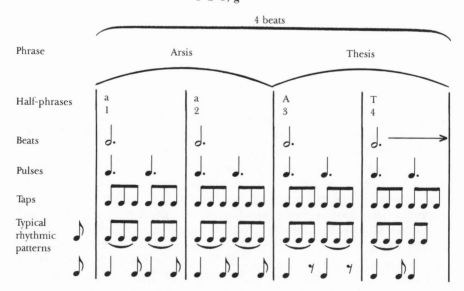

Fig. X-4: Alternate Model for the Giga I Dance Rhythm
I–2–3, $\frac{6}{8}$

clue to tempo, though more research needs to be done in this area.[18] With such a wide variety of time signatures, the performer must study each piece to determine the relationship of structure to measure lines.

One difficulty in studying gigas is that they do not appear to have any choreographic associations. The gigas in Baroque musical suites have not yet been associated by scholars with a particular dance. It seems likely that gigas in Italy were originally a spin-off from the jigs of English country dance fame,[19] but by the late seventeenth century gigas have a life quite apart from dance steps, as the works of Corelli and other Italian composers abundantly demonstrate.[20] Even though English country dancing was popular in Germany throughout the eighteenth century, during Bach's life and afterward, any connection between these dances and the gigas in his suites has yet to be established. Gigas appear to be more of a purely instrumental excursion than does any other Baroque dance except the allemande.

Another difficulty in studying gigas is that seventeenth- and eighteenth-century theorists who wrote about gigues and gigas did not fully account for the different types of pieces which appear under these titles. Theorists, writers, and musicians of Bach's time distinguished between French gigues and Italian gigas, but none was able to account for the diversity of instrumental composition which appears under these titles. The best attempts were made by Mattheson, Rameau, and Montéclair.

Johann Mattheson mentions four dance types under the category gigue:

> the common one (English gigues, characterized by an ardent and fleeting zeal, a passion which soon subsides); the Loure (slow, proud and arrogant); the Canarie ("must have great eagerness and swiftness" and also "a little simplicity"); and the Giga:
> Finally the Italian *Gige*, which are not used for dancing, but for fiddling (from which its name may also derive), force themselves to extreme speed or volatility; though frequently in a flowing and uninterrupted manner: perhaps like the smooth arrow-swift flow of a stream.[21]

Since Mattheson gives no musical examples it is difficult to know exactly what pieces he means by "English gigues" and "Italian *gige*." However, he does associate Italian gigas with a type of fast-driving instrumental piece for violin, which may refer to some gigas found in Corelli and, later, in works of Bach.

Another writer who offered distinctions among gigues was Jean-Philippe Rameau. In a discussion of gigue rhythms in his 1722 *Treatise on Harmony* he gives several musical examples, though, again, not of particular pieces. In an effort to reduce to a minimum the multiplicity of meter signs used in gigues and gigas, he presents four theoretical examples, at the same time comparing them with the French gigue (Ex. X-10).[22] The "Italian Gige," according to Rameau, may have two, three, or four ter-

Ex. X-10: Jean-Philippe Rameau's theoretical examples for Gigue and
Giga. a. French gigue; b., c., d. Italian gige.

nary beats per measure, and may begin at the beginning or in the middle
of the measure. His point is a good one; he presents both the pulse- and
the tap-level rhythms, leaving the grouping of pulses into beats up to
each composer.

Another type of distinction among gigues appears in the music of several
eighteenth-century composers. Montéclair's *Cinquième Concert*[23] includes a
gigue in the French style, which is full of strongly dotted rhythms, and one in
the Italian style, which proceeds in fluid, running eighth notes (Ex. X-11).
The latter is not a giga I, however, but a giga II, since the tripleness is on the
pulse not the tap level. Montéclair gives no example of giga I, and it is true
that this type rarely appears in the music of French composers. The distinctions made by Montéclair, Mattheson and Rameau seem valid but none ac-
counts for all or even most of the gigas.

The performance style of giga I is difficult to formulate because the
length and shape of the phrases are quite unpredictable. However, numerous sources provide information about tap-level groupings. In Corelli's giga (Ex. X-9) slurs consistently join the groups of three eighth
notes. Other gigas by Corelli (e.g., Op. 4, No. 4) use a 2 + 1 grouping for
tap-level eighth notes, implying a slightly slower tempo. The theoretical
example by Rameau (Ex. X-10) shows both ternary and 2 + 1 groupings
of eighth notes, though it is not possible to determine whether the pieces
are giga I or giga II, since so little music appears in the example. Bach
inherited a form which was already full of variety and not well explained
by theorists.

Ex. X-11: Two gigue styles in Michel Montéclair, *Cinquième Concert*, from *Concerts à deux Flutes Traversières sans Basses* (early eighteenth century. a. Gigue a la maniere Françoise; b. Gigue a la maniere Italienne.

BACH'S GIGA I

Bach wrote fifteen giga I pieces. All are soloistic excursions for virtuoso performers, and all but two are for the keyboard: in BWV 1010 for solo cello and in BWV 1068 for orchestra. One finds pieces similar to the ones already described, with joyous affect created by long phrases, few internal cadences, and a rapid tempo; much contrapuntal writing occurs, and five of the pieces are fugues. Bach uses a great variety of time signatures and, presumably, tempi. Since so little information is available on the performance style of giga I, most of the comments in this section simply describe structure and style in these pieces.

The earliest gigas, from the Weimar period, are somewhat experimental. The shortest one, in the Overture in F major for keyboard (BWV 820), could be either giga I or giga II. The simplicity of the harmony and texture and the absence of sixteenth notes implies a fairly fast tempo, which would make it a giga I; however, a slower tempo, projecting the qualities of giga II, is also a possibility.

In Partie in A major (BWV 832), the giga has the structure I–2–3, and almost all the tap-level eighth notes are slurred by threes. The harmony changes twice per measure except for the cadence measures (4, 8, 12, 16, 22, 28, and 34), where a single harmony lasts through the whole measure.

The keyboard Concerto in C major (BWV 977) is probably an arrangement of a concerto by Vivaldi or some other Italian composer. The giga has the metric structure II–2–3. It has balanced phrases except for measures 27–35 and is not imitative. A few sixteenth notes are used, but they function as ornaments, not as a lower level of meter. A few slurs group three eighth notes together (measures 23–24).

Concerto in G minor (BWV 975) is another concerto arranged for keyboard, this one definitely by Vivaldi (Op. 4, No. 6). The giga (II–2–3) has an unrelenting energy created by continuous ternary figures throughout its sixty measures. In form it is a single movement without the usual two reprises, and in texture it is nonimitative. Long cadences characterize this piece, in that the thesis harmony lasts a long time; e.g., measures 8–9, 17–18, 37–39, and 58–60.

The gigas in English Suites II, III, IV, and VI use many of the same techniques, but in a far more imaginative way. In Suite II (BWV 807) Bach achieves a wonderful swing and drive in the giga (I–2–3), sweeping the listener along with trills (e.g., measures 7, 9, and 11) which push each sequence to a higher pitch. It could be giga II if one chose to articulate and emphasize the trills broadly in a slower tempo, though most performers will not want to sacrifice the excitement of a fast tempo. Both strains begin with a four-measure phrase but never return to it again. The overall form is unusual in gigues: AA (first strain) BB (second strain) AB (entire piece again, without repeats).

The giga of English Suite III (BWV 808; II–2–3) has a lilting movement similar to that of BWV 807 but is imitative: both strains begin with a subject stated three times, and the subject of the second strain is an inversion of the first. In fact, this piece might become a fugue were it not for the fact that in both strains the third voice eventually drops out, and a two-part texture continues to the end. Only one interior cadence arrests the flow, the phrygian cadence in measure 11; measures 24 and 28 illustrate Bach's technique of avoiding cadences. A few ornaments decorate these spots—one preceding the phrygian cadence, one leading to the final cadence, and two in measures 28–29—giving extra life to the chromatic lines. The general lack of ornamental signs suggests a facile, fluent execution with little ritard at the end.

The giga in English Suite IV (BWV 809) is a two-voice, imitative piece with the structure II–2–3. It is both joyful and playful, recalling a pastoral idea by the hunting horn theme (measure 1) and by several ornamented pedal points in the style of a bagpipe drone. The two voices toss the hunt motif back and forth by sequences and repetition, sometimes alternating and sometimes playing it in concert. The few weak internal cadences (measures 35 and 43) do not impede the continuous movement.

In English Suite VI (BWV 811) we find one of Bach's great virtuoso giga-fugues (II–2–3), a challenge and a joy for any ambitious performer. The $\frac{12}{16}$ time signature is indicative of a fast tempo in which the ternary groups are to be played "lightly and without the least pressure," if we accept Kirnberger's interesting comments on a similar fugue by Bach in $\frac{6}{16}$ (*Well-Tempered Clavier*, Book II, Fugue XI in F major, BWV 880):

> If this fugue is to be performed correctly on the keyboard, the notes must be played lightly and without the least pressure in a fast tempo; this is what $\frac{6}{16}$ meter requires. [24] On the violin, pieces in this and other similarly light meters are to be played just with the point of the bow; however, weightier meters require a longer stroke and more bow pressure. The fact that these and several other meters that we shall list are considered superfluous and obsolete today [i.e., 1776] indicates either that good and correct execution has been lost or that an aspect of expression which is easy to obtain only in these meters is entirely unknown to us. [25]

The subject of this giga-fugue for three voices is a melodic wedge that moves away from a pedal point. The wedge becomes an inverted subject in the second strain. Virtually no internal cadences disturb the great energy accumulated by this subject and by the trills which decorate the pedal points. If one believes Kirnberger and performs everything with a light touch, the pedal points seem to shimmer and the suspensions glide almost effortlessly. Bach may have received his inspiration for this giga from a similar one by Buxtehude, a fugue also in $\frac{12}{16}$. [26]

The giga from the E♭ major cello suite (BWV 1010), with metric structure II–2–3, is the only giga I for a solo stringed instrument. The bowings, which come from the P 26 manuscript, join all the eighth notes in groups of threes. Formally, Bach makes this rather sprawling giga cohesive by the frequent return of the opening motive (measures 11–12, 19, 27–28) and the liberal use of echo effects, which exploit the timbres of the instrument.

Another giga-fugue in three voices appears in the Fifth French Suite in G major (BWV 816). It is similar to that in BWV 811, with the same structure, II–2–3; an inverted subject in the second strain; and the $\frac{12}{16}$ meter, suggesting a light touch in a rapid tempo. The movement in this rollicking giga is continuous, and the articulation of the form is clarified only by the subject entries. It makes an exuberant climax for a suite of dances, sweeping the listener along in a merry chase.

The Leipzig Partitas for keyboard, from *Clavier-Übung I*, contain elegant gigas which are at the same time challenging and problematic. The First Partita, in B♭ major (BWV 825), confronts us with a giga in common time (II–2–3) with implied triplets. Why didn't Bach simply notate this piece in $\frac{12}{8}$? Kirnberger offers an answer to this question, discussing the difference between $\frac{9}{8}$ with three triple beats and $\frac{3}{4}$ with triplets:

> Triplets in a $\frac{3}{4}$ measure should be performed differently than eighth notes in a $\frac{9}{8}$ measure; the former are very light and do not have the slightest accent on the last note, while the latter are performed more heavily and with somewhat more importance to the last note. Also, the [$\frac{3}{4}$ measure] never carries, or certainly very seldom, a new harmony on the last note while the [$\frac{9}{8}$ measure] does very often. And further, the former allows no "Brechung" in sixteenth notes, while the latter does very often. Were both types of measures not differentiated from each other through special properties, then all *Gigues* in $\frac{6}{8}$ could also be set in $\frac{2}{4}$ measure. Everyone can easily understand how illogical this is when, for example, a Gigue in $\frac{12}{8}$ or $\frac{6}{8}$ is set in c or $\frac{2}{4}$ measure.[27]

A comparison of this giga with the giga of Partita III (BWV 827), notated in $\frac{12}{8}$, immediately reveals the difference in style of composition and performance of the two pieces. Unlike BWV 827, the BWV 825 giga does not have a harmony sounded with the last note of the triplet and it does not have arpeggiated sixteenth notes; following Kirnberger, it should be played lightly "without the slightest pressure on the last note." Thus Bach's meter sign, c instead of $\frac{12}{8}$, tells the performer how to render this delightful giga. Its very simplicity and nonchalance, enhanced by a kind of *stile brisé* (broken-chord style), might tempt one to take it too quickly, reducing its easy gracefulness to a blur of sound verging on the aggressive.

The giga from the Partita III (II–2–3) is a more complex dance than that of Partita I. It is another three-part giga-fugue in which the subject is inverted in the second strain. The subject, which centers around the note A, begins as a broken-chord figure and a mordent (measure 1, pulses 1–2) and sounds well if all the pulses are articulated cleanly. The figuration of the subject is brilliantly exploited in sequence after sequence, building tension even though the harmonies hardly ever depart from the tonic, dominant, and subdominant.

Partita IV (BWV 828) contains a giga unique in all of Baroque music—it is in $\frac{9}{16}$, giving it two levels of tripleness below the beat (I–3–3). Handel wrote gigas in $\frac{24}{16}$ and $\frac{12}{16}$,[28] and Kuhnau wrote one in $\frac{9}{8}$,[29] but only Bach, to our knowledge, used $\frac{9}{16}$ for a giga. Kirnberger again has advice to performers on the interpretation of this sign:

> $\frac{9}{16}$ meter of three triple beats that is derived from $\frac{3}{8}$ was used in many ways by the older composers for gigue-like pieces that are to be performed extremely quickly and lightly. But it no longer occurs in contemporary music; $\frac{9}{8}$ meter appears in its place.[30]

Even though Kirnberger speaks of three beats to the measure, it is fair to say that most performers will feel the measure as one beat, a unique metric scheme for gigas and, in fact, all of Bach's dances. Cadences occur at irregular intervals and are at best fleeting. But Bach has made this giga even more intriguing. It is a loosely knit three-part fugue in which the subject is six measures long and begins with a dotted eighth note tied over to the second pulse. Furthermore, the second strain begins with a new subject, which is then combined with the main subject!

The giga from the E minor Partita (BWV 830) is the most problematical of all. Like the giga II from the D minor French Suite (BWV 812; see below), it is written in common time and all its meter levels are duple (IV–2–2); no tripleness is evident. Several meter signs occur among the different sources for this piece: ¢ in the Anna Magdalena Bach *Clavierbüchlein* of 1725, and 𝇍 in *Clavier-Übung* I (1731). The obvious question is whether to play the notation as written or to resolve it (somehow) so that tripleness is heard (see below, "Gigues Notated in Duple Meter").

Again Bach writes a three-part fugue with an inverted subject in the second strain, but that is its only similarity with other gigas; it is basically an anomaly. The extremely angular subject, made up of seconds, thirds, and diminished sevenths, creates a tormented affect. The piece ends with the bass assuming the place of the upper voice, standing the whole structure on its head. It is a magnificent ending for Bach's published Opus 1.

The last giga I by Bach is for orchestra, from the Overture in D major (BWV 1068). It has the metric structure I–2–3. It is scored for three trumpets, timpani, two oboes, strings, and continuo. The trumpets and oboes enhance the already joyful character of this giga by adding brilliance and color to the lines, and the opening fanfare returns with particular exuberance in the winds.

The cheerfulness of this giga seems related to the Corelli piece in Ex. X-9. Bach, also, writes a giga with a strong sense of balance and fairly frequent cadences. The opening strain falls into phrases of 4 + 4 + 16 measures, the last created by the unexpected evaded cadence in measure 18. The second strain has 8 + 4 + 4 + 8 + 4 + 20 measures, with the last extended phrase produced by a deceptive cadence on VI in measure 65.

Bowings stress groups of three eighth notes, since the harmony does not change within the ternary group. The only sixteenth notes are in measure 23, but they are purely ornamental and are slurred to the following eighth note.

BWV 817

GIGA II

Bach's most complex, exploratory, and challenging gigues are in the category we designate "giga II." They are complex because there is another metric level below the tripleness. Figs. X-5, X-6, and X-7 present the metric structures of giga II, all of which have triple groupings of eighth notes on the pulse level and duple groupings of sixteenth notes below that. It is difficult to find German examples of giga II outside of Bach's works; a few occur among compositions by Pachelbel, Buxtehude, Erlebach, and Froberger. The giga II comes mostly from French composers; see "Gigue a la maniere Italienne" by Montéclair (Ex. X-11), which uses fluid, running eighth notes with a generous mixture of sixteenths.

Exx. X-12 and X-13 each show a giga II by François Couperin. The gigue for viole (Ex. X-12) has numerous ornaments, frequent harmonic changes, and varied groupings of eighth notes. For example, in measure 1 the first three pulses are slurred together; the slurring in measure 2 is different; and the final measure of the strain has a third type of grouping, joining four eighth notes. In the "La Milordine" gigue (Ex. X-13) the composer writes in fingering to illustrate how to make a descending legato line out of the seemingly disjunct figuration often found in giga II. The bass in this passage is phrased so as to form counter-rhythms against the upper voice; modern performers might not think to project such counter-rhythms in a giga II without Couperin's explicit reminder. Again, a moderate tempo is necessary for such subtlety to be evident to the listener.

It is worthwhile at this point to review Table V (p. 145). All three dances—French gigues, giga I, and giga II—generally have a lively or

Fig. X-5: Model for the Giga II Dance Rhythm

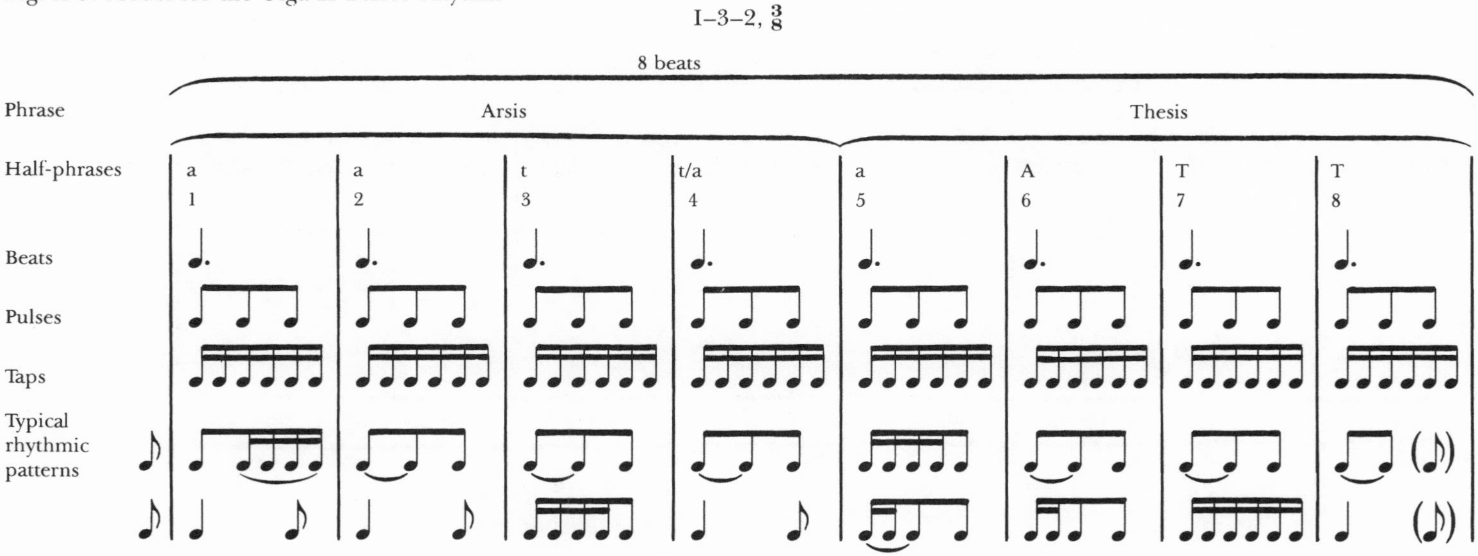

I–3–2, $\frac{3}{8}$

Fig. X-6: Alternate Model for the Giga II Dance Rhythm   II–3–2, 6, 8

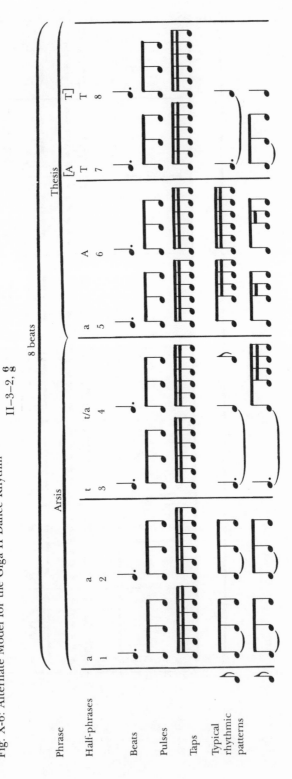

Fig. X-7: Alternate Model for the Giga II Dance Rhythm
IV–3–2, $\frac{12}{8}$

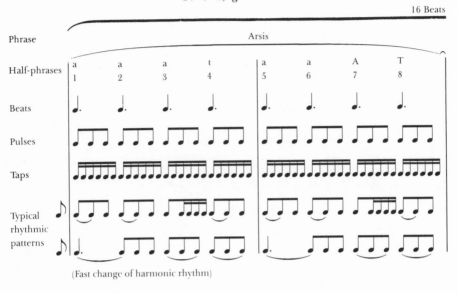

(Fast change of harmonic rhythm)

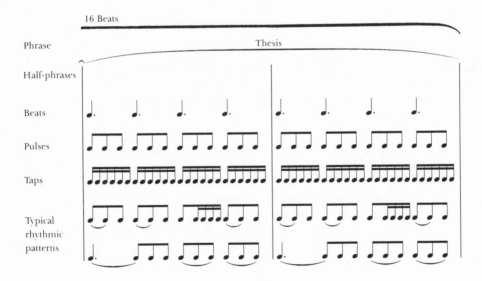

Ex. X-12: Gigue by François Couperin, *Pièces de Viole* (1728), measures 1–4 and 15–18.

joyful affect, long phrases of unpredictable length, imitative texture, and a paucity of internal cadences. French gigue and giga II share additional characteristics, including a common metric structure with tripleness at the tap level and harmonic change within the triple pulses, the use of moderate tempo with some ornamentation, and variety in the grouping of sixteenth notes by slurs. French gigue and giga II are different because of the "sautillant" figure, which prevails in the former but is only rarely heard in the latter.

Giga I and giga II also have several characteristics not shared with French gigues. In general, gigas are longer and more complex pieces than French gigues. Texturally, one often finds fugues or quasi-fugal procedures, usually with the subject inverted in the second strain. Both gigas appear under a large variety of time signatures.

Both French gigue and giga I have characteristics unique to themselves. The French gigue features the already mentioned "sautillant" figures. Giga I alone has tripleness on the tap level, no harmonic change within triple groups, slurs covering ternary figures only, and a slower tempo with an "illusion of quickness" because of the speed of the many notes. On the other hand, giga II has no unique characteristics, that is, qualities which do not occur either in giga I or French gigue.

Therefore, one may postulate that French gigue and giga I had comparatively separate origins, but that giga II pieces were derived historically from one or both of the other types. As such, giga II is the farthest from actual dancing or any choreographic associations at all, except as they might have

Ex. X-13: Opening of Gigue "La Milordine," from **Couperin:Pièces** (1713).

Gracieusement et légérement

come from the French gigue or giga II. Giga II, then, is more of an instrumental excursion than any other Baroque dance type except the allemande.
It is easy to see why Bach was attracted to it, even though his German contemporaries were not.

GIGA II IN BACH'S MUSIC

Among Bach's works there are more pieces which are giga II than giga I.
Twenty pieces of the giga II type survive if one counts the lute arrangement
(BWV 1006a) of the Third Partita for solo violin (BWV 1006) and the *double*
in the Partita for lute (BWV 997). Most of the giga II pieces are more complex, with more careful detail, grander scope, and longer length than those

which are giga I. Included among the giga II type are a four-voice fugue (in BWV 965) and three three-voice fugues (in BWV 810, 812, and 829). Eight of the pieces begin with a balanced phrase structure, while the rest do not. All those of the giga II type are entitled "gigue" or "gique."

The three earliest giga II pieces, from the Weimar years are all in $\frac{12}{8}$ time with the structure IV–3–2. The longest of Bach's giga II pieces is in the keyboard Sonata in A minor (BWV 965), which is fashioned after a 1687 sonata by Reinken. It is a four-voice fugue with a long and extremely sequential subject. Against this Bach writes chromatic counter melodies and episodic material with written-out mordents and other ornamental figures designed to highlight syncopations. The two strains are equal in length, with the subject of the second strain an inversion of the initial subject. Because of the fast harmonic rhythm and chromatic nature of the harmony, a moderate tempo is most appropriate. No major internal cadences break up the forward motion of the intense chromaticism.

The giga in the Suite in E minor (BWV 996) is a complex dance for lute, composed of almost constantly running sixteenth notes in arpeggio or *tirata* figures. The texture changes freely from two- to three-part writing, with occasional four-voice chords. Chromatic modulations and sequential figures keep a constant forward momentum, which is difficult for even the most accomplished of lute players.

The giga in the Sonata in E minor for violin and continuo (BWV 1023) has only a few sixteenth notes and would be a giga I except for the many harmonic changes on the tap level. This piece challenges the soloist because of the similarity of the figuration throughout; the only bowings indicated are slurs, which frequently group three eighth notes together. Dynamic contrasts are one possible solution.

Pieces of the giga II variety occur in English Suites I and V. In the former (BWV 806), in E minor, the giga (II–3–2) is graceful and effortless but at the same time relentless; the imitative, two-part texture never ceases in the constant forward motion of its sixteenth notes. The only relief comes just before the ends of phrases, when a hemiolia shifts the meter from $\frac{6}{8}$ (♩. ♩.) to $\frac{3}{4}$ (♩ ♩ ♩); careful articulation of these hemiolias gives us a chance to "catch our breath," so to speak. Another distinctive feature of this piece is the recurring rhythmic figure ♫ ♪ , an ornamented syncopation which occurs frequently in both voices. Unlike most gigas, there are numerous cadences (measures 4, 12, 16, 21, 25, 35, and 40); some of these would be enhanced by ornamentation such as the *double cadence* (for example, in measures 3–4 and 20).

The giga of the Fifth English Suite (BWV 810), with structure I–3–2, is a three-part fugue with an inverted subject in the second strain. But why does Bach notate it in $\frac{3}{8}$ instead of $\frac{6}{8}$? One possiblity is that he avoids the idea of beats grouped in twos, which is associated with dance music. The piece has "swing," especially if one articulates the subject, ♫♫♫♫ | ♫. ♫. ♫. ♫ , but it is not bound to regularly recurring cadential patterns, as is a dance. The subject begins in conjunct sixteenth notes and then bursts forth in disjunct, chromatic movement. No internal cadences block the flow of notes in the second strain, as Bach intensifies this giga by the use of suspensions, a pedal point (measures 35-37), and harmonic sequences. This is an exciting, dynamic piece!

Giga II for Solo Stringed Instruments

Giga II appears in four of the six suites for solo cello and two of the partitas for solo violin, all of which were composed during Bach's tenure in Köthen. Apparently Bach favored giga II over giga I for these unusual solo excursions, since only one giga I has survived for solo cello (in BWV 1010) and none for solo violin.

It is the bowings of the gigue in Suite I (BWV 1007) which firmly fix this piece as a giga II (II–3–2). Taken from the Anna Magdalena manuscript, they present the cellist with varied ways to group the ternary figures—sometimes $1 + 2$ (measure 1), sometimes $2 + 1$ (measures 9-11), and sometimes with a written-in slide, which may occur as in measure 3 (♫♫♫) or as in measure 28 (♫♫♫). Additional performance indications from this manuscript include staccato eighth notes in measures 2 and 7, three-note slurs at the beginning of the second strain and a slurred *tirata* figure in measure 33. The presence throughout of four- and eight-measure phrases, clearly ending in internal as well as final cadences, recalls the pleasurable regularity of the dance.

Balanced phrasing with numerous internal cadences is also a characteristic of the giga in D minor in Suite II for cello (BWV 1008). It has the metric structure I–3–2. Here, too, the bowings require a highly articulate style of performance, though it is quite different from that of the giga in BWV 1007. In contrast to BWV 1007, in BWV 1008 the level of the tap is expressed by the almost constant sixteenth notes, most of them grouped in twos or threes. All three-note slides are phrased as they were in BWV 1007, as are almost all groups of three conjunct sixteenth notes (e.g., measure 10). The dupleness of the tap level is expressed by numerous two-note groupings among the sixteenth notes, though other groupings also occur.

The giga in Suite III (BWV 1009) in C major (I–3–2) is truly a *tour de force* of solo string writing and will be a stimulating challenge for any performer. It is a joyful piece in which Bach apparently delighted in making the cellist negotiate wide leaps. The Italian style of string writing, with its rapid-fire pedal points (measures 21–31), sequences, repetitions, and echo patterns (measures 21–26, 33–44, and 81–88), sustains our interest throughout. Internal cadences are carefully avoided. The bowings, many of which are unlike those of the previous gigas for solo cello, again require careful articulation. Sixteenth notes are bowed in two-note groupings in all the pedal-point sections.

The giga from the Sixth Cello Suite (BWV 1012, in a scordatura tuning[31]) has a very wide range and the metric structure II–3–2. The piece is a veritable catalogue of virtuoso string techniques, also with meticulous bowings taken from the Anna Magdalena manuscript. Pedal points are articulated in the 2 + 1 rhythm (e.g., measures 5–8), although numerous groups of six sixteenth notes to the bow also occur and help to emphasize the level of the beat (e.g., measures 15–16). It is interesting to note that these groupings never straddle the bar line. Another technique is a kind of tremolo figure (measures 24–36 and 65–66) in which double-stops are used. Triple- and quadruple-stops also appear on occasion. Clearly, this masterfully stylized giga should be played at a moderate tempo so that the joyous affect projects through the many technically demanding passages.

The violinist has little chance to rest in the giga from Partita II for solo violin (BWV 1004), which has the structure IV–3–2. In fact, the constant sixteenth notes pose a real problem, which is similar to the challenge of the "Bourée Anglaise" in the Sonata for solo flute (BWV 1013): how can the headstrong flow of notes be articulated and grouped artistically? Fortunately a great variety of bowings can be derived from the autograph manuscript, P 967. These bowings also offer possibilities for some of the places in which no bowing is indicated. Help in forming the overall shape of each strain comes from Bach in the form of written-in terrace dynamics (*piano* and *forte* indications). Occasional harmonic reference points (e.g., measure 3, beat 1; measure 5, beat 3) also aid in articulating the structure, partly compensating for the general lack of internal cadences. Arpeggios and *tiratas* augment the virtuoso character of this stimulating work.

The giga in Partita III for solo violin (BWV 1006), in the structure II–3–2, offers fewer problems. It is a charming, buoyant, good-humored piece featuring four- and eight-measure phrases cast in strains of equal length. Again there are arpeggio and *tirata* figures and several internal cadences, with a few bowings written in. This is Bach's shortest giga. Bach must have liked it, for he arranged it for another instrument, possibly the lute-harpsichord. Though a recent authority deems it unplayable on the lute,[32] this version (BWV 1006a) hints at what might have been Bach's intentions in the solo violin piece; one finds echo effects (measures 6–7), explicit harmonies, and imitative texture (measures 13–14 and 29–30). It would be interesting to try incorporating these features into BWV 1006. An inherent gracefulness shines through both versions, possibly prefiguring the well known gigue from the E major French Suite (see below).

Giga II in the French Suites

The intense, problematic giga in the D minor French Suite (BWV 812) is notated in duple meter. (We discuss the special problems of this notation below.) This interesting and strenuous piece is a three-part fugue in which the subject of the second strain is an inversion of the opening subject. The only internal cadence comes in the second strain (measures 21–22) and is phrygian.

Balance is important in the giga from French Suite III (BWV 814) with metric structure I–3–2, though not in the sense of balanced, four-measure phrases. Rather, balance shines through because each 34-measure strain begins imitatively, with voices one measure apart; each of the two voices is equal in importance, each strain has one major cadence at about the halfway point (measures 16 and 52), the four major cadences are all approached by figures which succeed well in a hemiolia articulation, and musical ideas are often echoed from one voice to the other. Articulations gleaned from gigas in the solo cello suites will clarify the rhythms of this piece—opportunities abound for two-note groupings (e.g., measures 9-10, upper voice) as well as for a 4 + 2 arrangement (measures 5–8). This seamless piece elegantly unfolds with only a few musical ideas, making varied articulation of the rhythms essential. Upbeats should be sharply articulated; long notes may be embellished by trills.

The Italian style rings like a bell in the "gique" (II–3–2) from the E♭ major French Suite (BWV 815). Its sixty measures, in two unequal strains, shift back and forth between two- and three-voice texture, with a few five-note chords thrown in for special effect (measure 33). Although the first strain opens with three statements of the rollicking subject, the piece is only pseudo-fugal. The good-natured intensity builds with the help of harmonic sequences, long trills, and the introduction of sixteenth notes toward the end of each strain. Again, varied articulations borrowed from the bowings in the gigas in the cello suites will enhance the rhythms, especially in places where the two voices are both busy, such as measure 25, in which the lower voice could be played ♫♩♫♩ against the upper voice's ♩♫♫♩♫♫ .

Balance is also a delightful feature in the well-known giga from the E major French Suite (BWV 817), with structure II–3–2. The simple musical materials are developed within two strains of equal length: the first comprises three eight-measure phrases, though longer ones come in the second one. A two-voice texture flows throughout in imitative fashion without ever becoming too complex or challenging. Varied articulations, derived from bowings in the cello suites, will enhance the already cheerful affect. The ternary pulses often sound best in a 2 + 1 articulation. Long notes (e.g., in measures 17, 19, and 20) may be ornamented with a trill or a *port de voix*, though in those preceded by a note from below the ornament should begin on the lower note (for example, in measure 29 the trill sounds best if approached from E♯, not a G♯). The long trill in measure 35 could be approached from either below or above. A stunning though graceful ending will occur if the hemiolia in measure 47 is carefully articulated with no ritard.

The gigue in the keyboard Suite in A minor (BWV 818) contains many of the same features as the giga II type in the French Suites. It has a metric structure of II–3–2. The imitative texture moves mostly in three voices, creating two strains of equal length with one clear internal cadence in each strain. Numerous ornaments enliven the forward movement, and varied articulations will add even more spice.

The Leipzig Giga II Pieces

Two giga II pieces have survived from Bach's Leipzig days, both in the metric structure II–3–2. The "gique' from the Fifth Partita for keyboard (BWV 829) is a mature piece and is without doubt the most spectacular of the four giga II fugues. The subject begins with gusto (Ex. X-14). This fugue achieves remarkable fluidity with its sequences and wonderful chains of suspensions (measures 23–25). Both major cadences are feminine with double appoggiaturas. In the second strain we expect the usual inverted subject but instead are greeted with something new, into which Bach incorporates a familiar giga rhythm with *Vorschläge* explicitly indicated (Ex. X-15, measure 2). The last few measures of the piece establish Bach as the complete master of the giga II.

The giga from the Partita in C minor for lute (BWV 997) was published some time between 1737 and 1741 but may well have been composed much earlier. It is the only giga II with a *double,* the only one in which the "sautillant" pattern for the French gigue is occasionally interspersed, and the only one in which all the phrases are either four or eight measures long. Numerous French *agréments* are woven into the texture or indicated by symbols, contributing to an affect of stately grace. The *double* spins out the material in arpeggiations, tiratas, and broken-chord figures in such an interesting manner that it could stand as a perfect giga on its own.

Ex. X-14: Subject of Gique, from J. S. Bach, Partita V, BWV 829.

Ex. X-15: Second strain of Gique from Bach, Partita V.

GIGUES NOTATED IN DUPLE METER

Two of Bach's gigues are notated entirely in duple meter—that is, all the metric levels contain duple not triple groupings of notes. They are the gigues in the French Suite in D minor (BWV 812) and in the Sixth Partita in E minor (BWV 830). The problem is whether to perform them exactly as they are notated or to change some of the rhythms so that tripleness is evident on the pulse or the tap level. This is not a trivial problem, since strikingly different performances result from the choice between dupleness and tripleness.

The problem exists not only in Bach's music but in the gigues of numerous earlier and contemporaneous composers such as Denis Gaultier, Arcangelo Corelli, Froberger, Kuhnau, Böhm, and Johann Mattheson; the practice goes back well into the seventeenth century and is not an innovation of Bach's. Musicologists have discussed the subject in print for over twenty years but there is no consensus.[33] The 1986 *New Harvard Dictionary of Music* ends the "Gigue" article by stating that "gigues notated in duple simple meter may call for interpretation in triplets," but this offers no guidance for decisions the performer must make. The following is a summary of arguments on both sides of the issue.

Two lines of argument favor a performance with triplets, one based on a study of notational practices reaching as far back as the sixteenth century, the other relying on the statements of theorists and writers of the seventeenth and eighteenth centuries. Michael Collins makes the most persuasive and carefully documented statement of this position.[34] He considers the binary notation of some seventeenth- and eighteenth-century gigues as an archaic practice stemming from the sixteenth century. Composers sometimes wrote duple notation while they actually expected the music to be performed in triplet figures. Collins terms this "resolved hemiolia," which means that the notation represents resolutions by the composer of ternary figures into binary ones. The implication is that the performer must resolve the notation back into what the composer had in mind. The evidence for this theory, though complex, has been accepted by many musicologists, including Donington and Ferguson.

One of the strongest forms of evidence Collins offers is the fact that several gigues by Froberger appear in some sources in duple meter and in others in triple.[35] Ex. X-16 shows two manuscript versions of the same gigue, the first in duple meter in the hand of the composer, the second from a later source and in a different hand. Collins believes that the second version is "someone else's idea of how Froberger's gigues ought to be notated"; in other words, it is simply a different method of notation rather than a rhythmic transformation of the piece. Other examples from Froberger appear in Collins's article.[36]

The second line of argument in favor of a resolution to triplets is derived

Ex. X-16: Opening of two versions of a Gigue by Johann Jacob Froberger, from *Orgel- und Klavierwerke* (mid-seventeenth century). a. from Suite XXVIII; b. from Suite XV.

a.

b.

from the writings of theorists of the seventeenth and eighteenth centuries. For example, Sébastien de Brossard states:

> GIGA or Gicque or Gigue . . . this is a tune ordinarily for instruments, which is written almost always in triple time, and is full of dotted and syncopated notes which make the tune gay and, so to speak, jumping, etc. See SALTARELLO. The Italians usually indicate the movement of the gigue in $\frac{6}{8}$ or $\frac{12}{8}$ time for the violins and sometimes with the sign of C or quadruple measure for the bass. The bass is played then as though it were dotted.[37]

Of the ten gigas in Corelli's trio sonatas, Opus 2 and Opus 4, four have some notational reference to common time. In the giga of Opus 2, No. 9, where all the parts have the meter sign C three consecutive eighths are marked as triplets. In the giga of Opus 4, No. 4, the middle voice is marked C and the upper and lower are in $\frac{12}{8}$; all groups of three eighth notes in the middle voice are marked as triplets in order to coincide with those of the other parts. Following Brossard, the eighth notes of the middle voice would be "assimilated" with those in the other two voices so that they coincided rhythmically, rather than clashing, as the notation at first appears to indicate. In the gigas of Opus 4, Nos. 7 and 12, the upper voice is in $\frac{12}{8}$ and the middle and lower voices are in C; no triplets occur in the lower voices since there are no eighth notes. More examples of this type of assimilation appear in Donington[38] and Ferguson.[39]

Another seventeenth-century writer who offers help is Bénigne de Bacilly. In his *L'Art de Bien Chanter* of 1679 he associates the use of intensified dotted rhythms with an early type of gigue.[40] The term "en gigue" referred to the practice of performing a duple-meter allemande with dotted rhythms so that it became a gigue. Several duple-meter pieces among the lute works of Ennemond and Denis Gaultier are entitled "allemande giguée" or "allemande ou gigue." The lutenist Perrine (d. after 1698), who was the first person in France known to transcribe lute pieces into standard keyboard notation, wrote about two allemandes by Denis or Ennemond Gaultier that "this piece can be played *en gigue";* following each one is a transcription of the allemande into a gigue, now entitled "gigue," with the even eighth notes of the allemande changed to dotted eighth- and sixteenth-note figures. Of course, this is not evidence for "tripleness," but it does illustrate a practice by which a performer altered the equality of even eighth notes to some form of inequality in order to transform an allemande into a gigue.[41]

None of the seventeenth- and eighteenth-century writers who discuss the gigue, either as a dance or as stylized dance music, refer to it as a piece in duple meter; if meter is mentioned, it is always with some degree of tripleness, so that one may feel confident that tripleness on at least one metric level was an essential characteristic of the gigue. Johann Walther refers to gigues *notated* in duple meter: "They [fugues composed in gigue style] may also be composed in common time [*schlechten Tacte*]."[42] However, he is speaking of composition, which may or may not refer to performance. The only meter signs Walther gives at the beginning of his article on the gigue are $\frac{3}{8}$, $\frac{6}{8}$, and $\frac{12}{8}$; none are duple.

Finally, there is the interesting comment by Kirnberger, quoted on p. 162 above, on distinguishing between triplet eighth notes in $\frac{3}{4}$ time and normal eighth notes in $\frac{9}{8}$ time. At the end of his statement, Kirnberger clearly takes the position that gigues should not be written in common time because the performer will naturally resolve duple figures into triple ones, resulting in an incorrect performance.

What are the arguments in favor of performing Bach's two gigues in duple meter exactly as they are written? The strongest one is that the evidence given above is not conclusive, but only suggestive; and since there is no consensus, a performance in duple meter may be as correct as one using tripleness. A second argument lies in the aesthetic impact of the music which results from duple meter—a more angular, dynamic, and aggressive affect may be created. A third line of thought contends that duple-meter gigues are a unique genre and should not be made to sound like all the other gigues.

Although we believe that the historical evidence so far discovered favors changing "duple" gigues to some form of triple meter, individual performers must make their own decisions. For those who decide to experiment, the question becomes "How do I do it?" Often there is more than one way to incorporate tripleness, and performances will inevitably vary. Exx. X-17 and X-18 present our resolutions of the gigues from BWV 812 and 830 and may serve as a guide for the adventurous.

Ex. X-17: Gigue by J. S. Bach, BWV 812.

Ex. X-18: Gigue by J. S. Bach, BWV 830.

CHAPTER 11
The Loure and the Forlana

The loure and the forlana have many similarities. Both make charming but infrequent appearances in Baroque suites of the early eighteenth century, and both come to this stylized dance music via the aristocratic French theater—opera and ballet productions by Campra, Lalande, Destouches, Desmarets, J.-Ph. Rameau, and their contemporaries. Both have a metric structure of II–3–2, both have an upbeat and employ the "sautillant" rhythm found in the French gigue, and both are associated with pastoral affects and the pastoral tradition. They differ in phrase structure, which is unbalanced in the loure but very balanced in the forlana; in tempo, which is slow in the loure and moderate in the forlana; and in texture, which is often contrapuntal in the loure but is generally homophonic or melody and accompaniment in the forlana. Though the origins of both dances are unknown, it seems likely that they are different. The forlana was associated by some eighteenth-century writers with the "folk" dance and music of Venice, but the loure appears to go no farther back in history than the French theater works of Lully, with the earliest titled piece in *Les Fêtes de l'Amour* of 1672.[1] Two loures and one forlana survive in the works of J. S. Bach.

BWV 1006

THE LOURE

Numerous French writers referred to the loure as a "slow gigue,"[2] and this description is apt providing one understands that it signifies a slow "French gigue" and not a slow giga I or II (see chapter 10). Most loures are notated in $\frac{6}{4}$, though a few may be found in $\frac{3}{4}$, in which case one may imagine every two measures joined together into $\frac{6}{4}$. As Fig. XI-1 shows, loures often use the "sautillant" rhythm ♩. ♪♩ almost continually, a characteristic shared with the French gigue. The slow tempo of the loure, however, gives it a more-languid quality than the gigue; it moves with a subtle energy which can be majestic,

Fig. XI-1: Music and dance in the opening of "Gigue lente," *Entrée a deux, dancée par Mr. Dumirail et Mlle. Victoire al'Opera d'Hésionne,* from Louis-Guillaume Pécour, *Recueil de Dances* (Paris, 1704), p. 109; music by André Campra, *Hesione* (1704), II, 4.

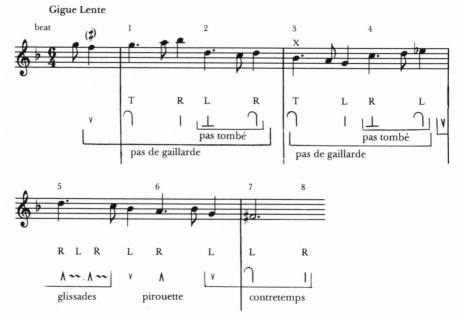

while the gigue moves quickly and with obvious energy and drive. These qualities of the loure are created in part by the unpredictability of the phrases—each of a different length and more often five or seven measures long than four or eight—and by the almost hypnotic repetition of the slow-moving "sautillant" rhythm. Though the character of the loure is seldom specified by theorists, Johann Mattheson mentions, in a section devoted to the gigue, that loures, "slow and dotted, exhibit a proud and arrogant nature, on account of which they are beloved by the Spanish."[3] While "proud and inflated" is less than complimentary, it does imply a majestic dance rather than one of moderate affect, such as a gavotte or a minuet.

Fig. XI-1 presents the opening music and dance of a French theatrical entry of the early eighteenth century, the "Air des Graces" from *Hésione*, the 1700 *tragédie lyrique* by André Campra. It shows the loure to be unusual as a dance, with two step-units to the measure, not just one as in most of the other French Court dances. Furthermore these step-units are complex, not simple, and they normally contain difficult movements, which only the best dancers can perform well—*entre-chats*, *battements*, and *pirouettes* of more than one complete turn. The dancer often has as many as six separate steps to a measure, requiring not only virtuosity but a quiet nobility in order to avoid clutter and busyness. Nobility in this case translates into a firm grasp of several simultaneous levels of rhythm as well as an understanding of the inner organization of the long phrases.

Although almost all loures preserved in notation are theatrical pieces, the most famous one is the ballroom dance *Aimable Vanqueur*. It was first published in 1700 and has been republished many times; some versions in later-eighteenth-century Spanish publications interpolate ornamentation into both the music and the dance.[4] John Hawkins mentions this piece in 1776, by which time the loure's popularity as a characteristic French dance had declined:

> The LOUVRE is a mere dance-tune; the term is not general, but is applied singly to a French air, called L'aimable Vainqueur, of which Lewis XIV was extremely fond; the French dancing masters composed a dance to it, which is well known in England.[5]

Fig. XI-2 shows the metric structure of the loure (II–3–2) consisting of two slow beats to the measure, with the tripleness of the "sautillant" figures on the pulse level and duple taps below that. Although all music theorists and most dance theorists who describe beating time in the loure specify two beats per measure. Feuillet's *Chorégraphie* (1700) calls the loure a dance in "quadruple time" with four beats to the measure.[6] This is probably not in contradiction to other theorists, but merely a way to classify the French dances in relation to each other. Feuillet separates the duple-meter dances which have one step-unit to the measure (bourée, rigaudon, gavotte, and gigue) from those with two step-units per measure (loure and entrée grave). Kellom Tom-

Fig. XI-2: Model for Loure and Forlana Dance Rhythm
II–3–2, $\frac{6}{4}$*; IV–3–2, $\frac{6}{8}$

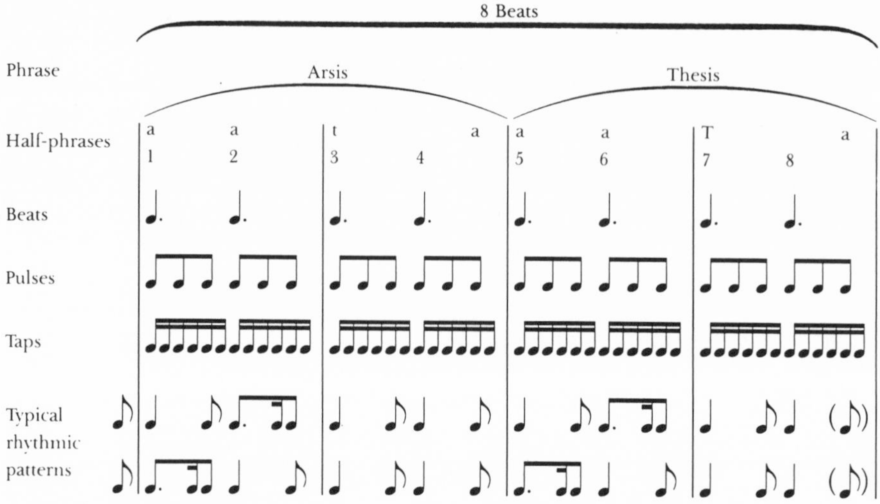

*In most loures, the beat is ♩. in $\frac{6}{4}$.

linson, writing from London in 1735, talks of the loure as a dance in "quadruple meter" which has two slow beats per measure.[7]

The loure of Ex. XI-1 illustrates many of the characteristics described
above. A "heavy slowness" is indicated by the word "Pesamment," possibly
reminding the performer to keep the feeling of two dotted half-note beats to
the measure even though the tempo is slow enough for six quarter-note
beats. The phrase is of an unpredictable length, unbalanced, with frequent
use of the "sautillant" figure; syncopations are frequently used (measures 1–
4); one might articulate a hemiolia in measure 3. Ex. XI-2 shows the first
strain of a loure for several instruments by J. S. Bach's Saxon contemporary
Telemann. A sense of heaviness and perhaps the majestic quality mentioned
by Mattheson are implied by the indications for separate bowing in measures
1–2, and by the appogiaturas of measures 3–4.

BACH'S LOURES

The well-known loure from Partita III for solo violin (BWV 1006) challenges
the performer to maintain the sense of two beats to the measure in a slow
tempo. The "sautillant" rhythm helps toward this end by reminding the listener of a gigue, though increasing ornamentation as the piece goes on
threatens to obscure this reference. Bach's loure is more balanced than
French loures since each strain begins with a four-measure phrase, each

Ex. XI-1: Opening of Loure by François Couperin, *Les Goûts-réunis ou nouveaux concerts* (1724).

Ex. XI-2: Opening of orchestral Loure by Georg Phillipp Telemann, *Musique de Table* (1733), Ouverture in E minor.

made up of two-measure segments. BWV 1006a contains a lute version of this piece, an octave lower but in the same key, with differently notated ornamentation (e.g., in measure 10); performers will find it useful to compare the two versions.

Bach's other surviving loure is in the G major French Suite (BWV 816); it is mistakenly titled "Bourrée II" in some editions. What is most striking is that all the phrases are carefully balanced (4 + 4 and 4 + 4), without the elusive unbalanced quality of the French loures. The contrapuntal texture in (mostly) two voices is elaborated by skillfully placed Italian ornamentation (e.g., measures 5–6), which succeeds best if performed lightly. Maintaining two beats to the measure again challenges the performer, but once more it will help if one brings out the "sautillant" rhythm of the gigue. The upbeat should be articulated with a separation before the first full measure, where an appoggiatura emphasizes the downbeat (first strain) and may be added to it (second strain). The dots over the notes in the upper voice in the second half of measure 7 are reminiscent of Telemann's separate bowings (Ex. XI-2, measures 1–2) and may be incorporated as well in measure 15.

BWV 1006

THE FORLANA

The haunting strains of a forlana linger in the mind even after the piece is over, an illusion created by the balanced, segmented phrases and the rondeau-form repetitions, which are important hallmarks of the style. Historically, the forlana was an energetic, lusty courtship dance popular in Venice in the early eighteenth century, according to the eminent musicologist Paul Nettl.[8] Possibly this ferocious energy is of Slavic origin; Venice controlled the Slavic region of Friulia, and during the seventeenth century Slavic colonists moved onto Venetian plains and eventually into Venice itself. By the eighteenth century there are references to a forlana dance popular with gondoliers and street people, accompanied by mandolins, castanets, and drums.

André Campra first popularized forlanas in France by including them in his ballets, beginning in the 1690s. A forlana entry in *L'Europe galante* (1697) endured throughout the eighteenth century because its music became the accompaniment for a beloved ball dance (Fig. XI-3). In Scene 4 of *Carnaval de Venise* (1699), forlanas are danced by a troupe of Slavs, Armenians, and gypsies; and there are forlanas in *Les Fêtes Vénitiennes* (1710). Composers for the stage, including Mouret, Lalande, and J.-Ph. Rameau, continued to use forlanas, as did composers of stylized dance music, including Montéclair, François Couperin, and J.-B. Senaillé-le-fils.[9] Untitled pieces derived from

Fig. XI-3: Music and dance in *La Forlana,* **Pécour:1700Recueil,** p. 62; music by André Campra, *L'Europe galante* (1697), III, ii.

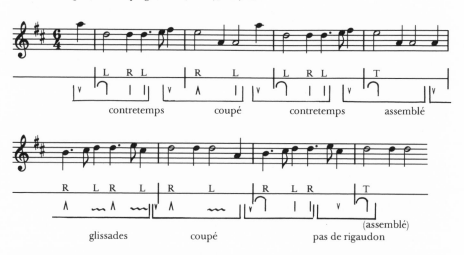

the forlana may be found in the later chamber music of Mondonville (trio sonata Op. 2, No. 2, third movement [1734]) and LeClair (violin sonata Op. 4, No. 3, third movement [1730] and Op. 9, No. 3, second movement [1738]). J. S. Bach seems not to have been much attracted to the forlana, since only one survives among his works.

The character of the forlana is "gay" according to Rousseau[10] and Compan,[11] and the tempo is moderate or moderately fast.[12] We suggest a tempo of ♩. = MM 69–80. Borin presents an example from *L'Europe galante,* which he marks "Vîte."[13] Grassineau groups forlana with other dances using the "sautillant" rhythm such as the gigue. Pastoral affects are common in forlanas, usually created by a drone bass.

The forlana dance rhythm (Fig. XI-2) consists of a harmonic-rhythmic phrase which begins with an upbeat, is eight beats long (four measures), and is notated in either ♮ or ♮ time. A primary thesis occurs on beats 7 and 8 and a secondary thesis on beats 3 and 4. Since the four-measure phrase is often repeated, a satisfying point of repose may not actually occur until measure 8. Forlanas are most often set in rondeau form.

Fig. XI-3 shows the music and dance in *La Forlana,* which was probably the most popular forlana danced in the eighteenth century. It was first published in 1700 and republished many times, including at least once in the 1770s.[14] Use of repetition and balance in the tune is evident by the two-measure segments, but the dance also uses this technique since each four-measure phrase ends with an *assemblé,* or jump onto both feet together (measures 4 and 8). This is a lively dance, as the many hops, leaps, and *pas de rigaudon* attest; there is one step-unit to the bar, with rhythms of ♩. ♩. and ♩ ♩ ♩. most commonly used. Forlanas were enjoyed not only in theatrical performances—five choreographies have been preserved in notation—but also at aristocratic balls as social dances. Nine *danses à deux* survive for ball dancing, as well as numerous forlana contredanses for four or eight persons.

Montéclair's forlana (Ex. XI-3) offers a nice contrast of styles, coming between the allemande and a passacaille in his Sixth Concert. The first eight measures present the dance rhythm clearly and illustrate the qualities of balance and rhyme so important in this music. The composer indicates an ornament on beat 3 to mark a minor thesis, and then holds the dominant over beats 7 and 8 in order to indicate a more important articulation of the rhythm. He then repeats the phrase with a change of ending so that a satisfying thesis occurs on the tonic in measure 8. These eight measures reappear within and at the end of the dance.

The last movement of François Couperin's *Concert Royal* in E minor is a forlana, a masterpiece of the genre. Wilfred Mellers calls it "one of Couperin's most personal conceptions."[15] The first four measures (Ex. XI-4a) show Couperin's creative barring, which ensures that the thetic points will fall only on beat 8. The composer's meticulous articulation marks set off the smaller group of 2 + 4 + 4 beats in the pattern. In the fourth (and final) couplet (Ex. XI-4b) Couperin surprises the listener with "Notes égales et coulées" (equal notes with slurs). The melody lilts between the interval of a second and a fourth with a drone accompaniment swaying back and forth on the interval of a sixth, finally returning to the by now unforgettable rondeau.

Ex. XI-3: Opening of Forlana by Michel Montéclair, *Sixième Concert à deux Flutes Traversières sans Basses* (early eighteenth century).

Ex. XI-4: Forlane by François Couperin, *Concert Royal*, No. 4. a. measures 1–4; b. final couplet.

BACH'S FORLANA

Bach's only forlana is placed at about the midpoint of his orchestral Suite in C major (BWV 1066). It is not in rondeau form but simply in two strains, each repeated. A pastoral affect is quickly made evident by the drone bass and the softly murmuring inner voices with eighth notes grouped by twos. The melody, taken by violins and oboes in unison, is similar to that quoted by Borin from Campra's *L'Europe galante*. All thetic points occur on beats 7 and 8 except for an extension beginning at measure 17. The bass movement changes from an octave drone to the "sautillant" rhythm of the upper voices, and the inner parts join with this in measure 22. The swirling motion of this piece may remind some listeners of the rippling water in Venetian canals.

BWV 817

CHAPTER 12

The Polonaise

The passion and fierce nationalism of Chopin's sixteen polonaises have colored our perception of this type of music ever since the early nineteenth century, when they began to be composed. However, Polish dances appeared in European music at least two hundred years earlier, attested to by pieces entitled "polnischer Tanz" and "polacca" in several late sixteenth-century keyboard tablatures. In the seventeenth century the French term "polonaise" came to designate pieces which embodied some aspects of "Polish style" or which were reminiscent of authentic Polish music; most of these pieces were by composers living outside of Poland. By the eighteenth century numerous polonaises were composed as instrumental pieces characterized by strong rhythms, which emphasize a certain beat or pulse, often the downbeat of a measure.[1] These rhythms include ♫ and ♫♪; in addition, the thesis or cadence measure may be specially accented with a feminine cadence using the rhythm ♫♫♩ .

The absence of upbeats in polonaises of this type further intensifies the overall affect of strength and virility. Johann Mattheson wrote:

> The beginning of a polonaise, taken in the strict sense, has something peculiar, in that it begins neither with the half note in upbeat, as the gavotte; nor even with the last quarter of the meter, as a bourrée: but straightway quite bluntly and as the French say, *sans façon* commences confidently on the downbeat. . . . [2]

Friedrich II, king of Saxony, where Bach lived, was also king of Poland, and many relationships existed between the peoples of these two contiguous areas. In particular, there are reports of a Court dance known as the polonaise performed at Dresden at least by 1708. According to Józef W. Reiss and Maurice J. E. Brown, "The court polonaise . . . was played by musicians in the galleries of the great reception halls while the assembly, dressed in great splendour, danced it below in processional figures whose character suggested the name 'martial dance.' "[3] The eighteenth-century polonaise is probably a descendant of the instrumental accompaniment to these ceremonial, aristocratic, processional dances. Much later in the century music theorists still referred to it as "ceremonious."[4] Unfortunately, no records of either the dance or its accompaniment have survived, and information about the polonaise must be derived from the writings of such German music theorists as Mattheson, Marpurg, and Kirnberger and from the music itself.

In *Der vollkommene Capellmeister* (1739) Johann Mattheson first describes the polonaise in his discussion of "Tone-Feet" and their variation, which he calls *rhythmopöia*.[5] The examples he chose to illustrate this phenomenon are unique. In showing how chorale melodies could be turned into dances by altering their rhythm, he transformed the chorale "Ich ruf zu dir" (Ex. XII-1) into polonaises, in duple time, using the spondee (– –), and in triple time, using the iamb (⌣ – –).[6] He called these two dances *Vortanz* and *Aufsprung*. In another portion of the treatise Mattheson described polonaises in "even and uneven meters."[7] He believed that the dances in common time were those danced in Poland, and those in triple meter, which we describe here, were the German stylized version. He ascribed an affect to the polonaise of "frankness and a free manner,"[8] although, like many other of Mattheson's pronouncements about affect, it is impossible to know exactly which pieces he was referring to.

Kirnberger discussed the tempo of the polonaise, which he said was somewhere between that of a sarabande and a minuet.

> The *polonaise,* which is faster than a sarabande and one-third slower than a minuet—so that a time span of eight measures in a polonaise is equal to twelve measures of a minuet—also tolerates only sixteenths as the fastest notes.[9]

A tempo slower than the minuet seems reasonable, since numerous sixteenth notes often appear in polonaises. From this we derive our model dance rhythm (Fig. XII-1), with a metric structure of III–2–2 in which there are three quarter-note beats to the measure and sixteenth notes form the tap level. Based on music we have observed, a model polonaise rhythm consists of a harmonic-rhythmic phrase twelve beats in length (four measures), with a primary thesis created by a feminine cadence (or syncopation) on beats 11–12 and a preliminary thesis similarly created on beats 5–6.

Ex. XII-1: Polonaise example, **Mattheson:Vollkommene.** a. Chorale "Ich ruf zu dir"; b. Polonoise 1; c. Polonoise 2.

Ex. XII-2 shows the beginnings of two polonaises by G.-Ph. Telemann, a composer who spent much of his creative life in Saxony, where he might have been exposed to Polish music and dance. In Ex. XII-2a the downbeat is accented by four sixteenth notes grouped by twos, with further accents created by the ♫ rhythm in measure 3. Telemann often preceded this type of dance with a duple-meter overture, also in Polish style (Ex. XII-2b). No information is available on performance style, but one might infer sharply accented beats from the strong affect of the dance described by Reiss and Brown as "martial."

Ex. XII-2: Two polonoises by Georg Phillipp Telemann. a. Opening of Polonoise for flute or violin and bass; b. Opening and later excerpt from Ouverture à la Polonoise in D minor for keyboard.

Fig. XII-1: Model for the Polonaise Dance Rhythm
III–2–2, $\frac{3}{4}$

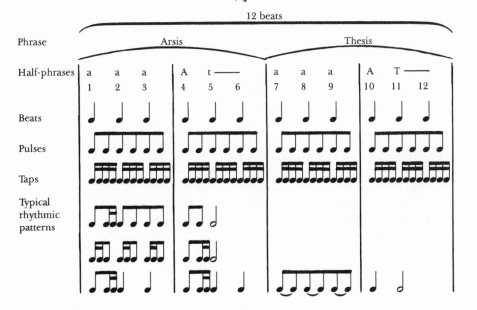

BACH'S POLONAISES

Only three titled pieces by Bach have survived, one for keyboard and two for orchestra, but all are beautiful examples of this rare addition to the dance suite (the polonaise in the *Clavierbüchlein* for Anna Magdalena Bach is not by J. S. Bach). The polonaise in the First Brandenburg Concerto (BWV 1046) is actually one of the "couplets" in a minuet in rondeau form, which brings the concerto to a close (see discussion of BWV 1046 in chapter 5). In several ways it is unlike the description offered above; e.g., it is in $\frac{3}{8}$ time, which implies a fast tempo (not slow) and it has an upbeat. However, it does have an accented downbeat on thesis measures 16, 24, and 32, and emphatically accented pulses in measures 25–28, the only part of the piece marked "forte." The solo violin, with sixteenth notes bowed by twos, as in Ex. XII-2a, is supported by a musette-style drone bass in the lower strings. Long notes, such as in measures 4–6, might be ornamented by a trill or a mordent.

The dance from the Sixth French Suite (BWV 817) appears to be more in the style of other eighteenth-century polonaises, with no upbeat, theses strongly accented by four sixteenth notes, and other accents implied by rhythms such as ♫♩ and ♩♫ . If performed with strong accents in a moderately slow tempo (slower than a minuet) and no tempo fluctuation, one might be able to recreate the spirit of a noble, martial, ceremonial dance. Bach has indicated ornaments, either written-out or by sign, for most of the thetic portions of the piece; one might also add a mordent to the long notes in measures 6 and 13–14. The notated turns (e.g., measure 12) will be clear to the listener if they are slurred as a group of four sixteenth notes.

The polonaise from the B minor orchestral suite (BWV 1067), seems to recall, more than the other two, the ceremonial yet festive instrumental dance accompaniment played "in the galleries of the great reception halls, while the assembly, dressed in great splendour, danced it below." A slow tempo is mandated by the inclusion of a *double* with ornamental thirty-second notes; the melody is full of sharply dotted rhythms, which create a "martial" affect; and feminine cadences abound. The distinctive rhythm of measure 1 is repeated incessantly except in thetic measures, enhancing the strong affect. One can almost imagine the stunning *double* actually accompanying stately dancing, with the by now familiar rhythms of the tune taken by low strings, the inner voices gone, and the flute soaring above. Articulations and ornamentation from the original music may be used in the *double;* they will not interfere with the flute elaboration because the difference in range of the two parts keeps them separate and distinct from each other. The majestic strength and exuberance of this piece will ultimately lead to the polonaises of Chopin, where they become a symbol of national heroism and chivalry.

BWV 1004

BWV 582

CHAPTER 13
The Chaconne and the Passacaglia

The structure of chaconnes and passacaglias is strikingly different from that of the other Baroque dances used by Bach. Whereas the other dances use bipartite form or (less often) rondeau form, chaconnes and passacaglias unfold by means of continuous variations. By the early eighteenth century some French and German composers were writing long, complex, emotionally charged pieces under these titles. With no natural limitation as to length, they felt free to invent elaborate compositions using a wide variety of techniques within the same piece, including strong contrasts in instrumentation, dynamic level, texture, ground bass pattern, mode and key, repetition scheme, melody, harmony, rhythm, and occasionally even meter.

It is difficult to list the identifying characteristics of chaconnes and passacaglias because there are so many exceptions. For example, most chaconnes and passacaglias are in triple meter (metric structure III–2–2) but several occur in duple meter,[1] and it is not uncommon to find a temporary shift to duple meter within a long piece.[2] The continuous variations of these two dances are based on a four-measure phrase with an identifiable or fixed-bass pattern. However, in many pieces the "fixed" bass changes as the piece progresses; and occasionally one finds an eight-measure fixed-bass pattern.

Repetition schemes vary also; in numerous pieces every phrase is performed twice, but in some the opening phrase or phrases form a discrete section of music which recurs from time to time, as in a rondeau.

Equally difficult is the task of drawing up a list of features which distinguish chaconnes and passacaglias from each other. On the issue of tempo, for example, many French theorists state that chaconnes are generally faster than passacaglias,[3] but Johann Mattheson believed the opposite, perhaps from his own experience or perhaps in error.[4] Brossard said in 1703 that the melody of the passacaille was more expressive and tender than that of the chaconne, a subjective statement repeated by many lexicographers who followed him, including Richelet (1732), Furetière (1743), Rousseau (1768), and Lacombe (1759).[5] Some writers believed that chaconnes were more often in a major key and passacailles in a minor key, but so many exceptions exist that this idea cannot be relied upon.[6]

The history of the chaconne and the passacaglia has been explored in depth by musicologist Richard Hudson, whose articles in *New Grove* discuss their connections with guitar music, song, and dance in Spain and Italy in the early seventeenth century. French composers adopted both dances into theatrical presentations as early as 1658 (Jean-Baptiste Lully's *Alcidiane*), and at least one chaconne or passacaglia is included in most French theatrical works of the late seventeenth century and well into the eighteenth. Several of these theatrical choreographies have been preserved in the Feuillet dance notation: fourteen chaconnes and six passacailles offer insight into the character and quality of movement of these dances. All of the surviving passacailles and most of the chaconnes were created for theatrical use, chiefly by Louis-Guillaume Pécour, ballet master and choreographer of the Paris *Opéra* from 1687 to 1729. The chaconnes are more numerous and varied; they include two ball dances for court celebrations of the English king or queen[7] and three solo entries for a male Harlequin, complete with information on head and arm gestures and rules for moving the hat.[8] The additional illustration in the Harlequin dances was necessary since these gestures were not part of the standard repertoire of movements in the French noble style but represent a kind of character dancing. Many chaconnes and passacaglias are quite long, some over one hundred measures. The form of both music and dance usually consists of a gradual, persistent increase in complexity, finally coming to a high point and then diminishing to a quiet ending.

Perhaps as a remnant of Spanish influence one finds an example of castanets used with chaconne music in Feuillet's *Chorégraphie* (Fig. XIII-1). The castanets add an exciting rhythmic dimension to the performance; in addition to the rhythms of the music (in the melodic notes and harmonic changes) and the rhythms of the dance (in the dance steps as well as in the arm, head, and body movements) there are the rhythms in the beating and shaking of the castanets. Fig. I-2 shows a dancer with castanets.

As an even further dimension of performance one may consider the idea

LA DANCE

Ayant ainfi conçû toutes chofes, on Nottera l'Air, aprés quoy on marquera la batterie des Caftagnettes au deffous en forme de Partition, en forte que chaque Mefure de la batterie fe rapporte juftement à celle de l'Air qui eft notté au deffus.

EXEMPLES.

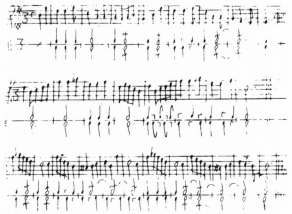

Fig. XIII-1: Castanets used in a Chaconne, from **Feuillet:Chor** (1700), p. 101; music by Jean-Baptiste Lully.

of pantomime in dance and the extended opportunity for expressive gestures which the long chaconnes and passacailles offer. One of the most extraordinary dancers of the eighteenth century was Marie Sallé (1707–1756), a choreographic innovator in the realm of dramatic dance who was also one of the most famous mimes of French history. One of her passacaille performances is reported by Cahusac in 1754:

> Mlle. Sallé . . . had the courage to use a very ingenious episodic action in the *passacaille* of *L'Europe galante*. She . . . appeared in the midst of her rivals with the grace and desire of an Odalisque who has designs on the heart of her master. Her dance was formed of all the beautiful attitudes that such a passion would engender. It became more animated by degrees. One read in her expressions a succession of feelings: she vacillated between fear and hope; but, at the moment when the Sultan gives his handkerchief to his favorite Sultana, her countenance, her glances, all her carriage rapidly assumed a new form; she tore herself from the stage with a despair reserved only for those tender souls who have experienced such an overwhelming rejection.[9]

This description is strangely reminiscent of the mimed sarabande of Pomey's dictionary, described in chapter 7 above.[10] It underlines the fact that pantomime was an important element of some theatrical dancing, and suggests an avenue of exploration for performers of music of this period. Other connections between the sarabande and the chaconne include an identical metric structure, the predominant use of a four-measure basic phrase, and a similar tempo (though the sarabande is usually somewhat slower). In addition one often finds some of the typical sarabande rhythms such as the "syncopation module" and the hemiolia (see Fig. VII-3). Jacques Ozanam, author of one of the earliest French dictionaries to include music, stated that the two dances were quite closely related: "The chaconne is a sarabande composed of several *couplets* almost always developed upon the same subject, which is normally found in the bass."[11] In Denis Gaultier's *La Rhétorique des Dieux* (1664–72) dances are often entitled "Chaconne ou Sarabande," lending further credence to the connection mentioned by Ozanam.

BACH'S CHACONNES AND PASSACAGLIAS

In contrast to the wealth of information about the chaconne and the passacaglia in France, there is no firm evidence concerning these dances in Germany at the time of Bach. Thus our discussion of his contributions will focus more on structure than on performance practices, showing how he used his genius in a dance variation form. Throughout his life Bach was continually interested in the concept of improvisation and variation. His legacy, therefore, of only two titled chaconnes and one titled passacaglia seems small until one grasps the monumental nature of these pieces.

The concluding piece in Cantata 150 is a Ciaccona in B minor, "Meine Tage in den Leiden," performed by the chorus, solo bassoon, two violins, and continuo. It is set in $\frac{3}{2}$, and the absolutely consistent ground bass, built on a rising pentachord taking up four measures, is heard twenty-two times. Although the configuration of the pattern never changes, the harmony does (see Fig. XIII-2). The structure is striking for its three groups of four measures each, which may be symbolic of the Trinity. The ground is embellished by ever-changing Italianate figuration in the vocal and instrumental parts, which include variations on the ground itself by the bassoon. The litany of the chaconne ground may have been chosen by Bach to illuminate the textual references to God as "my faithful shield" and to Christ as "he who now stands beside us." This glorious choral work may even retain a vestige of the dance rhythm if the tempo is not too slow.

Dance as a premise is only a distant memory, however, in the gigantic Ciaccona that concludes the Fourth Sonata for solo violin (BWV 1004). It is a very sophisticated piece and surpasses, in our opinion, all previous examples of the variation chaconne. The premise is a four-measure ostinato bass which is varied either melodically—into a chromatic descending tetrachord, descending diatonic tetrachord, or a variation of the two—or harmonically, as in the first arpeggio section. The overall key structure is minor–major–minor. The variations usually appear in pairs, as in the Lully chaconne (Fig.

Fig. XIII-2: Harmonic structure of J. S. Bach, "Ciaccona," BWV 150, No. 7.

```
12  +  4  +  8  +  4  +  8  +  4  +  4  +  4  +  4  +  36
 b    →D    D   →f♯    f♯   →A   →E    E   →b        b
⏟        ⏝        ⏝                            ⏟
12        12        12                          3 × 12
```

XIII-1). Unlike Lully, however, Bach writes repeat sections which subtly enhance the content of the original phrase, leading one to speculate whether Lully also intended such elaboration but did not explicitly indicate it. Bach's chaconne juxtaposes the French and Italian styles: French in those chordal sections which highlight the sarabande syncopation module ♩ '♩ and dotted rhythms, and Italian in the virtuoso passages with a seemingly infinite variety of diminutions. The French sections require the imaginative addition of agréments. Bach's bowings, taken from the autograph manuscript P 967, appear in the Neue Bach-Ausgabe edition.

The Passacaglia in C minor for organ (BWV 582) is constructed on *two* intertwining four-measure melodies; measure 4 establishes the dominant and measure 8 the tonic. The first half of the theme is from André Raison's "Christe, Trio en Passacaille" (1687) and may account for the elaborate French *agréments* of the opening variations.[12] There are twenty variations in two groups of ten, which in turn may be viewed as groups of $5 + 5 + 5 + 5$ variations. The central caesura is signaled by the ground moving to the upper voice at Variation 11, and the final five variations, beginning at Variation 16, begin with the ground again in the pedal.

The first five variations are a grand blend of Italian and French figuration: Variations 1 and 2 capitalize on the "sarabande syncopation module," and Variations 4 and 5 exploit various Italian *passaggi* and *tremoletti*. Variations 6–10 (especially 6–9) are characterized by the Germanic figure common in allemandes, ♪♫♫♩. The last ten variations contain a wealth of textures, including three distinctive ways to fashion arpeggio figures (Variations 14–16), triplet patterns (Variation 17), *tremoletti* and *passaggi* (Variation 18), and again the three-note allemande figure (Variations 19 and 20). After this magnificent drive to the end, and a moment's suspension in time, Bach launches into the fugue, using as the subject a portion of the passacaglia theme.

APPENDIX A

Titled Dances by J. S. Bach

Inclusive dates, e.g., "1715–25," indicate that the work was written during that period; "?1714" means possibly in that year; and a year in parentheses, e.g., "1735 (24)," indicates an earlier copy of the same work. When two cities are separated by a slash, e.g., "Weimar/Köthen," it is not certain where the work was written; when there is a dash between them, e.g., "Weimar–Leipzig," the work was written some time during the entire period. Capital letters indicate major keys, lower-case letters minor keys.

Bourées

BWV	Date	Place	Work	Instrument	Meter Sign	Number
822	unknown	unknown	Suite in g [arr. from another composer]	Klavier	¢	1
820	1708–14	Weimar	Overture in F	Klavier	¢	1
832	1708–14	Weimar	Partie in A	Klavier	¢	1
996	1708–17	Weimar	Suite in e	Lute	¢	1
806	1715–25	Weimar–Leipzig	English Suite I in A	Klavier	2	2
807	1715–25	Weimar–Leipzig	English Suite II in a	Klavier	2	2
1066	by 1724–25	Köthen/Leipzig	Overture in C	Orchestra	¢	2
1069	c. 1729	Köthen/Leipzig	Overture in D	Orchestra	c	2
1002	1720	Köthen	Partita I in D	Solo violin	¢	2 (with *double*)
1006	1720	Köthen	Partita III in E	Solo violin	2	1
1006a	1720	Köthen	Partita III in E	Arr. for lute	2	1
1009	c. 1720	Köthen	Suite III in C	Solo cello	¢	2

BWV	Date	Place	Work	Instrument	Meter Sign	Number
1010	c. 1720	Köthen	Suite IV in E♭	Solo cello	¢	2
1013	early 1720s	Köthen	Partita in a ("Bourrée anglaise")	Solo flute	2/4	1
816	1722–25	Köthen/Leipzig	French Suite V in G	Klavier	¢	1
817	c. 1724	?Leipzig	French Suite VI in E	Klavier	2	1
819	c. 1722	Köthen	Suite in E♭	Klavier	¢	1
1068	1729–31	Leipzig	Suite in D	Orchestra	¢	2
831	1735 (33)	Leipzig	Overture in the French Style in b	Klavier	2	2
1067	1738–39	Leipzig	Suite in b	Orchestra	¢	2

Gavottes

BWV	Date	Place	Work	Instrument	Meter Sign	Number
822	unknown	unknown	Suite in g [arr. from another composer]	Klavier	¢	1
808	1715–25	Weimar–Leipzig	English Suite III in g	Klavier	2	2
811	1715–25	Weimar–Leipzig	English Suite VI in d	Klavier	2	2
1066	1717–25	Köthen/Leipzig	Suite in C	Orchestra	¢	2
1069	1717–23	Köthen/Leipzig	Suite in D	Orchestra	c	1
202	?1718–23	Leipzig	Cantata "Weichet nur, betrübte Schatten," No. 9	Soprano aria	2	1
1006	1720	Köthen	Partita III in E	Solo violin	¢	1
1006a	1720	Köthen	Partita III in E	Lute	¢	1
1011	c. 1720	Köthen	Suite V in c	Solo cello	¢	2
1012	c. 1720	Köthen	Suite VI in D	Solo cello	¢	2
815	1722–25	Köthen/Leipzig	French Suite IV in E♭ (Gavotte I)	Klavier	2	1
815a	1722–25	Köthen/Leipzig	French Suite IV in E♭ (Gavotte II)	Klavier	2	1
816	1722–25	Köthen/Leipzig	French Suite V in G	Klavier	¢	1
817	c. 1724	?Leipzig	French Suite VI in E	Klavier	c	1

BWV	Date	Place	Work	Instrument	Meter Sign	Number
995	1727–31	Leipzig	Suite in g [arr. from BWV 1011]	Lute	¢	2
1068	1729–31	Leipzig	Suite in D	Orchestra	c	2
830	1731 (25 + 30)	Leipzig	Partita VI in e	Klavier	¢	1
831	1735 (33)	Leipzig	Overture in the French Style in b	Klavier	2	2

Minuets

BWV	Date	Place	Work	Instrument	Meter Sign	Number
1033	?	?	Sonata in C	Flute (probably unaccompanied)	$\frac{3}{4}$	2
822	?	?	Suite in g [arr. from another composer]	Klavier	$\frac{3}{4}$	3
820	1708–14 or earlier	Weimar	Overture in F	Klavier	$\frac{3}{4}$	2
1071	1713	Weimar	Sinfonia in F (early version of BWV 1046)	Orchestra	$\frac{3}{4}$	2
809	1715–25	Weimar/Leipzig	English Suite IV in F	Klavier	3	2
173a,4	1717	Köthen	Cantata, "Durchlaucht'ser Leopold" (tempo di minuetto)	Duet for soprano and bass	$\frac{3}{4}$	1
1006	1720	Köthen	Partita III in E	Solo violin	$\frac{3}{4}$	2
1006a	1720	Köthen	Partita III in E	Arr. for lute	$\frac{3}{4}$	2
1007	c. 1720	Köthen	Suite I in G	Solo cello	$\frac{3}{4}$	2
1008	c. 1720	Köthen	Suite II in d	Solo cello	$\frac{3}{4}$	2
841	c. 1720	Köthen	Minuet I from Clavier-Büchlein of W. F. Bach	Klavier	$\frac{3}{4}$	1
842	c. 1720	Köthen	Minuet II from Clavier-Büchlein of W. F. Bach	Klavier	3	1

BWV	Date	Place	Work	Instrument	Meter Sign	Number
843	c. 1720	Köthen	Minuet III from Clavier-Büchlein of W. F. Bach	Klavier	3/4	1
929	1720	Köthen	Trio in g from Clavier-Büchlein of W. F. Bach	Klavier	3/4	1
1046	by 1721	?Köthen	Brandenburg Concerto I in F	Orchestra	3/4	2
1066	by 1724–25	Köthen/Leipzig	Suite in C	Orchestra	3/4	2
812	1722–25	Köthen/Leipzig	French Suite I in d	Klavier	3/4	2
813	1722–25	Köthen/Leipzig	French Suite II in c	Klavier	3/4	1
814	1722–25	Köthen/Leipzig	French Suite III in b	Klavier	3/4	2
815a	1722–25	Köthen/Leipzig	French Suite IV in E♭	Klavier	3/4	1
817	c. 1724	?Leipzig	French Suite VI in E	Klavier	3/4	1
818a	c. 1722	Köthen	Suite in a	Klavier	3/8	1
819	c. 1722	Köthen	Suite in E♭	Klavier	3/4	2
825	1731 (26)	Leipzig	Partita I in B♭	Klavier	3/4	2
828	1731 (28)	Leipzig	Partita IV in D	Klavier	3/4	1
829	1731 (30)	Leipzig	Partita V in G (Tempo di Minuetto)	Klavier	3/4	1
1069	c. 1729	Köthen/Leipzig	Suite in D	Orchestra	3/4	2
1067	c. 1738–39	Leipzig	Suite in b	Orchestra	3/4	1

Passepieds

BWV	Date	Place	Work	Instrument	Meter Sign	Number
1066	by 1724–25	Köthen/Leipzig	Overture in C	Orchestra	3/4	2
810	1715–25	Weimar–Leipzig	English Suite V in e	Klavier	3/8	2
829	1731 (30)	Leipzig	Partita V in G	Klavier	3/8	1
831	1735 (33)	Leipzig	Overture in the French Style in b	Klavier	3/8	2

Sarabandes

BWV	Date	Place	Work	Instrument	Meter Sign	Number
821	1708–14	Weimar	Suite in B♭	Klavier	3/4	1
823	1708–14	Weimar	Suite in f	Klavier	3/4	1
832	1708–14	Weimar	Partie in A	Klavier	3/4	1
965	before 1710	?Weimar	Sonata in a (after Sonata I in Reinken's 1687 *Hortus Musicus*)	Klavier	3/4	1
996	1708–17 or earlier	Weimar	Suite in e	Lute	3/2	1
806	1715–25	Weimar–Leipzig	English Suite I in A	Klavier	3/4	1
807	1715–25	Weimar–Leipzig	English Suite II in a	Klavier	3/4	1 (with additional *agréments*)
808	1715–25	Weimar–Leipzig	English Suite III in g	Klavier	3/4	1 (with additional *agréments*)
809	1715–25	Weimar–Leipzig	English Suite IV in F	Klavier	3/4	1
810	1715–25	Weimar–Leipzig	English Suite V in e	Klavier	3/4	1
811	1715–25	Weimar–Leipzig	English Suite VI in d	Klavier	3/2	1 + *double*
1002	1720	Köthen	Partita I in b	Solo violin	3/2	1 + *double*
1004	1720	Köthen	Partita II in d	Solo violin	3/4	1
1007	c. 1720	Köthen	Suite I in G	Solo cello	3/4	1
1008	c. 1720	Köthen	Suite II in d	Solo cello	3/4	1
1009	c. 1720	Köthen	Suite III in C	Solo cello	3/4	1
1010	c. 1720	Köthen	Suite IV in E♭	Solo cello	3/4	1
1011	c. 1720	Köthen	Suite V in c	Solo cello	3/4	1
1012	c. 1720	Köthen	Suite VI in D	Solo cello	3/2	1

BWV	Date	Place	Work	Instrument	Meter Sign	Number
1013	early 1720s	Köthen	Partita in a	Solo flute	3/4	1
812	1722–25	Köthen/Leipzig	French Suite I in d	Klavier	3/4	1
813	1722–25	Köthen/Leipzig	French Suite II in c	Klavier	3/4	1
814	1722–25	Köthen/Leipzig	French Suite III in b	Klavier	3/4	1
815	1722–25	Köthen/Leipzig	French Suite IV in E♭	Klavier	3/4	1
816	1722–25	Köthen/Leipzig	French Suite V in G	Klavier	3/4	1
817	c. 1724	?Leipzig	French Suite VI in E	Klavier	3/4	1
818	c. 1722	Köthen	Suite in a	Klavier	3/4	1
818a	c. 1722	?	Suite in a (var. of BWV 818)	Klavier	3/4	1 + *double*
819	c. 1722	Köthen	Suite in E♭	Klavier	3/4	1
995	1727–31	Leipzig	Suite in g, after BWV 1011	Lute	3/4	1
825	1731 (26)	Leipzig	Partita I in B♭	Klavier	3/4	1
826	1731 (27)	Leipzig	Partita II in c	Klavier	3/4	1
827	1731 (25 + 27)	Leipzig	Partita III in a	Klavier	3/4	1
828	1731 (28)	Leipzig	Partita IV in D	Klavier	3/4	1
829	1731 (30)	Leipzig	Partita V in G	Klavier	3/4	1
830	1731 (25 + 30)	Leipzig	Partita VI in e	Klavier	3/4	1
831	1735 (33)	Leipzig	Overture in the French Style in b	Klavier	3/4	1
997	1737–41	Leipzig	Partita in c	Lute	3/4	1
1067	c. 1738–39	Leipzig	Suite in b	Orchestra	3/4	1

Courantes

BWV	Date	Place	Work	Instrument	Meter Sign	Number
996	1708–17 or earlier	Weimar	Suite in e	Lute	3/2	1
806	1715–25	Weimar–Leipzig	English Suite I in A	Klavier	3/2	2 + 2 *doubles*

BWV	Date	Place	Work	Instrument	Meter Sign	Number
807	1715–25	Weimar–Leipzig	English Suite II in a	Klavier	3/2	1
808	1715–25	Weimar–Leipzig	English Suite III in g	Klavier	3/2	1
809	1715–25	Weimar–Leipzig	English Suite IV in F	Klavier	3/2	1
810	1715–25	Weimar–Leipzig	English Suite V in e	Klavier	3/2	1
811	1715–25	Weimar–Leipzig	English Suite VI in d	Klavier	3/2	1
1011	c. 1720	Köthen	Suite in c	Solo cello	3/2	1
819	c. 1722	Köthen	Suite in E♭	Klavier	3/2 [6/4]	1
812	1722–25	Köthen/Leipzig	French Suite I in d	Klavier	3/4	1
814	1722–25	Köthen/Leipzig	French Suite III in b	Klavier	6/4	1
818	c. 1722	Köthen	Suite in a	Klavier	3/4	1
818a	c. 1722	Köthen?	Suite in a	Klavier	3/2	1
1066	by 1724–25	Köthen/Leipzig	Suite in C	Orchestra	3/2	1
826	1731 (27)	Leipzig	Partita II in c	Klavier	3/2	1
828	1731 (28)	Leipzig	Partita IV in D	Klavier	3/2	1
995	1727–31	Leipzig	Suite in g, after BWV 1011	Lute	3/2	1
831	1735 (33)	Leipzig	Overture in the French Style in b	Klavier	3/2	1

Correntes

BWV	Date	Place	Work	Instrument	Meter Sign	Number
821	1708–14	Weimar	Suite in B♭	Klavier	3/4	1
965	?	?	Sonata in a [after Reinken's *Hortus Musicus*, 1687]	Klavier	3/4	1
1002	1720	Köthen	Partita I in b	Solo violin	3/4	1 + *double*
1004	1720	Köthen	Partita II in d	Solo violin	3/4	1
1007	c. 1720	Köthen	Suite I in G	Solo cello	3/4	1
1008	c. 1720	Köthen	Suite II in d	Solo cello	3/4	1

BWV	Date	Place	Work	Instrument	Meter Sign	Number
1009	c. 1720	Köthen	Suite III in C	Solo cello	$\frac{3}{4}$	1
1010	c. 1720	Köthen	Suite IV in Eb	Solo cello	$\frac{3}{4}$	1
1012	c. 1720	Köthen	Suite VI in D	Solo cello	$\frac{3}{4}$	1
1013	early 1720s	Köthen	Partita in a	Solo flute	$\frac{3}{4}$	1
813	1722–25	Köthen/Leipzig	French Suite II in c	Klavier	$\frac{3}{4}$	1
815	1722–25	Köthen/Leipzig	French Suite IV in Eb	Klavier	$\frac{3}{4}$	1
816	1722–25	Köthen/Leipzig	French Suite V in G	Klavier	$\frac{3}{4}$	1
817	c. 1724	Leipzig?	French Suite VI in E	Klavier	$\frac{3}{4}$	1
825	1731 (26)	Leipzig	Partita I in Bb	Klavier	$\frac{3}{4}$	1
827	1731	Leipzig	Partita III in a	Klavier	$\frac{3}{4}$	1
829	1731 (30)	Leipzig	Partita V in G	Klavier	$\frac{3}{8}$	1
830	1731 (25 + 30)	Leipzig	Partita VI in e	Klavier	$\frac{3}{8}$	1

French Gigues

BWV	Date	Place	Work	Instrument	Meter Sign	Number
822	?	?	Suite in G minor [arr. from another composer]	Klavier	$\frac{6}{8}$	1
823	1708–14	Weimar	Suite in f (fragment)	Klavier	$\frac{3}{8}$	1
1011	c. 1720	Köthen	Suite V in c	Solo cello	$\frac{3}{8}$	1
813	1722–25	Köthen/Leipzig	French Suite II in c	Klavier	$\frac{3}{8}$	1
995	1727–31	Leipzig	Suite in g, after BWV 1011	Lute	$\frac{3}{8}$	1
831	1735 (33)	Leipzig	Overture in the French Style in b	Klavier	$\frac{6}{8}$	1

Giga I

BWV	Date	Place	Work	Instrument	Meter Sign	Number
820	1708–14 or earlier	Weimar	Overture in F	Klavier	$\frac{6}{8}$	1
832	1708–14 or earlier	Weimar	Partie in A	Klavier	$\frac{6}{8}$	1
977	1713–16	Weimar	Concerto in C	Klavier	$\frac{12}{8}$	1
975	1713–16	Weimar	Concerto in g [after Vivaldi, Op. 4, No. 6]	Klavier	$\frac{12}{8}$	1
807	1715–25	Weimar–Leipzig	English Suite II in a	Klavier	$\frac{6}{8}$	1
808	1715–25	Weimar–Leipzig	English Suite III in g	Klavier	$\frac{12}{8}$	1
809	1715–25	Weimar–Leipzig	English Suite IV in F	Klavier	$\frac{12}{8}$	1
811	1715–25	Weimar–Leipzig	English Suite VI in d	Klavier	$\frac{12}{16}$	1
1010	c. 1720	Köthen	Suite VI in E♭	Solo cello	$\frac{12}{8}$	1
816	1722–25	Köthen/Leipzig	French Suite in G	Klavier	$\frac{12}{16}$	1
825	1731 (26)	Leipzig	Partita I in B♭	Klavier	C	1
827	1731 (25 + 27)	Leipzig	Partita III in a	Klavier	$\frac{12}{8}$	1
828	1731 (28)	Leipzig	Partita IV in D	Klavier	$\frac{9}{16}$	1
830	1731 (25 + 30)	Leipzig	Partita VI in e	Klavier	$\Phi, \frac{2}{1}, \text{¢}$	1
1068	1729–31	Leipzig	Overture in D	Orchestra	$\frac{6}{8}$	1

Giga II

BWV	Date	Place	Work	Instrument	Meter Sign	Number
965	?	?	Sonata in a minor [after Sonata I in Reinken's *Hortus Musicus*, 1687]	Klavier	$\frac{12}{8}$	1
996	by 1717	Weimar	Suite in e	Lute	$\frac{12}{8}$	1
1023	1714–17	Weimar	Sonata in e	Violin and continuo	$\frac{12}{8}$	1
806	1715–25	Weimar–Leipzig	English Suite I in A	Klavier	$\frac{6}{8}$	1
810	1715–25	Weimar–Leipzig	English Suite V in e	Klavier	$\frac{3}{8}$	1
1007	c. 1720	Köthen	Suite I in G	Solo cello	$\frac{6}{8}$	1
1008	c. 1720	Köthen	Suite II in d	Solo cello	$\frac{3}{8}$	1
1009	c. 1720	Köthen	Suite III in C	Solo cello	$\frac{3}{8}$	1
1012	c. 1720	Köthen	Suite VI in D	Solo cello	$\frac{6}{8}$	1
1004	1720	Köthen	Partita II in F	Solo violin	$\frac{12}{8}$	1
1006	1720	Köthen	Partita III in E	Solo violin	$\frac{6}{8}$	1
1006a	late 1730s	Köthen	[arr. of BWV 1006]	?Lute-harpsichord	$\frac{6}{8}$	1
812	1722–25	Köthen/Leipzig	French Suite I in d	Klavier	c or ¢	1
814	1722–25	Köthen/Leipzig	French Suite III in b	Klavier	$\frac{3}{8}$	1
815	1722–25	Köthen/Leipzig	French Suite IV in E♭	Klavier	$\frac{6}{8}$	1
817	c. 1724	?Leipzig	French Suite VI in E	Klavier	$\frac{6}{8}$	1
818	c. 1722	Köthen	Suite in a	Klavier	$\frac{6}{8}$	1
829	1731 (30)	Leipzig	Partita V in G	Klavier	$\frac{6}{8}$	1
997	1737–41	Leipzig	Partita in c	Lute	$\frac{6}{8}$	1 + *double*

Loures

BWV	Date	Place	Work	Meter Sign	Number	Instrument
1006	1720	Köthen	Partita III in E	$\frac{6}{4}$	1	Solo violin
1006a	1720	Köthen	Partita III in E	$\frac{6}{4}$	1	Arr. for lute
816	1722–25	Köthen/Leipzig	French Suite V in G	$\frac{6}{4}$	1	Klavier

Forlana

BWV	Date	Place	Work	Meter Sign	Number	Instrument
1066	1717–25	Köthen/Leipzig	Suite in C	$\frac{6}{4}$	1	Orchestra

Polonaises

BWV	Date	Place	Work	Meter Sign	Number	Instrument
1046	by 1721	?Köthen	Brandenburg Concerto I in F (couplet in Minuet)	$\frac{3}{8}$	1	Orchestra
817	c. 1724	?Leipzig	French Suite VI in E	$\frac{3}{4}$	1	Klavier
1067	c. 1738–39	Leipzig	Suite in b	$\frac{3}{4}$	1 + *double*	Orchestra

Chaconnes and Passacaglia

BWV	Date	Place	Work	Instrument	Meter Sign
150, No. 7	c. 1708–09	Mühlhausen or Weimar	"Meine Tage in den Leiden" (Ciaccona)	Chorus	$\frac{3}{2}$
1004	1720	Köthen	Sonata IV in d (Ciaccona)	Solo violin	$\frac{3}{4}$
582	?1708–12 (or later)	?Weimar	Passacaglia in c	Organ	$\frac{3}{4}$

Appendix B

Untitled Dance Music by J.S. Bach

(A Partial List)

Bourées

Keyboard:
   WTC I, Fugue III, in C♯, BWV 845
   WTC II, Fugue XII, in f, BWV 881
   Organ Fugue in c, BWV 537
   Organ Fugue in g, BWV 542
Instrumental:
   Musical Offering, BWV 1079, Trio Sonata, 2d mvt.
   Sonata in E for flute, BWV 1035, 2d mvt.
Orchestra:
   Brandenburg Concerto II, 1st mvt.
   Concerto in g for harpsichord, BWV 1058, 1st mvt.
      (based on Concerto in a for violin, BWV 1041, 1st mvt.)
   Concerto in c for two harpsichords, BWV 1060, 3d mvt.
Sacred Vocal:
   Songs from G. C. Schemelli's *Musicalisches Gesang-Buch*
      (Leipzig, 1736) (e.g., BWV 446, BWV 449, BWV 469)
   Cantata 140, No. 4: "Mein Freund ist mein!"
   Cantata 202, No. 1: "Weichet nur"
   B Minor Mass, BWV 233, No. 2: "Laudamus te," from "Gloria"
Secular Vocal:
   Cantata 173a, No. 6: "So schau' dies holden Tages Licht"
   Cantata 173a, No. 7: "Dein Name gleich der Sonnen geh"
   Cantata 211, No. 10: "Die Katze lässt es mausen nicht"
   Cantata 212, No. 2: "Mer hahn en neue Oberkeet"
   Cantata 212, No. 24: "Wir gehn nun wo der Tudelsack"
   Cantata 216: "Mit Lachen und Scherzen"

Gavottes

Keyboard:
   WTC II, Prelude XII, in f, BWV 881
   WTC II, Fugue XIII, in f♯, BWV 882
   French Suite in b, BWV 814: Anglaise
   Trio sonata in G for organ, BWV 530, 1st mvt.
Sacred Vocal:
   Magnificat in D, BWV 243: "Quia fecit mihi magna"
   Cantata 64, No. 5: "Was die Welt in sich hält"
   Cantata 130, No. 5: "Lasz, o Fürst der Cherubinen"

Cantata 176, No. 3: "Dein sonst hell beliebter Schein"
Cantata 194, No. 5: "Hilf, Gott dasz es uns gelingt"
Secular Vocal:
Cantata 173a, No. 3: "Leopold's Vortrefflichkeiten"
Cantata 213, No. 13: "Lust der Völker"

Minuets

Keyboard:
Partita III, BWV 827: Burlesca (called "minuet" in
Clavierbüchlein of Anna Magdalena Bach, 1725)
Organ Prelude in F, BWV 556
Orchestra:
Concerto for Harpsichord and Orchestra, BWV 1054, 3d mvt.
Sacred Vocal:
Cantata 1, No. 5: "Unser Mund und Ton der Saiten"
Cantata 11, No. 10: "Ach ja! so komme bald zurück"
Cantata 25, No. 5: "Öffne meinen schlechten Liedern"
Cantata 65, No. 6: "Nimm mich dir zu eigen hin"
Cantata 77, No. 5: "Ach, es bleibt in meiner Liebe"
Mass in G, BWV 236, No. 3: "Gratias agimus tibi"
Magnificat in D, BWV 243, No. 2: "Et exultavit"
St. John Passion, BWV 245, No. 67: "Ruht wohl, ruht wohl" (chorus)
Secular Vocal:
Cantata 173a, No. 8: "Nim auch, grosser Fürst" (chorus)
Cantata 210, No. 2: "Spielet, ihr beseelten Lieder"
Cantata 211, No. 4: "Ei! wie schmeckt der Coffee süsze"
Cantata 212, No. 14: "Klein zschocher müsse so zart und süsze"

Passepieds

Keyboard:
WTC I, Fugue XI, in F, BWV 856
Goldberg Variations, BWV 988: Var. 19
WTC II, Fugue XXIV, in b, BWV 893
Sacred Vocal:
Cantata 49, No. 1: Sinfonia
Cantata 152, No. 1: Concerto, Part II
Cantata 182, No. 8: "So lasset uns gehen in Salem der Freuden" (chorus)
Secular Vocal:
Cantata 202, No. 7: "Sich Uben im Lieben"
Cantata 205, No. 11: "Zurükke, zurükke, geflügeltn Winde"
Cantata 213, No. 9: "Ich will dich nicht hören, ich will dich nicht wissen mag"

Sarabandes

Instrumental:
WTC I, Prelude VIII, in e♭, BWV 853

Goldberg Variations, BWV 988: Aria
Musical Offering, BWV 1079, Trio Sonata: "Largo"
Sacred Vocal:
    Cantata 6, No. 1: "Bleib bei uns"
    Cantata 27, No. 5: "Gute Nacht"
    Cantata 75, No. 3: "Mein Jesu soll mein Alles sein"
    Canata 91, No. 3: "Gott, dem der Erdenkeris zu klein"
    Cantata 96, No. 5: "Bald zur Rechten, bald zur Linken"
    Cantata 97, No. 7: "Hat er denn beschlosen"
    Cantata 135, No. 3: "Tröste mir, Jesu mein Gemüte"
    Cantata 153, No. 8: "Soll ich meinen Lebenslauf"
    Cantata 188, No. 1: "Ich habe meine Zuversicht"
    St. John Passion, BWV 245, No. 19: "Ach mein Sinn"
    St. Matthew Passion, BWV 244, No. 78: "Wir setsen uns mit Tränen nieder"
      (chorus)
    BWV 212, No. 8: "Unser trefflicher lieber Kammerherr"

Correntes

Keyboard:
    Invention X, in G, BWV 781
    Sinfonia No. 6, in E, BWV 792
    Sinfonia No. 13, in a, BWV 799
    Little Prelude in d, BWV 935

French Gigues

Keyboard:
    Organ Fugue in E, BWV 566, No. 2
    "Komm, heiliger Geist, Herre Gott," from 18 Chorales, BWV 652
    Solo Concerto in g, BWV 983, No. 3
    Goldberg Variations, BWV 988: Var. 7
Secular Vocal:
    Cantata 211, No. 8: "Heute noch, heute noch"

Giga I

Keyboard:
    Organ Fugue in G, BWV 577
    Partite diverse sopra "Sei gegrüszet, Jesu Gütig," BWV 768, No. 8
    WTC I, Prelude III, in C$\sharp$, BWV 848
    WTC II, Fugue IV, in c$\sharp$, BWV 873
    WTC II, Fugue XI, in F, BWV 880
    WTC II, Fugue XIX, in A, BWV 888
    Concerto, BWV 980, No. 3
Other Instrumental:
    Sonata No. 1 in g for Solo Violin, BWV 1001, No. 3
    Brandenburg Concerto III, BWV 1048, No. 3

Sacred Vocal:
   Cantata 66, No. 1: "Erfreut euch, ihr Herzen" (chorus)
   Cantata 192, No. 3: "Lob, Ehr' und Preis" (chorus)

Giga II

Keyboard:
   Organ Fugue in a, BWV 543, No. 2
   Organ Prelude in C, BWV 547
   Organ Fugue in C, BWV 564, No. 2
   Organ Fugue in F, BWV 590
   Invention IV in d, BWV 775
   Concerto for Solo Harpsichord, No. 3, BWV 974, 3d mvt.
   Concerto for Solo Harpsichord, No. 14, BWV 985, 1st mvt.
Instrumental Ensemble:
   Sonata for Viola da Gamba and Klavier, No. 2, in D, BWV 1028, No. 4
   Sonata for Viola da Gamba and Klavier, No. 3, in g, BWV 1029, No. 3
Orchestra:
   Brandenburg Concerto V, BWV 1050, No. 3
   Brandenburg Concerto VI, BWV 1051, No. 3
   Easter Cantata, BWV 249, No. 1: Sinfonia
Sacred Vocal:
   Cantata 40, No. 7: "Christen kinder, freuet euch"
   Cantata 49, No. 1: "Ich geh' und suche mit Verlangen"
   Cantata 79, No. 2: "Gott, der Herr ist Sonn' und Schild"
   Cantata 96, No. 1: "Herr Christ, der Gottes-Sohn" (chorus)
   Cantata 145, No. 5: "Merke, mein Herze"
   B Minor Mass, BWV 233, No. 2: "Gloria" (chorus)
   Easter Cantata 249, No. 3: "Kommt, eilet und laufet"
Secular Vocal:
   Cantata 207, No. 2: "Vereinigte Zwie tracht der wechselnden Saiten" (chorus)
   Cantata 208, No. 15: "Ihr lieblichste Blikke" (chorus)
   Cantata 214, No. 9: "Blühet, ihr Linden" (chorus)
   Cantata 215, No. 9: "Stifter der Reiche" (chorus)

Loures

Keyboard:
   WTC I, Prelude IV, in c#, BWV 849
   Fantasia in c, BWV 906

Polonaises

Keyboard:
   Partite diverse sopra "Sei gegeüszet, Jesu gütig," BWV 768, No. 10
Sacred Vocal:
   Cantata 184, No. 4: "Glück und Segen sind bereit"
Secular Vocal:
   Cantata 205, No. 13: "Zweig und Äste"

Cantata 212, No. 4: "Ach, es schmeckt doch gar zu gut"
Cantata 212, No. 6: "Ach, herr Schösser, geht nicht gar zu schlimm"
Cantata 212, No. 12: "Fünfzig Taler bares Geld"
Cantata 214, No. 3: "Blast die wohl gegriffnen Flöten"
Cantata 216, No. 7: "Heil und Segen"

NOTES

Works for which complete citations appear in the Bibliography are identified in the Notes by author and title only or by the abbreviations given in the Bibiliography.

PREFACE

1. "Denen Liebhabern zur Gemüths Ergoetzung verfertiget." The *Clavier-Übung* (Leipzig, 1731) is available in a facsimile edition of the copy in the Gemment Museum, Den Haag (The Hague, 1983).
2. Christoph Wolff, "Bach, Johann Sebastian," **New Grove,** Vol. I, sections 18–19, pp. 815–16.
3. E. Mohr, *Die Allemande* (Leipzig, 1932).
4. W. Danckert, *Geschichte der Gigue* (Leipzig, 1924).
5. Willi Apel, *Harvard Dictionary of Music,* 2d ed. (Cambridge: Harvard University Press, 1969).
6. Letter from Gesner to Marcus Fabius Quintilianus (1738), quoted in translation in **David/Mendel:Bach,** p. 231.

1. FRENCH COURT DANCE IN BACH'S WORLD

1. **Geiringer:Bach,** p. 11. Geiringer cites G. Fock, *Der Junge Bach in Lüneburg* (Hamburg, 1950).
2. **Geiringer:Bach,** p. 12.
3. For illustrations and detailed information on the technique and style of French Court dancing, consult **Hilton:Dance.**
4. Further information is available in Marie-Françoise Christout, *Le Ballet de Cour de Louis XIV* (1967).
5. Rebecca Harris-Warrick, "Ballroom dancing at the court of Louis XIV," p. 42.
6. See **Little/Marsh:Inventory** and **Hilton:Dance** for more information.
7. Shirley Wynne, "Complaisance: An Eighteenth-Century Cool."
8. **Taubert:Rechtschaffener,** Petermann *Nachwort.*
9. Renate Brockpähler, *Handbuch zur Geschichte der Barockoper in Deutschland.*
10. Christoph Weigel, *Abbildung der Gemein-Nutzlichen Haupt-Stände von dem Regenten biss auf die Künstler und Handwercker.*
11. Angelika Gerbes, "Gottfried Taubert on Social and Theatrical Dance of the Early Eighteenth Century," p. 11.
12. Brockpähler, *Handbuch zur Geschichte der Barockoper.*
13. For more information on French dancing at the Württemberg court, see Adrien Fauchier-Magnan, *Les Petites Cours D'Allemagne Au XVIIIième Siècle.*
14. André Pirro, "Remarques de quelques voyageurs sur la musique en Allemagne et dans les pays du nord, de 1634 à 1700," p. 334.
15. Ibid., p. 338.
16. For more information on these courts, see **Ecorcheville:Suites,** Vol. 1, chapter 3, "Les Oeuvres et leur Milieu."
17. **Ecorcheville:Suites.**
18. Background information on the Kroměříž library is available in **New Grove,**

article "Kroměříž ." It is likely that other pieces by Lully lie unrecognized under the name of another composer.

19. **New Grove,** article "Volumier."

20. Information on Dresden has been derived from Moritz Fürstenau, *Zur Geschichte der Musik und des Theaters am Hofe zu Dresden.*

21. We are indebted to Kurt Petermann, Leipzig dance historian and archivist, for bringing to our attention this work in the Leipzig Tanzarchiv der DDR.

22. **Feuillet:l700Receuil.**

23. Quoted by Friedrich Wilhelm Marpurg in *Historisch-kritische Beiträge zur Aufnahme der Musik,* Vol. I, 1754, as reported in **New Grove,** article "Volumier."

2. TERMS AND PROCEDURES

1. For references, see **Aldrich:Rhythm,** p. 16.

2. **Houle:Meter,** pp. 36–38; **Ellis:Lully,**Appendix B, p. 244.

3. **Houle:Meter,** pp. 33–61. Houle also points out the frequent disparity among eighteenth-century theorists on how to beat the measure, the difficulty of defining "beat," and the growing distinction between tempo and meter because of the changing function of time signatures in the eighteenth century.

4. See below, chapter 10.

5. For example, see the final figures of "Sarabande pour femme," **Feuillet:1700Receuil,** p. 24; "Entrée pour deux hommes" by Louis-Guillaume Pécour, *Recueil de Dances* (Paris, 1704), pp. 148–53.

6. Robert Donington, *Baroque Music: Style and Performance,* pp. 148 ff.

7. Irmgard Hermann-Bengen, *Tempobezeichnungen: Ursprung und Wandel im 17. und 18. Jahrhundert.*

8. See below, chapter 8, note 13 and accompanying text.

9. Thoinot Arbeau, *Orchésography.*

10. Robert Donington, *A Performer's Guide to Baroque Music,* p. 247.

11. **Hilton:Dance,** pp. 262–66.

12. **Houle:Meter,** chapter 2 and pp. 71–77; **Mather:Dance,** chapter 1 and pp. 126–28.

13. *Der Critische Musicus an der Spree,* quoted in **Donington: Interpretation,** p. 51.

14. **Kirnberger:Kunst,** part II, chapter 4, Tempo, I, p. 106; Beach translation, p. 376.

15. **L'Affilard:Principes,** Introduction, quoted in translation by Erich Schwandt, "L'Affilard on the French Court Dances," p. 390.

16. See, for example, **Tomlinson:Dancing,** p. 25.

17. Friedrich Wilhelm Marpurg, *Clavierstücke mit einem practischen Unterrich für Anfänger und Geübtere,* pp. 7–8; English translation by Edward Jenne.

> Von verschiednen Compositionsarten fürs Clavier, und
> der rhythmischen Anordnung eines Tonstückes.

> Ein jedes Tonstück besteht ordentlicher Weise aus Paragraphen, aus Perioden, und aus Sectionalzeilen.

> Jeder kleinere Theil einer Composition, der einige Tacte begreift, und durch einen Ruhepunct von dem folgenden abgesondert ist, heiszt eine Sectionalzeile. Zwo oder mehrer Sectionalzeilen, wovon die letztere insgemein mit einer halben Cadenz geendigt wird, machen einen Perioden, wovon der letzte mit einer ganzen Cadenz geendigt wird, machen einen Paragraph [Exempel, aus der *Jeannette*]. . . . Wenn wir den aus zwei Viertheilen bestehenden halben Tact, womit das Stück anfängt, vorüberlassen, und den folgenden ganzen Tact, als den ersten,

mit der Zahl 1, den darauf folgenden mit 2, und so weiter bezeichnen: so sind diese Ruhepuncte im zweyten, vierten, sechsten, und acten Tact, und zwar zum Anfange eines jeden Tacts, sehr deutlich zu empfinden. Der erste Ruhepunct geschicht mit den Noten e–d–c im Zweiten Tact; der zweyte mit h–a–g im vierten Tact, der dritte wieder mit den Noten des ersten, im sechsten Tact, und der vierte mit einer ganzen Note, die im siebenten Tact anfänget, und zum Anfang des achten zur Wirklichkeit kömmt. Da vier Ruhepuncte vorhanden sind: so sind auch folglich vier Sectionalzeilen vorhanden. . . . Die beyden ersten Section-alzeilen, . . . einer halben Cadenz vertritt, machen einen Perioden; und die beyden letztern, nemlich die dritte und vierte, machen wieder einen Perioden. Diese beyde Perioden zusammen genommen geben einen Paragraph. Ehe wir in der Erklärung der Jeannette fortfahren, will ich kürzlich zeigen, was eine ganze und halbe Cadenz, und was ein Absatz ist. . . . Die ganze Cadenz findet da Platz, wo der Basz von der Quinta Toni in den Grundton; der Diskant aber entweder durch die Secundam oder Septimam Toni in den Grundton geht. Die beyden letzten Noten aus dam Basse und Diskant machen das Intervall der Octave unter sich, und beyde müssen auf einen guten Tacttheil fallen, welches man den Einschnitt der Cadenz nennet. Exempel von der ganzen Cadenz findet man am Ende des Rondeau der "Jeannette," ferner am Ende des ersten und zweyten Couplet, und zum Anfange des vierten Tacts im dritten Couplet.

Die halbe Cadenz wird dadurch characterisirt, dasz der Basz aus Der Einschnitt musz, wie bey der ganzen Cadenz, auf einen guten Tacttheil fallen, z. E. [Ex. II-2]. Die beyden letzten Noten machen bey (a) und (b) das Intervall einer Quinte, und bey (c) einer 0ctave under sich.

Das Abzeichen der Abzätze ist, dasz die Oberstimme meistentheils eine Terz gegen den Basz macht. Sie werden sehr oft an die Stelle einer halben Cadentz gesetzt. . . . Ich komme zu dam ersten Couplet der Jeannette, wo ebenfalls, so wie im Rondeau, vier Ruhepuncte vorhanden sind; als im zweyten, vierten, sech-sten, und achten Tact. Sowohl der erste als zweyte Ruhepunctendiget sich auf eine Art, die in Ansehung der beyden letzten Noten nach dem vorhin gesagten eine halbe Cadenz zu bemerken scheinet. Es ist aber keine allhier, sondern nur ein blosser Absatz vorhanden. Denn der Einschnitt fällt nicht auf das erste, son-dern auf das zweyte Viertheil; und das zweyte Viertheil in einem zweytheiligen Tacte ist kein Tacttheil, sondern ein Tactglied, und zwar ein schlimmes Tactglied. Der dritte Ruhepunct in der ersten Hälfte des sechsten Tacts, wo der Einschnitt regelmäszig fällt, ob er gleich durch einen Vorschlag verzögert wird, kann so gut für eine halbe Cadenz, als für einen dieses, weil der Ruhepunct mit einer Terz geschicht. Uebrigens enthalten die beyden ersten Sectionalzeilen einen Peri-oden, und die beyden letzten auch. Wer die Länge des ersten Perioden bis zum dritten Ruhepunct ausdehnen vollte, wärde wegen der, nach der zweyten Sec-tionalzeile sich verändernden Modulation, soches unrechmäsziger Weise thun. Die beyden Perioden machen wieder einen Paragraph, und zwar den zweyten des Stückes aus.

Mit dem zweyten Couplet ist es just wie mit dem ersten beschaffen. Es endigt sich damit der dritte Paragraph des Stückes. Der zweyte Ruhepunct des dritten Couplets geschicht mit einer ganzen Cadenz; und der vierte mit einer halben; denn die Verzögerung des Einschnitts hebet das Wesen der halben Cadenz nicht auf. In diesam dritten Couplet findet sich bey der ganzen Cadenz in F der vierte Paragraph des Stückes, der zwar kurz, aber nichts destow niger ein Paragraph ist. Denn die Folge enthält nichts als einen eingeschobnen Perioden, der zur Vorber-eitung da steht, um wieder zu dem ersten Paragraphen zu kommen, womit das Stück schliesset.

18. "La Jeannette" appears only in Marpurg's book. The composer could have been either Louis-Nicolas Clérambault (1676–1749) or César-François-Nicolas Clér-ambault (d. 1760), according to David Tunley, in his article "Clérambault," in **New Grove.**

19. Marpurg, p. 22.

Gavotte, oder Gavote.

Die Gavotte ist ein Tonstück, welches in der geraden Tactart, und zwar im Zweyzweytheil gesetzet, mit zwey Viertheilen oder gleichgeltenden Noten im Aufschlage angehoben, aus ainer ungekünstelten leichten Melodie zusammen gesetzet, und in eine gerade Anzahl von Tacten, die von Absatz zu Absatz einen geraden Verhalt gegen einander machen müssen, eingeschränkt wird. Durch die gleichgeltenden Noten, womit die Gavotte anstatt der beyden Viertheile, im Aufschlage anheben kann, und welche die Anlage zum ganzen Metro machen, versteht man entweder vier Achttheile, (wovon auch das erste und dritte punctirt, und das zweyte und vierte in Sechzehntheile verwandelt werden kann;) oder ein punctirtes Viertheil mit einem darauf folgenden Achttheile; oder ein Viertheil mit zwey darauf folgenden Achttheilen, oder zwey Achttheile und ein Viertheil; oder endlich eine Weisse.

Keine Gavotte kann weniger als vier Tacte zu jeder Clausel, oder zu jedem Theile, haben. Insgemein nimmt man acht zu jedem Theile. Wenn der erste in eine Nebentonart schliesset: so lässet man insgemein den zweyten nur aus einem einzigen Paragraph bestehen; d.i. man weichet in selbigem in keine Nebentonart aus. Wenn aber die erste Clausel ihre Cadenz in den Hauptton machet, so wird, in der Mitte der zweyten Clausel, in einen Nebenton cadenziret.

Der Einschnitt der ganzen musz allezeit männlich seyn, wie es die Regel des Zweyzweytheiltacts erfordert; und die Einschnittsnote also, ohne Zergliederung des Niederschlages, den Wehrt der dazu gehörigen Weissen ausfüllen. Indessen erlaubet man, doch nur in Gavotten, die zum Tanze bestimmet sind, und alsdenn nur hauptsächlich bey einer Cadenz in der Mitte der zweyten Clausel manchesmahl einen weiblichen Einschnitt, das ist, einen Einschnitt auf dem zweyten Viertheil des zergliederten Niederschlages, z.E. [Ex. 11-3].

Das Metrum kann auf verschiedene Weise gebildet werden, mit herrschenden Viertheilen, oder mit herrschenden Achttheilen, oder vermischt. Man kann hin und wieder den Punct zu Hülfe nehmen, und was dergleichen Veränderungen mehr find, deren Wahl, so wie der Anfang im Auftact, von dem Character und der Bewegung abhänget, die man der Gavotte geben will. Denn die Gavotte kann zu allerhand Arten von Ausdrucken, frölichen und traurigen von verschiedenem Grade gebraucht, und also in einer mehr und weniger geschwindern, und mehr und weniger langsamen Bewegung ausgeführet werden.

Dieses Tonstück an sich gehöret unter die kleinen Tonstücke; das Tempo und Metrum davon aber hat bey grössern Sing- und Spielstücken Platz. Viele Rondeau pflegen gavottenmäszig gesetzt zu werden. Ein Exempel davon hat man an der Jeannette in dem ersten Theile dieser Clavierstücke. Zu merken ist annoch, dasz sich einige Tonmeister des Zweyvertheils, anstatt des Zweyzweytheils, bey der gavotte zu bedienen pflegen. Im Grunde ist es einerley, so lange das Zeitmaasz durch die dazu erforderlichen Wörter gehörig angezeiget wird. Doch erfordert es die Gewohnheit, bey der eigentlichen Gavotte den Zweyzweytheiltact zu gebrauchen.

20. Quoted in **David/Mendel:Bach,** pp. 323–24.

PART II

1. Bowing patterns, which are of great importance for an understanding of articulation in Baroque dances, are treated in detail in **Mather:Dance.** Rather than repeat the information here, we refer interested readers to that book.

2. For an introduction to the source problems in Bach's secular instrumental music, see Robert Marshall's excellent article, "J.S. Bach's Compositions for Solo Flute."

3. Natalie Jenne, "On the Performance of Keyboard Allemandes."

3. THE BOURÉE

1. Theorists who specify an affect for the bourée include **L'Affilard:Principes,** p. 33: a bourée is marked "fort légèrement"; **Dupont:Principes,** p. 34: "D. Quel est le gout de la Bourée / R. Elle se chante, fort légèrement"; **Rousseau:Dictionnaire; Compan:Dictionnaire:** "a deux tems gais"; **Quantz:Versuch,** p. 271: "lustig . . . ausgeführet" (Reilly translation, p. 291, "executed gaily"); Pierre Richelet, *Dictionnaire de La Langue Françoise,* 2 vols. (Amsterdam, 1732): "Ein lustiges Tanz oder Stück in der Musik"; Johann Leonard Frisch, *Nouveau Dictionnaire des Passages oder Neues Frantzösisch-Teutsches Wörter-Buch* (Leipzig, 1763).

2. "ihr eigentliches Abzeichen auf der ZUFRIEDENHEIT, und einem *Gefälligen Wesen* beruhe, dabey gleichsam etwas *unbekümmertes* oder *gelassenes,* ein wenig nachläsziges, gemächliches und doch nichts unangenehmes vermacht ist," **Mattheson:Vollkommene,** pp. 225–26.

3. "La Gigue doit se battre de même mouvement que la bourée & le Rigaudon," **Masson:Traité,** p. 8.

4. **Muffat:FP,** Strunk translation, Foreword.

5. **Christoph/Stössel:Lexicon,** p. 65: "Bourée ist ein langsamer Frantzössicher Tantz. . . . Es sind sonst lang im Gebrauch gewesene. . . ." The article speaks of the bourée as a dance for two, four, or eight persons, "leicht zu lessen, und lustig zu tantzen."

6. Wendy Hilton mentions ♩ = 80 MM as an approximate tempo for dancing many bourée choreographies. See **Hilton:Dance,** p. 266.

7. The most complete eighteenth-century discourse on bourée (and rigaudon) structure is found in F. W. Marpurg's *Clavierstücke mit einem Practischen Unterricht . . . ,* Vol. II, p. 23:

> Rigaudon. Bouree, or Bourree
>
> The Rigaudon and the Bouree may originally have been very different rhythmically and metrically. But today they are certainly not, and one finds that quite similar pieces will be called a Rigaudon by one master and a Bouree by another. Nevertheless, one should take the upbeat with two eighth notes and mix quarters and eighths in the note-organization [*Metro*] in order to characterize the Bouree; on the other hand, the Rigaudon is characterized by a quarter-note upbeat and as for the *Metro,* prevailing quarter notes. In regard to the meter, the rhythmical relationships of the measures, the number of measures for each section [Clause], and the close of the full cadence, [it is] the same as the gavotte.
>
> On the basis of what has been said above, the Rigaudon is explained as follows: the Rigaudon is a small composition which is in duple meter, and, to be sure, is set in ⅔ time, with a quarter-note upbeat. It is made of a simple melody in which quarter notes prevail, and is restricted to an equal number of measures, which, from section to section, are in direct proportion to each other. We can keep the previous explanation and change only "in which quarter notes prevail," and after that change the words "with a quarter-note upbeat" into "with two eighth-note upbeats": then you have a description of the Bouree.
>
> The Rigaudon and Bouree permit, after both their main reprises, a little additional reprise, which is generally used as a variation of the four last measures of the second section. One can compose all kinds of larger pieces in the style of the Bouree and Rigaudon. Both types are used exclusively to express joy in a greater or lesser degree. [Translation by Edward Jenne.]

8. **Freillon:Veritable,** p. 16.

9. *Ballet des Arts,* 1663 (LWV 18/6); *Ballet de la Naissance de Vénus,* 1665 (LWV 27/43); *Ballet de Flore,* 1669 (LWV 40/7).

10. **Ecorcheville:Suites,** Vol. II, p. 17.

11. **Quantz:Versuch,** Reilly translation, p. 291: "Eine *Bouree* und ein *Rigaudon* werden lustig, und mit einem kurtzen und leichten Bogenstriche ausgeführet. Auf jeden Tact kommt ein Pulsschlag."

12. Two bourées contain other types of phrases: *La Silvie* contains a single eleven-measure phrase; *La Nouvelle Bourgogne* has a phrase structure of 3 + 3 measures in both the music and the dance. See **Little/Marsh:Inventory** for further information.

13. *The New Grove Bach Family,* p. 207.

14. The slurs appear in the Bischoff edition of the English Suites in which these bourées occur. They are taken from the Gerber manuscripts, made during the time of Gerber's work with Bach, according to Bischoff. These slurs are useful models for the articulation of other Bach bourées.

4. THE GAVOTTE

1. **Bacilly:Remarques,** Caswell translation, p. 106.

2. **Dupont:Violon,** p. 39: "Elle se chante gracieuxement."

3. **Mattheson:Vollkommene,** p. 225; Harriss translation, p. 453.

4. **Freillon:Veritable,** p. 57: "Ce sont des airs plus graves et plus serieux, et dont les expressions sont plus touchantes."

5. **Grassineau:Dictionary,** p. 84.

6. **Rousseau:Dictionnaire,** entry "Gavotte": "Le mouvement de la Gavotte est ordinairement gracieux, souvent gai, quelquefois aussi tendre & lent."

7. Friedrich Wilhelm Marpurg, *Clavierstücke mit einem practischen Unterricht . . . ,* Vol. II, pp. 22–23: "Die Gavotte kann zu allerhand Arten von Ausdrucken, fröhlichen und traurigen von verschiedenen Grade gebraucht. . . . "

8. Jean-Jacques Rousseau, article "Gavotte": "sorte de danse dont l'air a deux reprises, chacune de quatre, de huit, ou de plusieurs fois quatre mesures à deux tems; chaque reprise doit toûjours commencer avec la second tems, et finir sur le premier. Le mouvement de la *gavotte* est ordinairement gracieux, souvent gai, quelquefois aussi tendre et lent."

9. **Démotz:Methode,** p. 169: "se battent à deux Tems grave."

10. **Muffat:FP,** Strunk translation, pp. 82 ff.

11. **Quantz:Versuch,** Reilly translation, p. 291.

12. **Dupont:Principes,** p. 30: "D. Quel est le gout de la gavotte? /R. Un peut plus lente, que la marche."

13. **Mattheson:Vollkommene,** p. 225; Harriss translation, p. 453.

14. **Montéclair:Principes,** pp. 36 and 50.

15. *IIIIe. Recüeil de danses de bal pour l'année 1705* (Paris, 1705): "c'est une maniere de branle a quatre que toutes sortes de personnes peuvent danser sans même avoir jamais appris" (Preface, 3 pages before p. 1).

16. **Saint-Lambert:Clavecin,** Harris-Warrick translation, p. 47.

17. **Freillon:Veritable,** p. 57: "Il n'en est pas de même des Gavottes. . . . Pour y bien réüssir, il les faut commencer sur le second temps de la mesure, qui se marque par un 2, et on les doit battre fort lentement."

18. **New Grove,** article "Gavotte."

19. See the comparison of French and Italian gavottes in **Montéclair:Principes,** pp. 36 and 50.

20. See above, text accompanying note 13.

21. Bowings may be studied in the facsimile edition, *Sei Solo a Violino senza Bassa accompagnato, Libro Prima, da Joh. Seb. Bach, 1720,* edited by Bernhard Sprengel, with

notes by Wilhelm Martin Luther, 2d ed. (Kassel:Bärenreiter, 1958). See also Joel Lester, "Problems in the Neue Bach-Ausgabe of the E Major Partita for Violin Alone."

22. **New Grove,** article "Violoncello."

23. Bach MS P 26, in the hand of Anna Magdalena 'Bach, now in Staatsbibliotek, Berlin; autograph facsimile in *Six Suites for Cello,* edited by Diran Alexanian.

24. David Boyden's article "Scordatura," in *New Grove Dictionary of Musical Instruments* (a revision, with new information, of material appearing in **New Grove,** in 1980), states that scordatura was "aimed primarily at tonal effects and secondarily at ease of fingering."

25. *New Grove Dictionary of Musical Instruments,* p. 806:

> In the late 17th and early 18th centuries the range of some cellos was extended upwards by a fifth string.
> Increasing musical demands also led to experiments with smaller instruments of the same compass as the cello, which could be played in the violin position. Several late 18th-century writers ascribed to [J. S.] Bach the invention of an instrument of this kind, the viola pomposa, with the tuning C–G–d–a–e′, and although Bach composed nothing that specifies its use there are good reasons not to confuse it with the violoncello piccolo for which he wrote parts in nine of his Leipzig cantatas. Whether the five-string cello for which Bach wrote his sixth unaccompanied suite (BWV 1012) was this same violoncello piccolo or simply a normal-sized cello with an extra e′ string is difficult to determine.

26. "Denen Liebhabern zur Gemüths Ergoetzung verfertiget." See above, Preface, note 1.

27. Robert Donington, *Baroque Music: Style and Performance,* p. 52.

5. THE MINUET

1. For a partial list of sources, see **New Grove,** article "Minuet."

2. For a recent study of social dance and its influence on music see Sarah Reichart, "The Influence of Eighteenth-Century Social Dance on the Viennese Classical Style."

3. **Ellis:Dances,** pp. 70–78.

4. **Mattheson:Orchestre,** pp. 193–99.

5. **Lecointe:Apologie,** Peyton translation, pp. 59 and 65.

6. **Brossard:Dictionaire:** "Minuetto, veut dire, menuet, ou Danse fort gaye, qui nous vient originairement du Poitou. On devroit à l'imitation des Italiens se servir du sign $\frac{3}{8}$ ou $\frac{6}{8}$ pour en marquer le mouvement, qui est toûjoure *fort gay & fort vîte;* mais l'usage de le marquer par un simple 3. ou *triple de Noires* a prévalu."

7. For example, Julia Sutton, "The Minuet: An Elegant Phoenix," p. 140.

8. Jean-Jacques Rousseau, article "Menuet":

> Menuet sort de danse que l'abbé Brossard prétend nous venir originairement du Poitou. Il dit que cette danse est fort gaie, et que le mouvement en est fort vîte. Ca n'est pas tout-à-fait cela. Le caractere du *menuet* est une noble et élégante simplicité, le mouvement en est plus modéré que vîte; et l'on peut dire que le moins gai de tous les genres de danse, usités dans nos bals, est le Menuet.

9. **Rameau:Maître,** chapters XXI–XXV; see also the analysis in **Hilton:Dance,** chapter 13.

10. Sutton disagrees with this idea, holding that music and dance phrases would

normally have coincided (pp. 121–25). However, abundant evidence points to dance and music phrases which frequently do not coincide. For example, the dancers sometimes added one step-unit to the Z figure, giving it fourteen measures (**Hilton:Dance,** p. 299). **Tomlinson:Dancing** (p. 137) remarks that dancers may begin within the strain of music after the bows so long as they do it at the beginning of a pair of measures. In addition, the number of steps in the circling figures is left up to the gentleman's preference (**Rameau:Maître,** chapter XXII).

11. **Hilton:Dance,** p. 294. For further examples of common cross-rhythms between minuet music and dance, see pp. 239–41.

12. See **Little/Marsh:Inventory** for more information.

13. **Mattheson:Vollkommene,** p. 224: "mässige lustigkeit."

14. Reichart, "The Influence of Eighteenth-Century Social Dance," chapter VII.

15. **Powell:Rhythmic,** pp. 157–59.

16. This manner of beating the minuet is described in several French sources, including **Loulié:Elements;** Jean Rousseau, *Methode Claire, Certaine et Facile* (Paris, 1683), pp. 34–35; and **L'Affilard:Principes,** pp. 39 and 45. **Masson:Traité** states:

> On peut battre à deux tems inégaux ces trois derniers Airs [chaconne, menuet, passepied], quoy qu'ils soient à trois tems; il est à remarquer qu'on met quelquefois trois noires pour un tems ou une blanche avec un point, ou trois croches seulement dans un tems, ou une noire avec un point, ou l'équivalent: Par exemple, de deux Mesures d'un Menuet les Maîtres de Danse n'en font qu'une à trois tems lents & égaux: Au contraire les Maîtres de Musique battent le Menuet à deux tems inégaux pour chaque Mesure; c'est-à-dire qu'ils restent au premier tems une fois davantage qu'au dernier.

Masson terms each movement of the arm a "beat"; with this terminology each measure of minuet music would have two unequal beats, the first twice as long as the second.

17. **Saint-Lambert:Clavecin,** p. 19.

18. For a detailed study of this complex issue, see **Houle:Meter.**

19. For example, **Tomlinson:Dancing,** pp. 142–52; **Taubert:Rechtschafener,** pp. 523–29 and 879–89.

20. **Loulié:Elements,** Cohen translation, pp. 61–62.

21. **Bacilly:Remarques,** Caswell translation, p. 199.

22. **Muffat:FP,** Strunk translation.

23. Kuhnau, Preface to *Neue Clavier Übung (1689)* [*pages unnumbered*]: "*hurtig.*"

24. **Tomlinson:Dancing,** p. 148.

25. **Borin:Musique,** p. 29. Mattheson and Kirnberger are in agreement.

26. Wendy Hilton reports that tempi of ♩. = MM 35 and ♩. = MM 38 (i.e., per measure) were comfortable in two minuets of contrasting tempi by L'Affillard. See **Hilton:Dance,** p. 299. This accords with tempi given in **L'Affilard:Principes.** See also Erich Schwandt, "L'Affilard on the French Court Dances," p. 399.

27. **Lecointe:Apologie,** p. 59.

28. **Saint-Lambert:Clavecin,** Harris-Warrick translation, p. 38.

29. **Ellis:Lully,** pp. 70–78.

30. See also the bowings in **Mather:Dance,** pp. 276–78.

31. Gaspard Le Roux, *Pieces de Clavessin* (Paris, 1705), edited by Albert Fuller (New York: Alpeg Editions, 1956), Suite V, pp. 33–34.

32. Robert L. Marshall, "J.S. Bach's Compositions for Solo Flute," pp. 468–69.

33. **Geiringer:Bach,** p. 270.

34. **NBA,** V/v, pp. 16–18.

35. Alfred Dürr, "The Historical Background and Composition of Johann Sebastian Bach's Clavier Suites."

36. This suite consists of Allemande, Courante, Sarabande, Bourée, and Minuet in its three manuscript sources, P 224, P 418, and P 1221; it was not published during Bach's lifetime or by Altnikol.

37. **NBA,** V/viii, p. 79.

38. Ibid., p. 99.

39. Hans Bischoff, ed., *Various Short Preludes and Fugues.*

6. THE PASSEPIED

1. **Brossard:Dictionaire:** "C'est un menuet dont le mouvement est fort vîte & fort gay."

2. The Praetorius example is reprinted in **New Grove,** article "Passepied."

3. **Türk:Clavierschule,** p. 402: "muntere."

4. **Walther:Lexicon:** "tändeln."

5. **Mattheson:Vollkommene,** Harriss translation, p. 460.

6. See the remarks on tempo in chapter 5.

7. **Freillon:Veritable,** p. 56.

8. **Quantz:Versuch,** Reilly translation, p. 291.

9. **Rousseau:Dictionnaire,** Waring translation, p. 313.

10. **Hilton:Dance,** p. 266.

11. **Ellis:Lully,** pp. 79 ff.

12. See Fig. V-1 for the relationship of dance and music.

13. Ibid.

14. **Little/Marsh:Inventory** contains more information.

15. **Mather:Dance,** pp. 285–86.

16. **Dupont:Violon,** p. 6: "Quelle remarque faite vous du coup d'archet du Paspied? Je remarque qu'il se joüe comme le Menuet excepté que l'on fait joüe les croches du Paspied comme les noires du menuet, et les doubles croches comme les croches du Menuet."

17. E.g., **Quantz:Versuch,** Reilly translation, p. 291; **Kirnberger:Kunst,** Beach translation, p. 397.

18. E.g., **Geiringer:Bach,** p. 329.

7. THE SARABANDE

1. For excellent coverage of early sarabande history, see Richard Hudson, article "Sarabande," in **New Grove.**

2. E. g., "Sarabande pour Femme," in **Feuillet:1700Recueil,** pp. 21–24; especially p. 21, measures 1–2 and 5–6, and p. 24.

3. Father François Pomey, "Description d'une Sarabande dansée," in *Le Dictionnaire Royal Augmenté* (Lyons, 1671), p. 22 (copy now in Bibliothèque municipale, Rodez). See Patricia M. Ranum, "Audible Rhetoric and Mute Rhetoric: the 17th-century French Sarabande." The passage appeared in both French and Latin; English translation by Patricia M. Ranum.

4. **Masson:Traité,** p. 7: "battre gravement"; **Niedt:Handleitung,** Mattheson, 1721, p. 105: "mit vielen *pas graves* ausgeführet; ob sie aber nur von hohen Standes Personen getantzet wird . . . "; **Walther:Lexicon:** "gravitaetische."

5. **Türk:Klavierschule,** p. 402: "hat einen ernsthaften mit Ausdruck and Würde verbundenen Charakter. . . . "

6. **Brossard:Dictionaire; Furietière:Dictionnaire,** 1701, 1727: "grave, lent, serieux."

7. Rémond de Saint-Mard, *Réflexions sur l'Opéra,* as quoted in **Anthony:FBM,** chapter 8, p. 103.

8. **Mattheson:Vollkommene,** p. 230.

9. James Talbot, manuscript notes in Christ Church Library, Oxford; Ms. 1187, c. 1690; quoted in **Donington:Interpretation,** pp. 326 and 335–36.

10. Wendy Hilton mentions this as a possible tempo for many sarabande choreographies. See **Hilton:Dance,** p. 266.

11. See François Couperin, third *Concert Royale:* "sarabande grave"; "Sarabande L'Unique," in *Pieces de Clavecin* II, Huitième Ordre: sarabande in two contrasting movements.

12. **Montéclair:Principes,** pp. 39–40.

13. Gaspard Le Roux, *Pieces de Clavessin* (Paris, 1705), edited by Albert Fuller (New York: Alpeg Editions, 1959); Suite I: "Sarabande grave"; Suite II: "Sarabande gaye."

14. See, for example, Oporto, Biblioteca Publica Municipal, Codice No. 1394 (for details, see **Little/Marsh:Inventory**).

15. **Mattheson:Vollkommene,** Harriss translation, p. 461.

16. *Pieces de Clavecin* II, Huitième Ordre.

17. See text accompanying note 3 above.

18. This freedom may explain why sarabande bowing patterns are inconsistent in the sources. See **Mather:Dance,** pp. 297–98 for patterns by Dupont and Montéclair.

19. **New Grove,** article "Sarabande," p. 492.

20. Reinken's sarabande appears in an appendix of P. Spitta, *Johann Sebastian Bach* (Berlin, 1880; English translation, 1889, reprinted New York: Dover, 1951).

21. **Kirnberger:Kunst,** Beach translation, p. 396.

22. **Quantz:Versuch,** Reilly translation, pp. 290–91.

23. See above, chapter 4, notes 24 and 25.

24. See above, chapter 4, note 25.

25 See **Mattheson:Vollkommene,** p. 353.

26. See below, chapter 9, note 12 and accompanying text.

27. Richard Hudson has noted the use of "rounded binary form" (repetition of the opening melody at the end of the second strain) in sarabandes by Buoni (1693) and other Italian composers. See **New Grove,** article "Sarabande," 2, i, p. 492.

28. See above, note 21 and accompanying text.

8. THE COURANTE

1. "On a comparé les évolutions de la courante aux ébats d'un poisson qui plonge, disparaît, et revient encore à la surface de l'eau." **Ecorcheville:Suites,** Vol. I, p. 66.

2. **Dupont:Musique,** p. 43: "D. Quel est le gout ou la maniere de chanter la courante? / R. Très gravement. . . . "

3. **Masson:Traité,** p. 7: "gravement."

4. **Walther:Lexicon:** "allerernsthaffteste."

5. **Rameau:Maître,** chapter XXVI.

6. **Compan:Dictionnaire,** article "Courante": "Cette Danse est trés grave, et inspire un air de noblesse."

7. **Mattheson:Vollkommene,** No. 123, p. 231: "Hoffnung."

8. **Quantz:Versuch,** Reilly translation, p. 291: "The entrés, the loure, and the courante are played majestically. . . . "

9. **Türk:Klavierschule,** p. 400: "ernsthaft."

10. For documentation, see chapter 5, notes 5 and 6 and accompanying text.

11. Editions de L'Oiseau-Lyre, pp. 39, 40, 95, 98, 255, 258.

12. Nicholas-Antoine Lebègue, *Les Pièces de clavessin,* Première Livre (Paris, 1677).

13. German and French in **Muffat:FS,** DTO, Vol. 4: "eylendshalber auzgenohmen die Noten. . . . , p. 22; "pour la vitesse du mouvement des notes. . . . ," p. 46. Cooper and Zsako translation, p. 228.

14. **Rameau:Maître,** chapter XXVI. Rebecca Harris-Warrick reports that the latest explicit reference she has found of Louis XIV dancing at a formal ball was in 1679, when he was forty-one years old. See "Ballroom Dancing at the Court of Louis XIV," p. 44.

15. **Taubert:Rechtschaffener,** pp. 570 ff. Much of Taubert's information concerning the courante has been translated and restated in Angelika Gerbes, "Gottfried Taubert on Social and Theatrical Dance of the Early Eighteenth Century," pp. 179–93. For a penetrating analysis of the five French courante choreographies and their relationship to music, see Wendy Hilton, "A Dance for Kings: The 17th-century French Courante."

16. **Taubert:Rechtschaffener,** pp. 579–90.

17. See chapter 2 for further discussion of the *tems de courante.*

18. They are *La Bourgogne, La Bocannes, La Courante,* and *La Duchesse* (see **Little:Inventory** for more information).

19. See **Little:Bourgogne** for more information on the Leipzig publication.

20. **Little:Contribution,** p. 118, note 5.

21. **Muffat:FS,** Cooper and Zsako translation, p. 228.

22. **Kirnberger:Kunst,** Beach translation, p. 394.

23. **Quantz:Versuch,** Reilly translation, p. 290.

24. Ibid., p. 291.

25. **Dupont:Musique,** p. 43: "D. Quel est le gout ou la maniere de chanter la Courante? / R. Tres gravement, et il faut destacher toutes les noires."

26. **Muffat:FS.**

27. Friedrich Wilhelm Marpurg, *Kritische Briefe Über die Tonkunst.* . . . , p. 26: "sondern von der *eigentlichen Tactart der Couranten* u. nach fränzösischer Art, welche zwar zu dem schweren Dreyzweytheil gehöret, aber der äusserlichen Form des Metri nach an verschiedenen Oertern, sehr vieles von dem Sechsviertheil entlehnt. Der Unterschied ist nur, dass diese Sechsviertheilpassagen im ordentlichen Dreyzweytheil gespielet werden müssen. Der seel. Herr Capellmeister Bach hat gnugsamächte Muster von diesem eigentlichen Courantentact hinterlassen. . . . "

28. See chapter 4, notes 24 and 25.

29. Alfred Dürr, "The Historical Background of the Composition of Johann Sebastian Bach's Clavier Suite," Part II, p. 57.

9. THE CORRENTE

1. *Orchestra or A Poem Of Dancing by Sir John Davies,* edited by E. M. W. Tillyard (London, Chatto & Windus, 1945; reprint, New York: Dance Horizons, [1977]).

2. Michael Praetorius, *Syntagma Musicum* (Wolfenbüttel, 1619): "Couranten haben den Namen à Currendo oder Cursitando, weil dieselbe meistentheils mit gewissen abgemessenen Sprüngen auff und nieder-gleich als mit lauffen im Tantzen

gebraucht werden" (Vol, III, p. 25). English translation in Hans Lampl, D.M.A. diss., University of Southern California, 1957, p. 69.

3. Cesare Negri, *Nuove Inventioni di Balli* (Milan, 1604), e.g., the dance "Balletto a due detto LA CORRENTE," p. 265.

4. Dance information on the corrente has been derived from **Aldrich:Rhythm,** pp. 94–100.

5. Ibid., pp. 80–81.

6. **New Grove,** article "Suite."

7. Thomas Mace, *Musick's Monument* (London, 1676; facsimile edition, Paris: Éditions du Centre National de la Recherche Scientifique, 1966), p. 129.

8. Bach, *Sei Solo a Violino senza Basso accompagnato.*

9. **Aldrich:Rhythm,** p. 99.

10. Bach MS P 26, in the hand of Anna Magdelena Bach, now in Staatsbibliotek, Berlin; autograph facsimile in *Six Suites for Cello,* edited by Diran Alexanian (Paris, 1929).

11. See chapter 4, notes 24 and 25.

12. See C.P.E. Bach, *Essay on the True Art of Playing Keyboard Instruments,* translated and edited by William J. Mitchell (New York: Norton, 1949), pp. 348–50.

10. THE GIGUE

1. **Furetière:Dictionnaire:** "Musique qui est gaye et eveillée."

2. Pierre Richelet, *Dictionnaire de la langue françoise,* 2 vols. (Amsterdam, 1732): "Composition de musique gaie et eveillée."

3. **Lacombe:Dictionnaire:** "remplé de notes pointées et syncopées qui rendent le chant gai et animé."

4. **Compan:Dictionnaire:** "tres gai."

5. **Christoph/Stössel:Lexicon:** "ist ein besonderes lustiges Instrumental-Stück."

6. **Türk:Klavierschule,** p. 401: "Ihr Character ist grösztentheils Fröhlichkeit."

7. **Brossard:Dictionaire,** article "Giga": "Giga, ou Gicque, ou Gigue. (Car les Etrangers, l'écrivent de ces trois manieres) est un air ordinairement pour les Instrumens, presque toûjours en triple qui est plein de Nottes pointées et syncopées qu'en rendent la chant gay, et pour ainsi dire *sautillant.*"

8. Jacques Ozanam, *Dictionnaire Mathématique,* p. 666: "La Gigue . . . qui se joüe vîte." **Neidt:Handleitung,** p. 98: "ist ein schneller Tanz." Johann Mattheson's revision of the Neidt's book is in his *Musicalischer Handleitung* (Hamburg, 1721); see p. 98. **Türk:Klavierschule,** p. 401: "musz die Bewegung geschwind seyn." But see **Grassineau:Dictionary:** "Giga, Gicque, or gigue, a jig, some of which are played slow, and others quick, brisk and lively, but are always in full measure, and in triple time; of some kind or other, usually $\frac{6}{8}$ or $\frac{12}{8}$." Grassineau is speaking of all types of gigue and giga, not just the French gigue.

9. **Hilton:Dance,** p. 266.

10. **Montéclair:Nouvelle,** pp. 16-17: "Le $\frac{6}{4}$ se bat à deux tems. Il faut la valeur de trois noires pour chaque tems. Le $\frac{6}{8}$ se bat à deux tems tres legers. Il contient deux mesures du Triple mineur, dont l'une se dit en frapant, et l'autre en levant."

11. **Montéclair:Principes,** p. 42.

12. **Masson:Traité,** p. 8: "La Gigue doit se battre de même mouvement que la Bourée et le Rigaudon."

13. **Dupont:Musique,** p. 36: "On passe viste les double croches, on se repose sur les croche pointée."

14. **Quantz:Versuch,** Reilly translation, p. 291.

15. **Geiringer:Bach,** pp. 288 and 294.

16. See chapter 4, notes 24 and 25.

17. *Fitzwilliam Virginal Book,* Vol. II: CXLIX (Nobody's Gigge); CLXXXIX (A Gigge. Doctor Bull's my selfe); CXC (A Gigge).

18. See chapter 2 for more discussion of problems concerning tempo in dance music.

19. John Playford, *The English Dancing Master,* contains numerous jigs for use in country dancing.

20. **New Grove,** article "Gigue."

21. **Mattheson:Vollkommene,** Harriss translation, p. 457.

22. Jean-Philippe Rameau, *Treatise on Harmony*(Paris, 1722); translated by Philip Gossett (New York: Dover, 1971), p. 177.

23. Michel Montéclair, *Concerts à deux Flutes Traversières sans Basses* (Paris: n.d.).

24. Kirnberger considers $\frac{12}{16}$ to be a combination of two $\frac{6}{16}$ measures; see **Kirnberger:Kunst,** Beach translation, p. 399.

25. Ibid., p. 388. Later Kirnberger adds (pp. 391–92):

> Although $\frac{12}{16}$ meter of [four] triple beats, which is derived from $\frac{4}{8}$ meter, is presently neglected and $\frac{12}{8}$ meter is always written instead, it is completely different from the latter in its greater lightness of execution. The elder Bach has certainly not written the fugue at (A) in $\frac{12}{8}$ [Fughetta in C minor, BWV 961] and the other at (B) in $\frac{12}{16}$ [Fugue in C♯ minor, BWV 873, WTC II] without good reason.
>
> Everyone will easily perceive the distinction between the two meters in these examples. The one at (A) designates a slower tempo and a more emphatic performance; furthermore, many sixteenth notes can be used in this meter. However, no shorter note values can be used in the one at (B), and the sixteenth notes are performed quickly and plainly without any emphasis. Handel, Bach, and Couperin have written many pieces in $\frac{12}{16}$ meter.

26. Dietrich Buxtehude, *Orgelwerke,* II, edited by Spitta, Seiffert, Kraft (Wiesbaden, n.d.), pp. 94–95.

27. **Kirnberger:Kunst,** II, p. 129 (our translation).

28. George Frideric Handel (London, 1733).

29. Johann Kuhnau, *Neue Clavier Übung,* erster Theil (Leipzig, 1689).

30. **Kirnberger:Kunst,** Beach translation, p. 397.

31. See chapter 4, notes 24 and 25.

32. See *The New Grove Bach Family,* edited by Stanley Sadie, Catalogue, p. 211.

33. Ray McIntyre, "On the Interpretation of Bach's Gigues"; Frederick Neumann, "External Evidence and Uneven Notes"; Michael Collins, "The Performance of Triplets in the 17th and 18th Centuries"; Robert Donington, *Baroque Music: Style and Performance,* pp. 53 and 63–64; Howard Ferguson, *Keyboard Interpretation,* pp. 89–96; Glen Wilson, Preface to *Clavier-Übung* I (The Hague: Mark A. Meadow, 1983).

34. Collins, "The Performance of Triplets."

35. J. J. Froberger, *Orgel- und Klavierwerke,* edited by G. Adler, DTO Vol. 13; Suite VII, pp. 20 and 71; Suite XV, p. 45; Suite XXVIII, p. 82.

36. Collins, pp. 296–98.

37. **Brossard:Dictionaire,** article "Giga." See note 7 above.

38. Donington, *Baroque Music: Style and Performance.*

39. Ferguson, *Keyboard Interpretation,* pp. 89–96.

40. **Bacilly:Remarques,** Reilly translation, pp. 232–35.

41. **Powell:Rhythmic** discusses the evidence (pp. 84–86) and reproduces one piece by Denis Gaultier in the two different versions.

42. **Walther:Lexicon.**

11. THE LOURE AND THE FORLANA

1. For further information see **New Grove,** articles "Loure" and "Forlana."

2. For example, **Tomlinson:Dancing,** p. 149: "As to *Tunes* of *triple Time* agreeing with *quadruple, viz. Louvres* or slow Jigs, . . . "; **Dupont:Musique,** p. 43: "L'orsqu'il y a audessus de l'air en Ecrit, loure, On doit chanter gravement au Contraire, l'orsqu'il est en Ecrit, Gigue, il faut chanter ou joüer legerement"; **Masson:Traité,** p. 8: "La Loure . . . doit se battre à deux tems égaux lentement; elle doit estre du même mouvement que la Mesure à deux tems lents. / Les Canaries & la Gigue . . . se battent à deux tems égaux: Il est bon de remarquer que les Canaries se battent un peu plus vite que la Gigue."

3. **Mattheson:Vollkommene,** No. 120, p. 228 (our translation): "Die *Loures* oder langsamen und punctirten zeigen hergegen ein *stoltzes, ausgeblasenes* Wesen an: deswegen sie bey den Spaniern sehr beliebt sind."

4. See **Little/Marsh:Inventory** for more details.

5. John Hawkins, *A General History of the Science and Practice of Music* (London, 1776), Vol. II, p. 705.

6. **Feuillet:Chor,** p. 87.

7. **Tomlinson:Dancing,** pp. 144 and 149.

8. Paul Nettl, article "Forlana," in *Musik in Geschichte und Gegenwart.*

9. E.g., Jean-Joseph Mouret, *Les Fêtes de Thalie,* 1714 and *Le Triomphe de Sens,* 1732; Michel-Richard de Lalande, *L'hymen champestre,* 1700; Jean-Baptiste Senailléee-le-fils, Aria in [Violin]Sonata No. 1, from *Deuxième Livre de Sonates,* 1712; see Exx. XI-3 and XI-4 for forlanas by François Couperin and Montéclair.

10. **Rousseau:Dictionnaire,** article "forlane": "Air d'une Danse de mesme nom commune a Venise surtout parmi des Gondoliers. Sa Mesures est à $\frac{6}{8}$; elle se bat gaiment, & la Danse est aussi fort gai."

11. **Compan:Dictionnaire,** article "forlane: "la Danse est aussi très-gaie."

12. **Rousseau:Dictionnaire; Compan:Dictionnaire; Türk:Clavierschule,** p. 400: "geschwinde Bewegung"; Johann George Sulzer, *Allgemeine Theorie der Schöner Künste,* 4 vols. (Leipzig, 1792-94): "sehr munterer Bewegung."

13. **Borin:Musique,** p. 57.

14. See **Little/Marsh:Inventory** for details.

15. Wilfred Mellers, *François Couperin and the French Classical Tradition* (New York: Dover, 1968), p. 250.

12. THE POLONAISE

1. For a provocative discussion of polonaise rhythms in the second half of the eighteenth century, see Sarah Reichart, "The Influence of Eighteenth-Century Social Dance on the Viennese Classical Style," pp. 107–32.

2. **Mattheson:Vollkommene,** Harriss translation, pp. 458–59.

3. **New Grove,** article "Polonaise."

4. **Türk:Clavierschule,** p. 402: "ein polnisches Natyional / Tanzstück im Dreyvierteltakte, von feyerlich gravitätischen Character." Johann George Sulzer, *Allgemeine Theorie der Schöner Künste,* 4 vols. (Leipzig, 1792–94).

5. **Mattheson:Vollkommene,** Harriss translation, p. 344.

6. Ibid., pp. 347–48.

7. Ibid., pp. 351 and 458.

8. Ibid., p. 459.

9. **Kirnberger:Kunst,** Beach translation, p. 216.

13. THE CHACONNE AND THE PASSACAGLIA

1. See, e.g., Handel's Passacaille in G minor (**New Grove** keyboard listing No. 255) and François Couperin's "La Favorite," subtitled "Chaconne a deux tems" (*Pièces de Clavecin,* Livre I, Ordre 3, 1713).

2. E.g., the *Passagalia of Venüs & Adonis* by Anthony L'Abbé contains a section in duple meter within the overall triple meter (see **Little/Marsh:Inventory** for more details).

3. E.g., L'Affilard's indications in 1705 are: chaconne, ♩ = MM 79; passacaille, ♩ = MM 53, as reported by Erich Schwandt in **New Grove,** article "L'Affilard." Even if both tempi seem excessively slow for modern performers, they do indicate that the chaconne is the faster dance.

4. **Mattheson:Vollkommene,** Harriss translation, pp. 465–66.

5. **Brossard:Dictionaire,** article "Passacaglia": "Passacaglia veut dire, Passacaille. C'est proprement une *Chacone.* Toute la différence est que le *mouvement* en est ordinairement plus *grave* que celuy de la *Chacone,* le chant *plus tendre,* et les expressions *moins vifves,* c'est pour cela que les *Passacailles* sont presque toûjours travaillées sur des *Modes meneuer.* C'est à dire, dont la *Médiante* n'est eloignée de la Finalle que d'une 3ce mineure." See also "Passacaille" articles in Pierre Richelet, *Dictionnaire de la langue françoise,* 2 vols. (Amsterdam, 1732) and in the dictionaries by Furetière, Rousseau, and Lacombe.

6. Richard Hudson, **New Grove,** articles "Chaconne" and "Passacaglia."

7. See **Little/Marsh:Inventory,** *The Favorite,* a chacone by Mr. Isaac, "Danced by her Majesty" (London, 1706) and *The Princess Ann's Chacone* by Anthony L'Abee "For His Majesties Birthday . . . 1719."

8. **Little/Marsh:Inventory:** *Chaconne for Arlequin* by Rousseau (manuscript, c. 1728); *Chaconne Darlequin* by De la Montagne (undated manuscript); and the anonymous *Entrée d'Arlequin* (undated manuscript).

9. Louis de Cahusac, *La Danse ancienne et moderne, ou Traité historique de la Danse* (The Hague, 1754), Vol. III, p. 154; quoted by James Anthony in "The Opera-Ballets of André Campra," Ph.D. diss., University of Southern California, 1964, pp. 492-93.

10. See chapter 7, note 3 and accompanying text.

11. Jacques Ozanam, *Dictionnaire Mathématique* (Paris, 1691), article "Chacone": "La Chacone est une *Sarabande* composée de plusieurs *Couplets* roulans presque tous sur le même sujet, qui se trouve ordinairement dans la *Basse.*"

12. For an example, see **NBA,** IV/vii, Anhang.

BIBLIOGRAPHY

Only books, articles, and editions cited in the text are listed here. Those that occur often are cited in the abbreviations following the full references.

Other abbreviations:
DTO   *Denkmäler der Tonkunst in Österreich*
JAMS   *Journal of the American Musicological Society*
MQ   *The Musical Quarterly*

Aldrich, Putnam. *Rhythm in Seventeenth-Century Italian Monody*. New York: W. W. Norton, 1966 [**Aldrich:Rhythm**].
_____. " 'Rhythmic harmony' as taught by Johann Philipp Kirnberger." In *Studies in Eighteenth-Century Music: A Tribute to Karl Geiringer on His Seventieth Birthday*, edited by H. C. Robbins Landon in collaboration with Roger E. Chapman. New York: Oxford University Press, 1970. Pp. 37–52.
Anthony, James R. *French Baroque Music from Beaujoyeulx to Rameau*. London: Batsford, 1973; 2d ed., rev., New York: Norton, 1978. [**Anthony:FBM**].
Anonymous [sometimes attributed to Johann Christoph and Johann David Stössel]. *Kurtzgefasstes Musicalisches Lexicon*. Chemnitz, 1737; reprint, 1749 [**Christoph/Stössel:Lexicon**].
Apel, Willi. *Harvard Dictionary of Music,* 2d ed. Cambridge: The Belknap Press of Harvard University Press, 1969.
Arbeau, Thoinot (Jehan Tabourot, pseud.). *Orchésography*. Langres: Jehan des Preys [1588]; 2d ed., 1589. English translation by Mary Steward Evans, New York: Kamin, 1948. Reprint with corrections, new introduction, and notes by Julia Sutton, and with Labanotation by Mireille Backer and Julia Sutton, New York: Dover, 1967.
Bach, Johann Sebastian. *Johann Sebastian Bach: Clavier-Büchlein vor Vilhelm Friedemann Bach*. Fascimile edition, edited and with a preface by Ralph Kirkpatrick. New Haven: Yale University Press, 1959.
_____. *Six Suites for Cello by J. S. Bach, in the hand of Anna Magdalena Bach*. Berlin, Preuzische Staatsbibliothek, Mus. Ms. Bach P 26. Edited by Diran Alexanian. Paris: Salabert, 1929.
_____. *Johann Sebastian Bach, Little Note Book for Anna Magdalena Bach Complete*. Preface by Arnold Schering, English translation by Kurt Oppens. New York: Kalmus, 1949.
_____. *Sei Solo a Violino senza Basso Accompagnato. Libro Prima, da Joh. Seb. Bach, 1720*. Berlin, Preuzische Staatsbibliothek, Mus. Ms. Bach P 967. Edited by Bernhard Sprengel, *Nachwort* by Wilhelm Martin Luther. Kassel and Basel: Bärenreiter, 1950.
_____. *Clavier-Übung von Johann Sebastian Bach, Op. 1, In Verlegung des Autoris*. Leipzig, 1731. Facsimile edition by Comission bey Boetil Seel hinderlassene Tochter, unter den Rathhause (reproduces the copy in the Gemment Museum, Den Haag). Preface by Glen Wilson. The Hague, 1983.
_____. *Werke*. Edited by Bach-Gesellschaft, 61 vols. in 44 (bound in 48 vols). Leipzig, 1851–99. Reprint, Ann Arbor: J.W. Edwards, 1947 [**BG**].
_____. *Neue Ausgabe sämtlicher Werke (Neue Bach-Ausgabe)*. Edited by Johann-Sebastian-Bach-Institut, Göttingen, and Bach-Archiv, Leipzig, ser. I-VIII. Kassel and Basle, 1954– [**NBA**].
_____. *Johann Sebastian Bach, 6 Partitas and Overture in French Style*. Edited by Hans

Bischoff, English translation by Gerturde Wedeen and Alexander Lipsky. New York: Kalmus, 1942.

———. *Johann Sebastian Bach, Six English Suites.* Edited by Hans Bischoff, English translation by Alexander Lipsky. New York: Kalmus, 1945. Reprint, Melville, N.Y.: Belwin-Mills, n.d.

———. *Johann Sebastian Bach. Various Short Preludes and Fugues.* Edited by Hans Bischoff. New York: Kalmus, 1946. Reprint, Melville, N.Y.: Belwin-Mills, n.d.

Bacilly, Bénigne de. *Remarques Curieuses Sur L'Art de Bien Chanter.* Paris, 1668; 4th ed., 1681. English translation by Austin B. Caswell as *A Commentary upon the Art of Proper Singing.* Brooklyn, N.Y.: Institute of Mediaeval Music, 1968 [**Bacilly:Remarques**].

Behrens, Samuel Rudolph. *L'Art de Bien Danser, Oder Die Kunst wohl zu Tantzen.* Leipzig, 1713. Reprint, in *Documenta Choreologica* 2; *Nachwort* and index by Kurt Petermann. Leipzig: Zentralantiquariat der DDR, 1977.

Borin [formerly attributed to Didier Saurin]. *La Musique Theorique, et Pratique, Dans Son Ordre Naturel: Nouveaux Principes Par Mr. XXXXX.* Paris, 1722 [**Borin:Musique**].

Boyden, David. Article "Scordatura." In *New Grove Dictionary of Musical Instruments,* edited by Stanley Sadie. London and New York: Macmillan, 1984.

Brockpähler, Renate. *Handbuch zur Geschichte der Barockoper in Deutschland. Die Schaubühne 62, edited by Carl Niessen.* Emsdetten/Westfalia: Lechte, 1964.

Brossard, Sébastien de. *Dictionaire de Musique, Contenant une explication des Termes Grecs, Latins, Italiens & François, les plus usitez dans la Musique.* Paris, 1703; 2d ed., 1705. Facsimile reprint, edited by Harald Heckmann, Hilversum: Knuf, 1965 [**Brossard:Dictionaire**].

Christoph and Stössel, attributed to. See Anonymous.

Christout, Marie-Françoise. *Le Ballet de Cour de Louis XIV 1643–1672.* Paris: A. et J. Picard, 1967.

Collins, Michael. "The Performance of Triplets in the 17th and 18th Centuries," JAMS 19/3 (1966):281–328.

Compan, Charles. *Dictionnaire de Danse. Contenant l'Histoire, les Règles et les Principes de cet Art, avec des Réflexions Critiques, et des Anecdotes Curieuses Concernant la Danse Ancienne et Moderne; le Tout Tiré des Meilleurs Auteurs qui ont Ecrit sur cet Art.* Paris, 1787 [**Compan:Dictionnaire**].

Couperin, François. *Pièces de Clavecin,* Vol. I. Paris, 1713 [**Couperin:PiècesI**]. Edited by Kenneth Gilbert, Le Pupitre XXI. Paris: Heugel, 1972.

———. *L'Art de Toucher le Clavecin.* Paris, 1717. Reprint with German translation by Anna Linde and English translation by Mevanevy Roberts, Wiesbaden: Breitkopf & Härtel, 1933.

———. *Concerts Royaux.* Paris, 1722. Reprint, vol. VII, Les Ramparts: Oiseau Lyre, 1932–33.

D'Alembert, Jean de Rond. *Eléments de Musique Théoretique et pratique suivant les Principes de M. Rameau.* Paris, 1752; reprints 1759–1779. Reprint, New York: Broude Bros, 1966. [**D'Alembert:Eléments**].

Danckert, W. *Geschichte der Gigue.* Leipzig, 1924.

Dandrieu, Jean-François. *Piéces de Clavecin Courtes et Facile de Quatre Tons Différents.* Paris, 1715–20 [**Dandrieu:Pièces**].

David, François. *Méthode Nouvelle ou Principes Généraux pour Apprendre Facilement la Musique, et l'Art de Chanter.* Paris, 1737; reprint, [1763].

David, Hans T., and Arthur Mendel, editors. *The Bach Reader.* New York, W. W. Norton, 1945; reprint, 1966 [**David/Mendel:Bach**].

Démotz de la Salle. *Méthode de Musique Selon un Nouveau Systême Très-court, Très facile & Très-sur.* Paris, 1728 [**Démotz: Méthode**].

Donington, Robert. *The Interpretation of Early Music.* New York and London: St. Martin's Press, 1963 [**Donington:Interpretation**]. 2d ed., London: Faber & Faber, 1965; rev. ed., 1974.

———. *A Performer's Guide to Baroque Music.* New York: Chas. Scribner's Sons, 1973.

———. *Baroque Music: Style and Performance.* New York: W. W. Norton, 1982.

Dupont, Pierre. *Principes de Musique par demandes et réponce.* Paris, 1713; reprinted four times by 1740 [**Dupont: Musique**].

———. *Principes de Violon par demandes et par réponce, par le quel toutes personnes, pourant aprendre d'eux-mêmes a jouer du dit instrument.* Paris, 1718; reprint, 1740 [**Dupont:Violon**].

Dürr, Alfred. "The Historical Background of the Composition of Johann Sebastian Bach's Clavier Suite," Parts I and II, *BACH* 16/1 (1985):53–68.

Ecorcheville, Jules. "Un livre inconnu sur la danse." In *Riemann-Festschrift Gesammelte Studien.* Leipzig, 1909; reprint, Tutzing: Hans Schneider, 1965. Pp. 288–93.

———. *Vingt Suites d'Orchestre du XVIIe Siècle français.* Berlin and Paris, 1906; reprint, New York: Broude Bros., 1970 [**Ecorcheville:Suites**].

Ellis [=Little], Helen Meredith. "The Dances of J.-B. Lully (1632–1687)." Diss., Stanford University, 1967 [**Ellis:Lully**].

Fauchier-Magnan, Adrien. *Les Petites Cours D'Allemagne Au XVIIIième Siècle.* Paris: Flammarion, 1958. English translation by Mervyn Savill as *The Small German Courts in the Eighteenth Century.* London: Methuen, 1958.

Ferguson, Howard. *Keyboard Interpretation.* New York and London: Oxford University Press, 1975.

Feuillet, Raoul-Auger. *Recueil de Dances, Composées Par M. Feuillet, Maître de Dance.* Paris, 1700, reprint 1709 and 1713. Facsimile reprint, New York: Broude Bros., 1968 [**Feuillet:1700Recueil**].

———. *Chorégraphie ou L'Art de Décrire la Dance, Par Caracteres, Figures et Signes Démonstratifs,* 2d ed. Paris, 1701; reprints 1709, 1713. Facsimile reprint, New York: Broude Bros., 1968 [**Feuillet:Chor**].

The Fitzwilliam Virginal Book, Vols. I and II, edited by J. A. Fuller Maitland and W. Barclay Squire. London: Breitkopf & Härtel, 1899. Reprint, New York: Dover, 1963.

Freillon-Poncein, J. P. *La Veritable Manière d'apprendre à jouer en perfection du Haut-Bois, de la Flute et du Flageolet. . . .* Paris, 1700 [**Freillon:Veritable**]. English translation by Catherine Smith. Diss., Stanford University, 1974.

Frescobaldi, Girolamo. *Toccate o partita d'Intavolatura.* Rome, 1635. English translation of "Al lettore" by Edward Dannreuther in *Musical Ornamentation,* Vol. I. New York and London: Novello, 1893–95. Pp. 48–49.

Furetière, Antoine. *Dictionnaire Universel, contenant Généralement tous les Mots François, Tant Vieux que Modernes, et les Termes des Sciences et des Arts.* Rotterdam, 1690. Reprint, Geneva: Slatkine, 1970 [**Furietière:Dictionnaire**]. Other editions 1701–1771.

Fürstenau, Moritz. *Zur Geschichte der Musik und der theaters am Hofe zu Dresden,* Vols. I and II. Dresden, 1861–62. Reprint, in one vol., Leipzig: Peters, 1971.

Galliard, J. E. *Observations on the florid Song.* London, 1742. (English translation of Pier Francesco Tosi, *Opinioni de' Cantori Antichi, e Moderni.* Bologna, 1723.)

Geiringer, Karl. *Johann Sebastian Bach. The Culmination of an Era.* New York: Oxford University Press, 1966. [**Geiringer:Bach**].

Gerbes, Angelika. "Gottfried Taubert on Social and Theatrical Dance of the Early Eighteenth Century." Diss., The Ohio State University, 1972.

Grassineau, James. *A Musical Dictionary. Being a Collection of Terms and Characters, As well Ancient as Modern; Including the Historical, Theoretical, and practical Parts of Music.* London, 1740. Facsimile reprint, New York: Broude Bros., 1966 [**Grassineau:Dictionary**].

Harris-Warrick, Rebecca. "Ballroom Dancing at the Court of Louis XIV," *Early Music* 14/1 (1986): 40–49.

Hermann-Bengen, Irmgard. *Tempobezeichnungen: Ursprung und Wandel im 17. und 18. Jahrhundert.* Münchner Veröffentlichungen zur Musikgeschichte, 1. Tutzing: Hans Schneider, 1959.

Hilton, Wendy. "A Dance for Kings: The 17th-century French Courante," *Early Music* 5/2 (1977):161–72.

———. *Dance of Court and Theater: The French Noble Style 1690–1725.* Princeton: Princeton Book Co., 1981 [**Hilton:Dance**].

Houle, George. *Meter in Music, 1600–1800: Performance, Perception, and Notation.* Bloomington: Indiana University Press, 1987 [**Houle:Meter**].

I. H. P. Maître de Danse, Oder Tantz-Meister. Leipzig, 1705.

Jenne, Natalie. "Bach's Use of Dance Rhythms in Fugues," *BACH* 4/4 (1973): 18–26; 5/1 (1974):3–8; 5/2 (1974):3–21.

———. "On the Performance of Keyboard Allemandes," *BACH* 10/2 (1979):13–30.

Kirnberger, Johann. *Die Kunst des reinen Satzes in der Musik, aus sicheren Grundsätzen hergeleitet und mit deutlichen Beyspielen erläutert.* Berlin and Königsberg, 1771 (Vol. I); 1776–79 (Vol. II) [**Kirnberger:Kunst**]; reprint of both volumes, 1793. Facsimile reprint, Hildesheim: Georg Olms, 1968. English translation of Vol. I and Vol. II, Part I, by David Beach and Jurgen Thym as *The Art of Strict Musical Composition.* Music Theory Translation series, 4. New Haven and London: Yale University Press, 1982.

———. *Recueil d'airs de danse caractéristiques, pour servir de modele aux jeunes compositeurs et d'exercice à ceux qui touchent du clavecin, avec un préface par J. Ph. Kirnberger. Partie I. Consistant en XXVI pieces.* Berlin: Jean Julien Hummel, [c. 1777].

Kuhnau, Johann. *Neue Clavier Übung,* erster Theil. Leipzig, 1689.

Lacombe, Jacques. *Dictionnaire Portatif des Beaux-Arts, ou Abrégé de ce qui Concerne l'Architecture, la Sculpture, la Peinture, la Gravure, la Poésie et la Musique. . . .* Paris, 1752; 4th reprint, 1766 [**Lacombe:Dictionnaire**].

L'Affilard, Michel. *Principes très-faciles pour bien apprendre la musique, qui conduirent promptement ceux qui ont du naturel pour le chant jusqu'au point de chanter toute sorte de musique proprement, & à livre ouvert.* Paris, 1694; 5th rev. ed., corrected and enlarged, Paris 1705 [**L'Affilard:Principes**]. Reprints to 1747.

Lecointe, Jean. *Apologie de la Danse: Son Antiquité, Sa Noblesse, et Ses Avantages. Avec une Dissertation sur le Menuet.* Paris, 1752 [**Lecointe:Apologie**]. English translation by J. Peyton as *An Apology for Dancing: shewing Its Antiquity Excellence and Advantages. With a Dissertation upon the Minuet.* London, 1752.

Lester, Joel. "Problems in the *Neue Bach Ausgabe* of the E Major Partita for Violin Alone," *Current Musicology* 18 (1972):64–67.

Little, Meredith Ellis. "The Contribution of Dance Steps to Musical Analysis and Performance: La Bourgogne," *JAMS* 28/1 (1975): 112–24 [**Little:Contribution**].

———. "French Court Dance in Germany at the Time of Johann Sebastian Bach: *La Bourgogne* in Paris and Leipzig." In *Report of the Twelfth Congress, International Musicological Society, Berkeley, 1977,* edited by Daniel Heartz and Bonnie Wade. Kassel: Bärenreiter, 1981. Pp. 730–34 [**Little:Bourgogne**].

———, and Carol Marsh. *La Danse Noble: An Inventory of Notated Dances and Sources.* New York: Broude Bros., 1991 [**Little/Marsh:Inventory**].

See also Ellis [=Little], Helen Meredith

Loulié, Etienne. *Eléments ou Principes de Musique, mis dans un Nouvel Ordre.* Paris, 1696. Reprints, Joachimsthal: Knuf, 1969; Geneva: Minkoff, 1971 [**Loulié:Elements**]. English translation by Albert Cohen as *Elements or Principles of Music.* Brooklyn, N.Y.: Institute of Mediaeval Music, 1965.

McIntyre, Ray. "On the Interpretation of Bach's Gigues," MQ 51/3 (1965):478–92.

Marpurg, Friedrich Wilhelm. *Der Critische Musicus an der Spree.* Berlin, 1749–50. Reprint, Hildesheim: Olms, 1970.

_____. *Historisch-kritische Beiträge zur Aufnahme der Musik,* Vol. I. Berlin, 1754. Facsimile reprint, Hildesheim: Olms, 1970.

_____. *Clavierstücke mit einem practischen Unterricht für Anfänger und Geübtere.* 2 vols. Berlin, 1762.

_____. *Kritische Briefe über die Tonkunst, mit kleinen Clavierstücken und Singoden begleitet von einer musikalischen Gesellschaft in Berlin,* Vol. II. Berlin, 1763. Reprint, Hildesheim: Olms, 1974.

Marshall, Robert L. "J. S. Bach's Compositions for Solo Flute," JAMS 32/3 (1979):463–98.

Masson, Charles. *Nouveau Traité des Regles Pour la Composition de la Musique.* Paris, 1697; 2d ed. 1699. Facsimile reprint edited by Imogene Horsley. New York: Da Capo, 1967 [**Masson:Traité**]. 3d ed., Paris, 1705. Facsimile reprint, Geneva: Minkoff, 1971.

Mather, Betty Bang. *Dance Rhythms of the French Baroque: A Handbook for Performance.* Bloomington: Indiana University Press, 1987 [**Mather:Dance**].

Mattheson, Johann. *Neu-Eröffnete Orchestre.* Hamburg, 1713 [**Mattheson:Orchestre**].

_____. *Der vollkommene Capellmeister.* Hamburg, 1739 [**Mattheson:Vollkommene**]. Facsimile reprint, Kassel: Bärenreiter, 1954. English translation by Ernest C. Harriss as *Johann Mattheson's "Der vollkommene Capellmeister": A Revised Translation with Critical Commentary.* Ann Arbor: UMI Research Press, 1981.

Mohr, E. *Die Allemande.* Leipzig, 1932.

Montéclair, Michel Pignolet de. *Nouvelle méthode pour apprendre la musique par les démonstrations faciles.* Paris, 1709 [**Montéclair:Nouvelle**].

_____. *Méthode facile pour apprendre à jouer du violon.* Paris, 1711–12 [**Montéclair:Violon**].

_____. *principes de musique.* Paris, 1736. Facsimile reprint, Geneva: Minkoff, 1972 [**Monteclair:Principes**].

Muffat, Georg. *Florilegium Primum.* Augsburg, 1695 [**Muffat:FP**]. Text in DTO I/2 (1894). English translation of Foreword in Otto Strunk, *Source Readings in Music History.* New York: Norton, 1950; reprint, 1965.

_____. *Florilegium Secundum.* Passau, 1698 [**Muffat:FS**]. English translation of Foreword in Otto Strunk, *Source Readings in Music History.* New York: Norton, 1950; reprint, 1965. English translation by Kenneth Cooper and Julius Zsako as "Observations on the style of playing airs de ballets in the French manner according to the late Monsieur Lully's method," in "Georg Muffat's Observations on the Lully Style of Performance," MQ 53/2 (1967):220–45.

_____. *Auserlesene Instrumental-Music.* Passau, 1701. English translation of Foreword in Otto Strunk, *Source Readings in Music History.* New York: Norton, 1950; reprint, 1965.

Neumann, Frederick. "External Evidence and Uneven Notes." MQ 52/4 (1966):448–64.

_____. *Ornamentation in Baroque and Post-Baroque Music, with Special Emphasis on J. S. Bach.* Princeton: Princeton University Press, 1978.

The New Grove Bach Family, edited by Stanley Sadie. London and New York: Norton, 1983.

The New Grove Dictionary of Music and Musicians, 20 vols. Edited by Stanley Sadie. London: Macmillan Publishers, 1980 [**New Grove**].

The New Grove Dictionary of Musical Instruments. Edited by Stanley Sadie. London, 1984.

New Harvard Dictionary of Music. Edited by Michael Randel. Cambridge and London: Belknap Press, 1986.

Newman, William S. *The Sonata in The Baroque Era.* 3d ed. New York: W. W. Norton, 1972.

Niedt, Friedrich Erhard. *Musicalische handleitung zur Variation des General-Basses.* Hamburg, 1721. Facsimile reprint, Buren: Knuf, 1976 [**Niedt:Handlitung**].

Ozanam, Jacques. *Dictionnaire Mathématique.* Paris, 1691. Abridged English translation by J. Ralphson, London, 1702.

Palisca, Claude. *Baroque Music.* Englewood Cliffs, N.J.: Prentice-Hall, Inc., 1968; rev. ed., 1981.

Pasch, Johann. *Beschreibung wahrer Tanz-Kunst.* Franckfurt, 1707. Facsimile reprint, with *Nachwort* and index by Kurt Petermann, in *Documenta Choreologica* 16. Leipzig: Zentralantiquariat der DDR, 1981.

Pécour, Louis-Guillaume. *Recueil de Dances, Composées Par M. Pécour. Pensionnaire des menus Plaisirs du Roy, & Compositeur des Ballets de l'Academie Royale de Musique de Paris. Et mises sur le papier Par M. Feuillet, Maître de Dance.* Paris, 1700; reprints, 1709, 1713. Facsimile reprint, New York: Broude Bros., 1968 [**Pécour:1700Recueil**].

Pirro, André. "Remarques de quelques voyageurs sur la musique en Allemagne et dans les pays du nord, de 1634 à 1700." In *Riemann-festschrift Gesammelte Studien.* Leipzig, 1909; reprint, Tutzing: Hans Schneider, 1965.

Playford, John. *The English Dancing Master.* London, 1651–1728. Annotated facsimile of 1651 edition by Margaret Dean-Smith. London: Schott, 1957.

Powell, Newman W. "Rhythmic Freedom in the Performance of French Music from 1650 to 1735." Diss., Stanford University, 1959 [**Powell:Rhythmic**].

————. "Kirnberger on Dance Rhythms, Fugues, and Characterization." In *Festschrift Theodore Hoelty-Nickel.* Valparaiso, IN: Valparaiso University, 1967. Pp. 65–76.

Quantz, Johann Joachim. *Versuch einer Anweisung die Flöte traversiere zu spielen; mit verschiedenen zur Beförderung des guten Geschmackes in der praktischen Musik, dienlichen Anmerkungen begleitet, und mit Exempeln erläutert.* Berlin, 1752 [**Quantz:Versuch**]. English translation by Edward R. Reilly as *On Playing the Flute.* New York: Schirmer Books, 1966. 3d ed., Breslau: 1789. Facsimile reprint, in Documenta musicologica 2, edited by H. P. Schmitz. Kassel: Bärenreiter, 1953.

Raison, André. *Livre d'Orgue.* Paris, 1688.

Rameau, Jean-Philippe. *Traité de l'Harmonie Reduite à ses Principes Naturels.* Paris, 1722. English translation by Philip Gossett as *Treatise on Harmony.* New York: Dover, 1971.

Rameau, P[ierre]. *Le Maître à danser.* Paris, 1725. Facsimile reprint, New York: Broude Bros., 1967 [**Rameau:Maître**]. English translation by Cyril W. Beaumont as *The Dancing Master.* London: Beaumont, 1931; facsimile reprint, New York: Dance Horizons, 1970.

Ranum, Patricia. "Audible Rhetoric and Mute Rhetoric: the 17th-century French Sarabande," *Early Music* 14/1 (1986):22–39.

Reichart, Sarah. "The Influence of Eighteenth-Century Social Dance on the Viennese Classical Style." Ph.D. diss., City University of New York, 1984.

Rousseau, Jean-Jacques. Articles "Gavotte" and "Menuet," in *Encyclopédie,* edited by Denis Diderot and Jean d'Alembert. Paris, 1751–72.

_____. *Dictionaire de Musique.* Paris, 1768. Facsimile reprint, Hildesheim: Olms, 1969; New York: Johnson, 1969 [**Rousseau:Dictionnaire**]. English translation by William Waring as *A Dictionary of Music.* London, 1771.

Saint-Lambert, Michel de. *Les Principes du Clavecin.* Paris, 1702. Facsimile reprint, Geneva: Minkoff, 1972 [**Saint-Lambert:Clavecin**]. English translation by Rebecca Harris-Warrick as *Principles of the Harpsichord.* Cambridge: Cambridge University Press, 1984.

_____. *Nouveau Traité de l'Accompagnement du Clavecin, de l'Orgue, et des Autres Instruments.* Paris, 1707. Facsimile reprint, Geneva: Minkoff, 1972. English translation by John S. Powell, Bloomington: Indiana University Press, 1991.

Saurin, Didier. See Borin.

Schmieder, Wolfgang. *Thematisch-systematisches Verzeichnis des musikalischen Werke Johann Sebastian Bachs.* Leipzig: Breitkopf & Härtel, 1950; reprint, 1981.

Schwandt, Erich. "L'Affilard on the French Court Dances," MQ 60/3 (1974):389–400.

Sutton, Julia. "The Minuet: an Elegant Phoenix," *Dance Chronicle* 8/3, 4 (1985):119–52.

Taubert, Gottfried. *Rechtschaffener Tanzmeister, oder gründliche Erklärung der frantzösischen Tantz-Kunst.* Leipzig, 1717 [**Taubert:Rechtschaffener**]. Facsimile reprint with commentary by Kurt Petermann in *Documenta Choreologica* 22. Leipzig: Zentralantiquariat der DDR, 1976.

Tomlinson, Kellom. *The Art of Dancing Explained by Reading and Figures: Whereby the Manner of Performing the Steps is Made Easy By a New and Familiar Method: Being the Original Work First Design'd in the Year 1724, And now Published by Kellom Tomlinson, Dancing-Master. In Two Books.* London, 1735 [**Tomlinson:Dancing**]. Facsimile reprint, New York: Dance Horizons, 1970; 2d ed. London, 1744.

Tosi, Pier Francesco. *Opinioni de' Cantori Antichi, e Moderni.* Bologna, 1723 [see J. E. Galliard].

Türk, Daniel Gottlob. *Clavierschule, oder Anweisung zum Clavierspielen für Lehrer und Lernende, mit kritischen Anmerkungen.* Leipzig and Halle, 1789. [**Türk:Clavierschule**]. Facsimile reprint, edited by E.R. Jacobi, *Documenta Musicologica* 23, Kassel: Bärenreiter, 1962. English translation by Raymond H. Haggh as *School of Clavier Playing.* Lincoln: University of Nebraska Press, 1983.

Walther, Johann Gottfried. *Musicalisches Lexicon, oder Musicalische Bibliothek.* Leipzig, 1732. Facsimile reprint, edited by R. Schaal, Kassel: Bärenreiter, 1953 [**Walther:Lexicon**].

Weigel, Christoph (publisher). *Abbildung der Gemein-Nutzlichen Haupt-Stände von dem Regenten biss auf die Künstler und Handwercker.* Regensburg, 1698. Facsimile reprint in Die Bibliophilen Taschenbücher 9, Dortmund: Harenberg, 1977.

Wynne, Shirley, "Complaisance: An Eighteenth-Century Cool," *Dance Scope* 5/1 (1970).

INDEX

MEREDITH LITTLE has taught at Stanford University and at the Aston Magna Academy. She is the author of numerous articles on Baroque music and dance, including 23 in the *New Grove*.

NATALIE JENNE, Professor of Music at Concordia University, River Forest, Illinois, is active as a harpsichord recitalist. She conducts workshops on Baroque performance practices and is the author of many articles on this subject.